MODES OF VALUE

MODES OF VALUE

A. H. Johnson

Philosophical Library
New York

TO
MY
SONS-IN-LAW and GRANDCHILDREN

Copyright, 1978, by Philosophical Library, Inc.,
15 East 40 Street, New York, New York 10016
All rights reserved
Library of Congress Catalog Card No. 77-79172
SBN 8022-2211-0
Manufactured in the United States of America

CONTENTS

SECTION FOUR   A REPRESENTATIVE SAMPLE OF
VALUABLE AND OF VALUE-OPPOSITE ENTITIES
—COMPARISONS

Preface

This book is an attempt to outline a philosophical approach to some major problems concerning value. It is based on an examination of comprehensive human experience.

I wish to express my gratitude to: The Canada Council for providing secreterial assistance; Dean John G Rowe, Faculty of Arts, University of Western Ontario for a generous subvention in aid of publication; Mrs. Pauline Campbell, of the Department of Philosophy for expert typing; my wife Helen for unfailing support, encouragement and extensive editorial activity.

I dedicate this book to my sons-in-law Albert H Oosterhoff and Hugh M. Kindred and to my grandchildren Michael Oosterhoff, Andrew Oosterhoff, Clea Kindred, Kerry Kindred. In various ways they have greatly aided my attempts to understand the nature and presence of value.

A.H. Johnson
University of Western Ontario
London, Canada

SECTION ONE

BACKGROUND

CHAPTER I

Introduction

I

We find ourselves in a world composed of many ingredients. Some of these occur many times, some do not. For example, there are many particular occurrences of food and of pain—but only one Socrates or Shakespeare. Among the many-occurrence *entities* is value.

In the course of subsequent discussion, the term "entity" is used instead of "person", "thing", "quality", etc. because of the convenience of its greater generality. It is used to refer to whatever is present to awareness, or is thought about (including imagined).

Obviously the term "entity" applies not only to *what* occurs many times but also to *each* of its particular occurrences. Consider an example: As I look at four pieces of kindling in my fireplace I am aware of four different *entities*—four different particular pieces of wood. However, I am also aware of *one entity*, namely wood, which occurs four different times. In this sense *wood* is a *many-occurrence* entity and *each piece* of wood is a *particular entity*,—a particular occurrence of a *many-occurrence* entity, wood. As has been noted, there are some particular entities which are not particular occurrences of many-occurrence entities. Consider for example the *distinctive* personality traits of Socrates or of Shakespeare.

The context usually indicates, with sufficient clarity, whether the

3

entity under discussion is many-occurrence or particular. In some cases qualifying terms are used in order to avoid possible misunderstanding.

It is appropriate in dealing with any entity, to rely on comprehensive experience. The term "comprehensive experience" is used to refer to awareness of all relevant entities in a situation, which are open to awareness. In this context a person is not influenced by prejudice, and pre-conceived conceptual schemes which distract attention from relevant data. Nor will he attempt to explain the non-imaginary in terms of the imaginary. Positively speaking, comprehensive experience involves awareness not only of all available relevant data, and the distinction of what is from what is not, but also of the danger of mistaken views, and the need to escape from such pitfalls.

In brief, on the basis of comprehensive experience, a person discovers the nature and status of what he is aware of, and of the entities he thinks about, but does not find present to awareness (e.g they are not seen or felt).

This book is primarily concerned with a number of related issues concerning value: (a) ways in which entities are valuable, (b) what entities are valuable.

II

It is essential to note that the value situation is complicated by the fact that there are several different *modes of presence* of value: i.e., entities are characterized by value in various ways: (1) intrinsically, i.e., as such, (2) when means, (3) because of the value of characteristics, (4) because of the value of entities which are its external[1] consequences,[2] (5) as possible, (6) as potential. Modes 2-6 are frequently referred to as "extrinsic". Here value is a characteristic which involves specific relation with other entities. Modes 1, 5 & 6 apply to all occurrences of an entity. Modes 2-4 do not. It is further essential to realize that modes 3 and 4 involve very fundamental qualifications. (See chapter 5, pp. 97-98, 102.) There are not six different sorts, or types, of value. Rather, one and the same entity, i.e., value, can be present in six different ways—that is to say: "modes of presence."

Let us now consider examples, and other clarifications, of the preceding comments: (1) morally good, beautiful, true[3], pleasure, as

4

such, are characterized by value, that is: intrinsically. (2) entities are valuable *when* they are functioning as means to ends. It is essential to realize that when one is considering the means characteristics of an entity one must identify carefully the end which is in relation to this specific entity. In other words, no entity has the characteristic means, as such. There are many entities toward which a specific entity cannot function as a means at all. There are four different varieties of the means relation, hence four different sorts of the mode: *valuable when means*. For example (a) a pen when used to write a note is functioning as an *instrument* and has value on that basis; (b) a cue strikes a ball and causes it to move. Therefore the cue has value because of its *causal* means function; (c) A smooth table top, when being used in the course of the game, is valuable as a *condition*; (d) a lighted cigar in the mouth of a billiard player, in the course of the game, since it is an ingredient in the total situation, has value as an *ingredient*. After all the general situation would not be what it is if the lighted cigar were not present. Of course the cue and the table are also ingredients in this situation. (3) A pen is valuable because it is characterized by beautiful and beautiful is characterized by value. (4) From a particular serving of food there result very beneficial consequences. Because of the value of these consequences, value accrues[4] to the food. In other words it derives value in the consequence mode. (5) Any pen, which is not now being used to write a note, is valuable in the *possible* mode. Namely it is such that it is possible that it may be used, and hence be valuable as an instrument, under certain conditions. (6) Any child, of good hereditary, living in a good environment, is valuable in view of his *potentialities*. He is capable of developing into a mature and superior, that is, valuable, sort of adult. Pen and child are valuable in the possible or potential mode because of values which they are capable of being characterized by—in other modes, 2-4.

Reference is made to particular occurrences of entities in the illustrations for modes 2-4 because, for example, not every pen is being used as an instrument at a certain time, or is beautiful. Nor does every occurrence of food have value because of beneficial consequences. With the exception of ingredient status, no entity unqualifiedly is valuable extrinsically, in modes 2-4. Only some particular occurrences are, in some cases only temporarily. Other particular occurrences are not valuable in these modes. In a sense, a many occurrence entity both is and is not valuable in some mode of the 2-4 sorts. However, every pen is valuable in the

5

possible mode and every child of a certain sort is valuable in the potential mode.

III

It may appear that there are additional modes of value,[5] not previously covered; (a) valuable because of "what it takes" to produce an entity, (b) the value of an entity depends on "what its presence eliminates". These however are not two new modes. Consider the following facts with reference to (a): there are cases of something being desired intensely. When great effort is put forth in order to obtain it, the effort shows the degree of desiring.[6] Effort does not bestow value on the entity sought. What satisfies desire has value, in the means mode, for example a building which satisfies desire for comfort. The value of the building also depends on its consequences—and on the characteristics. Consider next (b). This is actually a case of deriving value as a result of consequences—for example, a medical discovery is valuable because as a consequence pain is eliminated.

There is a third apparent additional mode of value (c): "valuable because of the value of its cause". For example, it may be contended that a painting by Rembrandt is valuable because of the value of Rembrandt as a human being in general, and as a great painter in particular. However, as a matter of fact, the painting has value on the basis of modes 2-5. If it is a very inferior work by Rembrandt this is not overbalanced by Rembrandt's excellence as a painter. Of course, it is likely that any painting by Rembrandt will be characterized by artistic excellence. But it is the characteristics of the painting, not the characteristics of the painter which are among the bases of the value of the painting.

(d) Another mode might appear to be involved when, for example, some article of furniture is considered to be valuable because it belonged to some person or period characterized by value. This might be termed "valuable by association" (in contradistinction from valuable because of value of external consequences). Valuable because of association would seem to apply to both past and present entities. However, there are decisive objections to this suggestion concerning a distinct mode of value. For example, the "object" which once belonged to a famous man may well be valuable because it is a means to recollection of that person and from the recollection comes pleasure as a consequence. Or, value may be due to the fact that one is interested in the great man and desires to

6

own one of his possessions. Hence insofar as such a devotee has the object, it satisfies this desire and thus has value on the means basis.

IV

Basic to the preceding discussion of the six modes in which entities are characterized by value, is the contention—a report based on comprehensive experience—that value is an entity in its own right. Specifically value (a) is not to be *identified with*, is not the "same as", another entity, (b) nor is *it*, that is its nature, generated by, or constituted by, any other entity. These points will now be discussed.

It is, of course, the case that value is a *characteristic* of various entities. Hence there is no occurrence of value unless there is occurrence of other entities of which it is a characteristic. However, (a) the nature of value is not identical with the entities which it characterizes. For example pleasure is characterized by value, but pleasure is one entity and value is another. There are many cases of value which are not cases of pleasure.

It (b) has been "argued", by some philosophers, that value is an entity generated by some other entity, for example, desire, or interest, or by resultant consequences. Thus for example, it is claimed that any object of any interest is characterized by value[7]—or that we desire things not because they are valuable, but they are valuable because we desire them.[8] However, it is found that there are many entities characterized by value which men do not desire, likewise concerning interest. Also the presence of pleasurable consequences is not the generating source of the entity value. Some valuable entities do not have pleasurable consequences. Further, there are many cases where persons are interested in, or desire, entities which are not valuable except as ingredients. Also, some entities which have pleasant consequences are not valuable, except as ingredients.

A careful examination of the facts indicates that frequently men desire and are interested in what they consider to be valuable. They derive pleasure from what they consider valuable. In brief: *mental states* are not, in comprehensive experience, found to have the generative function, or status of identity, assigned to them as far as value is concerned.

Other so-called generative sources, or identical entities, are introduced such as majority opinion. But here again it is obvious that in some cases majority opinion supports a valuable state of affairs, in others it doesn't. In some cases majority opinion is unaware of the presence of value. In some cases it is. In any case what "justifies" majority opinion?[9] The question remains open until, on the basis of comprehensive experience, a person realizes that value is a distinct entity, neither identical with nor derived from any other entity. In brief, the basic issue is not the occurrence of majority opinion etc.—rather it is a question of the presence, or absence, of the entity value as a characteristic.

The same general comments apply to other entities which are offered as being identical with, or generating cause of, value, for example: self development, reason, living according to nature, decreed by God, obligation, universalizability, contract.

Some philosophers, and others, attempt to identify value with such entities as fitting, harmonious, efficient, consistent, justice. It is the case that these entities are valuable intrinsically,[10] i.e., are characterized by value as such. But here again, one must avoid the mistake of claiming that an entity is the same thing as its characteristics. Specifically, value is one entity, fitting is another. So is harmonious, so is justice and so on.

In like fashion, it is the case that with reference to entities which are valuable when means, for example, when an entity functions as an instrument, it has the characteristic value. But here again two different entities are involved, the means function and the entity value. The *nature* of value is not the result of, or identified with, the means function. There are occurrences of value where there is no means function. To repeat when an entity functions as a means it has value in this mode, but the value as such is not generated by the means function. The same sorts of comments apply to entities valuable in other extrinsic modes.

In terms familiar to contemporary philosophers, it is here reported that value is a simple entity which is a characteristic of some other entities. Since it is not identical with other entities, nor does it have component parts, nor is its nature generated by any other entity, as far as comprehensive experience is concerned—its nature cannot be defined by reference to such reputed identical or generating entities or reputed parts. Thus a request for *some sorts* of definition, or criteria, of value can not be met. However, cases of its occurrence can be pointed to, or listed. In this sense a definition can be provided. Hence one can provide criteria in this sense. Further, one can show the sorts of situation in which value occurs as a characteristic.

It is here reported that value is an entity which is part of the "furniture of the universe", ultimately independent of man's initiative. It is neither a postulated, nor an other-worldly entity. Value is an entity of which people, relying on comprehensive experience, are aware. The process of finding and being aware is not a weird occult process. It is found to be in its nature: non-imaginary. Of course a person can imagine some situation and then consider what value it would have.

One cannot legitimately brush aside the status here assigned to value by assuming that because our language includes the word "value" therefore we have, in our gullibility, imagined that such an entity is present as an objective fact—but as a matter of fact it is not. By way of refutation, it is to be noted that "value" is not analogous to the term "mermaid". We have in use the word "value" because we are aware of the non-imaginary entity value, in so far as we rely on comprehensive experience.

It is here suggested that, in the case of value,[11] as in that of many other entities, some people deny the presence of what they are aware of, perhaps rather dimly,—because of some unfortunate conditioning. Hence their experience, in the sense the term is here used—is not comprehensive.

For example, an avant-garde artist may deny that there is any value in the works of Rembrandt. But his own behaviour indicates that he considers these paintings very valuable indeed. When no one is looking, he studies them carefully. Indeed some of Rembrandt's techniques are copied in the contemporary "officially critical" artist's work. In like fashion a male chauvinist may deny that Ms. Gloria Glitterbug is an efficient driver. But he is quite willing to entrust his life to her when she is driving through heavy and demanding traffic. This is not to be explained, in this case, by "blind infatuation" and hence an overwhelming desire to be with her at any cost!

The very important distinction between intrinsic and extrinsic requires further comment. There are many who accept some or all of what has been termed extrinsic modes of value, but refuse to admit that any entity is valuable intrinsically, i.e., apart from its relation to other entities. On the other hand, some persons, accepting the status of intrinsic value, claim that there is only one entity which is intrinsically valuable, for example only pleasure.

As a matter of fact, there are many entities which are found to be

9

intrinsically valuable: morally good, pleasure, true, beautiful and others to be mentioned in Chapters 2, 3 and 4.

Here as elsewhere the final appeal is to comprehensive experience. While the entities mentioned immediately above are valuable in some of the extrinsic modes, in some of their particular occurrences, and in other modes in all occurrences—they are also valuable as such, i.e., intrinsically. For example, the entity morally good has value over and above values based on the pleasurable consequences and causal function which it may have on occasion. (Also the possibility of value in some extrinsic modes, in all its occurrences.) In brief, a careful consideration of the entity *as such* indicates that it is characterized by value. The same general comments apply to other cases of intrinsically valuable entities, e.g., beautiful, true, pleasure. The facts are there for those who "can see". Purely abstract, or verbal, arguments are pointless when used by persons who attack comprehensive experience. In such cases one can only confront the doubter with specific cases and encourage more careful examination.

V

It is obvious that some of the entities discussed above, which are characterized by value, are in contrast with entities which are their *opposites*: for example, true-*false*; morally good-*morally evil*; beautiful-*ugly*; pleasure-*pain*. False, morally evil, ugly, pain, are characterized by what is sometimes termed "negative value", or "disvalue". These terms are open to various objections. For example, "negative value" appears to involve a contradiction: "Value" (something positive) and "negative". As a matter of fact, false, ugly, morally evil, pain, are not characterized by value intrinsically. But they are entities which are very definite, and in this sense positive, that is, entities which are present. The prefix "dis" means either (a) "opposite of", or (b) "absence of". More specificcally "absence of" in this context means either (i) "opposite of" or (ii) "neutral". To be absolutely clear, it seems necessary to use the apparently clumsy locution: "value-opposite". As in the case of value, so likewise with value-opposite—this entity is not the same as another entity nor is it, in its essential nature, generated by some other entity. Specifically, for example, value-opposite is not identical with pain. It is not generated by aversion.

Let us now consider briefly the six modes of presence of the entity: value-opposite:

(1) In examining false, ugly, morally evil, pain—it is found that they are characterized, as such, by *value-opposite*, i.e., in the intrinsic mode.

(2) There are entities which have the characteristic value-opposite, because they are *instruments*, or function as *causes*—in preventing or interfering with, the attainment of an end, or retention of, an entity. Further, there are entities which have the status of *conditions* relevant[12] to entities, which prevent, etc. the occurrence or retention, of entities. All such means-entities are characterized by value-opposite, for these "reasons". For example (a) a finger is used for tapping on a table, in a situation, and so serves as an instrument to prevent concentration by a person who is trying to study. The finger will thus be characterized by value-opposite with reference to the end: study with concentration; (b) a stick when jabbed in a person's stomach causes him to recoil and hence interfere with his forward motion; (c) the table is a condition in the situation involving a person tapping with his finger and hence disturbing the individual who is attempting to concentrate.

It was pointed out earlier that any entity, in any situation, has value as an ingredient. There is no parallel value-opposite characteristic involving ingredients. However, as will be noted later (see Chap. 5 p. 126) an entity which is an ingredient, in some cases derives value-opposite because of the value-opposite characteristics of an organic whole in which it is an ingredient. This derivation is in the consequence mode.

A careful examination of those entities reported to be characterized by value-opposite indicates that ultimately their preventing or interfering function is facilitating something. In other words, involved here are also cases of: "value when means". A more clear-cut and unambiguous case of "value-opposite" on the basis of preventing—the opposite of means value—would be situations where there is absence of entities which function as instrument, cause, ingredient or condition, in specific contexts.

(3) An entity which has characteristics which have the characteristic value-opposite, itself has the characteristic value-opposite on that basis, in most cases.[13] For example, a person whose behaviour is characterized

11

by morally evil will be characterized by value-opposite because that is the characteristic of his characteristic, namely morally evil.

(4) Value-opposite accrues to an entity in some cases[14] because of the value-opposite characteristic of its external consequences. For example, an item of food which results in poison engendered pain to a large number of people, has value-opposite accruing to it.

(5) Some entities are characterized by value-opposite in the possible mode. Thus, a stick is so characterized when it is not being used, because it is such that it can be used, for example, to push into someone's stomach and hence retard his progress towards some goal, and cause pain.

(6) There are some entities which are characterized by value-opposite in the potential mode. For example, a child of very bad heredity, brought up in an extremely poor environment, is potentially a mal-adjusted person or even a criminal and, on this basis is characterized by value-opposite in the potential mode.

It is very important to realize not only that the entity value, but also the entity value-opposite, its neither supernatural or non-natural. Each is part of the "world" which is open to human awareness—found, not created, or postulated, imaginatively.

Value and value-opposite are neither characterized by physical, mental or concept or physically based resultants.[15] However, in some cases, but not all, value and value-opposite are characteristic of entities which are characterized by physical or mental, etc.

The term "importance" is sometimes used as a synonym for "value". It is not employed in this fashion here because it covers both what is here termed "value" and also "value-opposite".

The question arises as to whether or not any *entity*, (i.e., any particular occurrence of a many occurrence entity, or a uniquely particular entity) is neither characterized by value or by value-opposite. The answer is: since any entity is an ingredient in some situation, thus every entity is on this basis characterized by value. It is well to note further, for example, that some entities are neither true or false and hence have neither value nor value-opposite in the context of this issue. Consider a fairy story. Also some entities do not have as consequence either pleasure or pain. Thus they are neither value or value-opposite with reference to the consequence mode in this context. Concerning instrumental and causal functions, some entities are neither in some situations, and on occasion are either valuable or value-opposite in others.[16] On the basis of such facts, the details of "value or value-opposite" can be "spelled out" concerning possible and potential modes. The complexity of detail need not concern us at this point.

VI

A very fundamental matter remains for introductory discussion. It is obvious that particular occurrences of entities differ in amounts of value. Comparisons are made. Some entities derive value in several ways. Hence there is a build-up to a total amount of (sum of) value. The same general state of affairs occurs with reference to value-opposite. Some particular occurrences of an entity are characterized both by value and value-opposite—with the balance falling on one side or the other.

In view of all these factors the problem arises as to *procedure* in: distinguishing varying amounts of value; comparing amounts of value; totalling amounts of value,—and likewise with reference to amounts of value-opposite. There is also the problem as to procedure in determining where the balance falls in cases where an entity is characterized by both value and value-opposite. One can deal with, for example, amounts of time, space, heat in terms of exact units of mathematical measurement. Exact mathematical statements of comparison can be made. For example, the distance from London, Ontario to Toronto is 120 miles. The distance from London to Sarnia is 60 miles—one half the first distance. On the other hand value does not lend itself to this exact mathematical treatment. Albert Schweitzer is more valuable than the pen which I am using in writing this statement—much more valuable—but an exact amount of value in numerical terms cannot be assigned either to the pen or to Schweitzer. Nor can one specify, with any claim to accuracy, that Schweitzer is, for example, 10001 times more valuable than my pen. To repeat, the entity value does not lend itself to the sort of measurement technique which is appropriate with reference to such entities as time, length, heat, etc.

In passing, it is relevant to note that value is not unique in this regard. Pleasure and interest are not such that one can set up a standard unit of measurement and apply it in strict mathematical fashion. The pleasure derived from eating an apple is less in value than that derived by a scientist in solving a complex research problem. This is clear enough.

But it is silly to claim that the first is accurately measured, for example, as 5 units of pleasure and the latter by 5000 hence is 1000 times more valuable. It is indeed the case that some devotees of mathematics claim that something approximating exact measurement is possible here. By reference to energy output and its duration one can, so it is claimed, set up exact mathematical measurement and comparison. This, however, has been shown to be a naive and erroneous oversimplification. Some very intense interests do not issue in energy output nor do they last long.

It must be emphasized that the absence of exact mathematical measurement with reference to value does not doom one to fumbling subjectivity and relativity, in dealing with the amount of value possessed by an entity, and in comparing amounts of value. As far as comprehensive experience is concerned: Schweitzer is found to be more vulnerable than my pen. This is an objective fact.

More specifically, a person who proceeds with care finds much more value characterizing Schweitzer than the pen. Thus this sort of comparison is regularly made with reference to numerous pairs of entities. One is found to have more value than the other. An exact mathematical technique is not required—even if it were possible—in order to make the comparison—nor indeed is any other less exact set of symbols and calculation technique. As a matter of fact, one can note the result of a process of totalling, i.e., coming together of several occurrences of value without engaging in mathematical (or other symbol) calculations. It is simply a case of: having observed, or been informed about, the joint presence of several individual occurrences of value, one becomes aware of the total value in the situation. In like fashion, one can strike a balance between amount of value and amount of value-opposite—i.e., discover on which side evaluation falls—here again without benefit of symbols and calculation techniques.

There is no mystery or scandal involved in these non-mathematical, or non-symbolic, approaches to the comparison etc. of amounts of value. What is reported here is the way things are in the realm of value. It is, of course, the case that the results of the non-symbolic process of comparison, totalling and striking a balance, are expressed in verbal symbols.

It is well to note that having compared the value of a large number of pairs of entities, one becomes increasingly aware of a hierarchical series. For example if A has less value than B and B has less value than C, the series running from minimum to maximum (in that series) is A, B, C. In

14

the context of a specific series of entities—for example the very complex one comprising the world—one is in a position to distinguish groups of entities which have slight value, those which have considerable value, those which have great value. It must be noted that there are variations of degree within each of these ranges of value (slight, considerable, great).

The subsequent discussion will serve to substantiate the immediately preceding remarks concerning comparison of amounts of value and related matters.

The pattern of comments concerning amounts of value can be paralleled with reference to value-opposite. However this seems unnecessary at this point.

SECTION TWO

INTRINSICALLY

CHAPTER 2

Simple Entities Which Are Intrinsically Valuable or Value-Opposite

I

The more detailed discussion of *modes of presence* of value and value-opposite, will begin with an examination of a number of entities which are valuable, or value-opposite, intrinsically.[1] This will serve to illustrate the status of: being intrinsically valuable or value-opposite. It will also clarify the nature of entities which are so characterized. This procedure is appropriate and necessary because, in many cases, extrinsic modes of presence of value and value-opposite involve such entities. For example, a picture which produces pleasure in a certain context, derives value extrinsically because of its intrinsically valuable consequences. Likewise food derives value-opposite from the pain it produces.

It will be recalled that entities are either simple or complex.

In this chapter attention will be focused on simple entities which are intrinsically valuable, or value-opposite. Since the same general pattern of analysis applies to both valuable and value-opposite simple entities, only valuable entities will receive detailed treatment.

It will be pointed out briefly, and avoiding unnecessary repetition, that these simple entities, as such, are neither identical with other entities nor are they derived from other entities. In view of the preceding discussion of the nature of value (Chapter I, pp. 8-10) it is not necessary to repeat the

19

argument that value which characterizes entities is not, as such, identical with another entity or derived from another entity. While this chapter shows that value characterizes some entities intrinsically, in section 4 it will be pointed out that some occurrences of these entities are also characterized by value in other modes.

II

(A) Prominent among simple entities which are valuable intrinsically is the entity: *beautiful*. Let us examine the nature of beautiful in the context of a particular occurrence.

Consider an object with specific color and shape and a specific arrangement of parts, for example, the fact of Miss Universe. It is characterized by: beautiful. The *presence* of beautiful depends on the entities which it characterizes. But they are not ingredients which constitute the *nature* of: beautiful. As far as comprehensive experience is concerned, beautiful is a simple entity. Hence it has no parts; nor is there sound evidence that such entities generate beautiful, in any sense. Equally erroneous is an attempt to equate beautiful with (or account for it, in terms of): object of desire, source of pleasure, what arouses aesthetic experience—and so on. An attempt to claim that different entities are the same, that is, identical, is simply to "fly in the face of facts." [2] In the context of comprehensive experience, on what other basis than the discovered presence, or absence, of the entity beautiful, can one legitimately report that one pattern of arrangement of specific entities is beautiful and another arrangement of specific entities is not beautiful? There is no external criterion, that is, something else in terms of which beautiful can be identified—the something else being either a repeated identical, or always accompanying, entity. One can, however, provide examples of entities which are characterized by beautiful.

Beautiful characterizes not only complex entities, such as the face of Miss Universe—but also simple entities, for example, some occurrences of green. It is important to note that the *pattern* of arrangement of Miss Universe's features, as such, is beautiful, so is the colour of her eyes.

The beauty of the complex entity her face, is not simply the sum of the beauty of its component ingredients. It is obvious that there are variations in degrees or amounts of, beauty. For example the face of Miss Universe is more beautiful than the green of her eyes. Corresponding to degree of beautiful there are degrees of value.

The fact that the entity beautiful is intrinsically valuable becomes obvious when one notes that quite apart from value derived from (i) a means function, (ii) characteristics other than value, (iii) consequences, (iv) possibilities—beautiful is characterized by value. Consider again the beauty of Miss Universe's face.

Careful examination reveals that even though the beauty of her face has a causal function (is valuable as means) and produces pleasure (a valuable consequence) and derives value on that basis, and has the possibility of more of the same—is valuable in these modes—these modes of value can be seen to be in addition to, the value of beautiful as such.[3] This becomes clear by contrast, when one considers the various modes in which a pen is valuable in the maximum case. It is valuable in all the relevant extrinsic modes but lacks one mode of value which is possessed by beautiful.

(B) *Pleasure*, like beautiful, does not have ingredients which constitute it. It is characteristic of a mind. Indeed, it is a mental entity.[4] Without a mind functioning in reaction to a stimulus, pleasure can not exist. There are certain sorts of situations which normally arouse a mind to generate pleasure. Nevertheless these entities are not ingredients of pleasure. They do not generate its nature, nor are they identical with it. The same is true of individual entities.

The same line of argument as in the case of beautiful above, i.e., demonstration by reference to relevant facts, can be used to show that pleasure is intrinsically valuable. But it need not be repeated here. The same comment applies to the other simple entities to be considered subsequently. Ultimately it is a case of being aware of the value of an entity as such, apart from its relations and related entities.

(C) Some mental images, or concepts, or propositions which function as reports concerning other entities—have the characteristic, *true* (accurate). The entity true is not always a characteristic of such entities when in the reporting relation to other entities. It is to be noted that the nature and characteristics of the entities reported determine whether or not a particular image, concept or proposition, which functions in the reporting relation, has, or does not have, the characteristic: true. Despite the fact that true is a characteristic of entities, as discussed above, these entities are not ingredient components of true. The entity true has no parts. Further, though the other entities, concerning which reports are made,

21

determine whether or not reporting entities are true, these facts are not ingredient components of true. In brief, true is neither the image, concept or proposition, or the reporting relation—nor the entities to which reference is made. Nor is it the sum of all of these. It is an *additional*[5] entity which characterizes the proposition, concept or image in the specified complex situation. Likewise its nature is not constituted by relations other than reporting accurately.[6]

Unlike beautiful and pleasure, there are no degrees of truth. For example, Miss Universe is more beautiful than Miss Skunk Hollow,—unless Miss Skunk Hollow *is* Miss Universe. Any true proposition is completely true, or not true at all. The phrase, "partial truth" does not imply a refutation of what has just been reported. In a complex situation, if there are accurate reports concerning some ingredients, and inaccurate, or no, reports concerning others—this is a case of lack of full coverage of all ingredients by a series of true (accurate) statements. In other words, some true statements concerning the structure are not available. There may, of course, be an increase in the number of true reports concerning the numerous ingredients of a complex situation. There are also ideas, etc. which have the status: "approximation to true". For example, the proposition "Mr. X is six feet tall" is an approximation to true if he is actually six feet three.

Incidentally, there are two senses in which there may be an increase in the amount of some entities such as those under discussion. There can be (i) an increase in degree (already discussed) or (ii) an increase in the number of occurrences of the entity. There is more of the entity beautiful in a situation composed of all the candidates for the Miss Universe title than where the victorious candidate is present alone.

(D) In the context of a specific situation some entities, for example concepts, emotions, overt actions—are characterized by: *fitting* (appropriate) in the sense that they meet the requirements of that situation, or measure up to a standard. Here again, as in the case of true, one is dealing with the characteristic of entities in the context of a relation to other entities. The requirements of an "environment", either natural or conventional, determine whether or not the specific concepts, emotions, actions which take place—or may take place) in relation to the situation—are characterized by fitting. It follows that an entity which is fitting in one situation will not be so characterized in another. For example, tackling a person in the context of one sort of a football game is fitting—

22

doing the same thing to a perfect stranger under normal conditions while walking on a street, is not.

It should be obvious, in view of the preceding discussion, that the concepts, emotions, actions (and situations) are not component ingredients of: fitting. Rather they are the entities which have the characteristic: fitting. It as such has no parts, and cannot be accounted for in terms of anything else.[7]

(E) A discussion of the entity *efficient* involves reiterating some of the same general points as in the discussion of fitting. It may seem that "fitting" and "efficient" are terms referring to the same entity. However, it should be noted that a person may be performing an action (in a situation) which is appropriate (fitting) but is not performing it efficiently. Further, the entity *efficient* "shows" variations in degree; *fitting* does not.[8]

There are other simple entities which are intrinsically valuable, namely (F) *consistent* and (G) *harmonious*. Both occur in the context of natural or conventional relations between two or more entities. As in the case of the other simple intrinsically valuable entities so far considered, these are not constituted by the entities and relations which they characterize, nor is their nature derived from or identical with any one of them. It must be stressed that there are no variations in degree of consistent and harmonious.

It may appear that consistent and harmonious are actually not two different entities but only one. Yet it should be obvious that a person's behaviour may be characterized by consistent without being characterized by harmonious. It may appear that both consistent and harmonious are included in: true. Is it not the case that when propositions are true they are also, in at least a sense, consistent and harmonious with the facts they report? However, fundamentally, harmony is present when the components of a situation are in a specific kind of mutually interacting patterned relation, while true is essentially a case of accurate report. Consistent characterizes a situation where one and the same principle is operative, in several cases. This is a different state of affairs from accurate reports, as such. A series of lies may be consistent and harmonious.

It is important to stress that consistency is essentially a matter of having the same pattern of procedure *in a specific situation*. Thus a person who always pays his bills behaves in a consistent fashion. However, a person who plays bridge while in a relaxation situation, and works hard at accountancy while in an employment one, is not inconsistent on the ground that in the latter he works and in the former he plays.

It will have been noted that "order" has not been mentioned as an entity which is intrinsically valuable. However, it should be obvious that fitting, consistent, harmonious involve order. However, some cases of order, for example causal sequences, are not valuable intrinsically.

Taking issue with some of the preceding reports, it may be contended that there *are* degrees of consistent, harmonious and fitting. However, on closer examination, it becomes clear that apparent support for these objections turn out to be a misinterpretation of what is actually the case. A person's behaviour (various behaviour entities) may be in some cases characterized by consistent or harmonious or fitting—in other cases not. Thus there are different percentages of occurrences of consistent or harmonious or fitting behaviour, but actually not degrees of them. When a particular behaviour entity is consistent it is consistent, when it is not it is not—likewise with reference to harmonious and fitting. There are, of course, degrees of approximation to consistent or harmonious or fitting. Further, for example, it is the case that in some situations, when harmony occurs, the situation is relatively simple—thus harmony is simple. In other cases it is the characteristic of a complex situation. The difference is not in degree of harmony but in degree of complexity of the situation.

(H) There remains for discussion a very important simple entity which is characterized by value intrinsically—namely *morally good*.

As in the case of beautiful, and "the others"—morally good is not identical with, or generated by, the entities which it characterizes. It is the characteristic of certain sorts of behaviour entities. There are degrees of morally good. All these matters will be discussed in Chapter 4.

III

It is relevant, at this point, to attempt to arrange the simple entities so far considered, in a scale of relative amounts of value, considering only the *intrinsic* mode. Thus for the time being discussion will "set aside" the fact that some entities, which are intrinsically valuable, also, on occasion (i.e., some particular occurrences of them) have values in other modes,—for example, when means or because of consequences. All

24

these complexities will be considered later after the nature of extrinsic value has been examined. Specifically, here initially we will be concerned only with the relative degree of intrinsic value of the following entities: morally good, beautiful, pleasure, true, fitting, efficient, consistent, harmonious. This is a significant issue for various reasons which will become evident as discussion proceeds.

It has been noted, in the preceding examination, that no ultimate bases for the identification of value are available, apart from the *experience* of value, in the context of comprehensive experience. The situation is the same with reference to amount of value. The following report is offered in this context.

It is important to be reminded, by way of background that there are different degrees of morally good, of beautiful, of pleasure. Hence there are corresponding differences in amount of value. In general, any occurrence of morally good has a higher degree of intrinsic value[9] than any occurrence of pleasure. In attempting to compare occurrences of morally good and beautiful no such "any occurrence" generalization is possible, as to the relative value status of those two entities in relation to each other; likewise beautiful and pleasure.

In order to clarify these comments, let us consider particular occurrences of the entities morally good, beautiful, pleasure, that is occurrences of these entities as they characterize particular occurrences of specific entities. This is done in order to indicate the relative degree of the intrinsic value of the characteristic entities under consideration.

An occurrence of morally good, as characterizing a particular occurrence of intense sympathy or concern for the welfare of others, love of a fellow man[10] is more valuable, for example, than the beauty of any face or any coin or any cathedral, or any landscape, or the pleasure derived from solving scientific problems or eating chocolates.

However morally good as characterizing occurrences of routine cooperation with friends or reciprocation of benefit has less value than the beauty of a great cathedral or the glory of a setting sun. Further, the beauty of an occurrence of love of a fellow man is equal in value to the morally good characteristics of such behaviour. However, the morally good characteristics of cooperation and reciprocation with reference to friends is superior in intrinsic value to that of any occurrence of pleasure. But the intense pleasure of high grade intellectual achievement is superior to the slight beauty of a mass produced gadget. But intense beauty is superior to slight pleasure.

Let us consider next the relative status of true with reference to morally good, beautiful, pleasure. It will be recalled that only true (among this group of four entities) does not have variation in degrees. Careful examination indicates that all cases of true are superior to all occurrences of pleasure. All cases of morally good are superior to all occurrences of true. The comparative relation of beautiful and true is more complex. It is this: A high degree of beautiful is superior in intrinsic value to true. However, a low degree of beautiful is inferior in status to true.

Turning to a consideration of other entities which are valuable intrinsically: it is very important to recall that while there are *no* degrees of the entities: fitting, consistent, harmonious, there are degrees of: efficient. These entities fall below morally good, a high degree of beautiful, and true in the following descending order (i.e., an occurrence of them): harmonious, a high degree of efficiency, consistent, fitting. A low degree of efficiency is at the bottom of the hierarchy, except in cases of a slight degree of beautiful.

Pleasure remains for further explanatory comment. Its status with reference to morally good, true and beautiful has already been discussed. It is now to be noted that a high degree of pleasure is superior to harmonious, efficient, consistent, appropriate. A low degree is inferior.

The process of ranking has been supported, in a few cases, by illustrations. Space does not permit a complete set covering all cases of these entities. It will perhaps be useful, in general, to consider a person characterized by the eight entities under consideration. This will, in the context of comprehensive experience, bring into focus their relative value. This scale of ranking, here outlined, is of course only a rough sketch. The distinction between intensive (high degree) and slight, is a very rough one. Borderline cases must be examined on an individual basis.

IV

It is found that as a matter of fact the entities: morally evil, ugly, pain, false, inappropriate, inefficient, inconsistent, discordant, are simple, i.e., they do not have component parts. However in many instances they do characterize complex entities. In such cases, they are not constituted by what they characterize, or by any relations or consequences.

What has been reported, in general, about simple entities which are valuable intrinsically, applies also to their corresponding opposite simple entities which are characterized by value-opposite, intrinsically. A repetition of detailed discussion is not necessary here. However, it is well to stress that the same general hierarchical pattern of relative status—is found in the case of morally evil, ugly, etc.—as with reference to morally good, beautiful, etc.

Any occurrence of morally evil, or "very ugly", or false has a higher degree of intrinsic value-opposite (i.e., is worse) than any occurrence of pain. In comparing occurrences of morally evil and ugly, no simple formula is available. For example, an occurrence of hatred of a fellow man is worse than the most ugly slum, or face, or garbage dump. However, the ugliness of such slum or face may be more value-opposite than the morally evil of some cases of non-cooperation or non-reciprocation. Any occurrence of morally evil is worse than any occurrence of false. Any occurrence of false is worse than a low degree of ugliness but has less intrinsic value-opposite than a high degree of ugliness. Below morally evil, "very ugly," and false in descending order of degree of intrinsic value-opposite are discordant, a high degree of inefficiency, inconsistent, inappropriate and a low (slight) degree of inefficient.

A high degree of (i.e., profound)[11] pain is worse than any degree of discord, inefficient, inconsistent, inappropriate. However, a low degree of pain is less intrinsically-value-opposite than the four entities.

CHAPTER 3

Complex Entities Which Are Intrinsically Valuable or Value-Opposite

In this chapter, *complex* entities which are intrinsically valuable, or intrinsically value-opposite, will be examined. As in the case of intrinsically valuable, or value-opposite, *simple* entities,—the question of extrinsic modes of value, or value-opposite, will be set aside for later discussion in Section 4.

As in the preceding chapter, attention will be focussed on entities which are characterized by *value* intrinsically. This is appropriate since the pattern of analysis is roughly the same for both intrinsically valuable and intrinsically *value-opposite* complex entities.

I

As background, it is essential to note that there are three main sorts of complex entities: (1) *organic whole*,[1] (2) *aggregation*, (3) those which are here termed "*operational resultant*".[2]

Complex entities have as distinguishable constituent ingredients: (i) components, (ii) relations of components.

(1) Organic wholes are complex entities which, because of the nature

28

of their components and the nature of the relations of their components—
have a genuine unity.

(2) In the case of *aggregations*, the nature of components is not an
essential factor. Any two or more entities may be the components of an
aggregation. Further, and fundamentally, the nature of the relation factors is such that there is no unity.

Let us consider physical examples. (1) A table is an organic whole. It is
composed of "legs" and a "top",[3] in a specific pattern of arrangement.
There is a distinctive unity of these ingredients. Its ingredients (component parts and the distinctive relations of the parts) of course involve
space and time. The table is a distinguishable entity which is the result of
the presence of its so-called components when they are in a specific
pattern of relationship. There is more in this situation than just various
shaped pieces of wood and a specific pattern of relation. The table is
typical of a sort of organic whole which may conveniently be termed a
"novel result". (2) The "legs" and the "top" "lying about" in a
carpenter's shop, before they are assembled, are a case of aggregation.
They are together in space and time, but they now lack the specific pattern
of arrangement which is involved in a table.[4]

(1) A pile of bricks, stacked neatly to form a cube is another case of a
physical organic whole of the novel result sort. On the other hand, (2)
merely dumping the bricks on the ground by tilting a truck body produces
an aggregation.

A more complex situation involving physical objects and other factors
as well, is the following: (2) When furniture is merely placed in a room by
movers in order to unload their van, this is very likely to be a case of
aggregation. (1) However, if the furniture is carefully arranged in the
room in accordance with aesthetic principles, an organic unity results.

The most obvious example of an organic whole of the novel result sort
is the human body—indeed any animal body. Here the components are in
very complex unified interrelation and pattern of relation. On the other
hand a severed arm lying beside its original possessor, constitutes an
aggregation on the basis of mere togetherness.

When a number of persons are working together as a unit for some
common cause, they constitute a society which is also the novel result
sort of organic whole. Consider for example a committee, a fraternal
society, a church, a business, a school institution. On the other hand, a

group of people sitting in a park, each "minding his own private business", constitutes an aggregation.

Examine next another sort of organic unity. It may be conveniently termed "reaction sequence". Consider: awareness of a table, pleasure when confronted by morally good behaviour. In each case, there is a distinct, unified, behaviour entity. The component entities are linked together by the relation of reaction. It is essential to note that this sort of organic whole differs crucially from the novel result sort. We have before us now components, for example, pleasure and morally good behaviour, in a reaction sequence—this is what the organic whole is—this and nothing more. On the other hand the bits of wood and their relations (in the case of the table) results in a new distinguishable entity which is an organic whole. The organic entity table is not the mere togetherness of components and relations. But this *is* all there is in the case of the reaction sequence sort of organic whole.

By way of contrast, the mere presence of a vague undirected feeling of malaise and random imagination image of a blue elephant together in time and, roughly speaking, mental space, constitute a group of mental entities which is an aggregation. It must be admitted that both of these cases involves an organic whole since there is awareness of the feeling or the imagination image. Nevertheless these entities, of which one is aware, constitute together an aggregation—not an organic whole, not one unified entity. It is to be noted that a *causal* sequence involving two physical entities, or two mental entities or one of each, is a case of an organic whole. This has the same general nature as the reaction sequences discussed above. The mere presence of otherwise unrelated entities of these sorts, would constitute an aggregation.

Many entities are components of a meaning relation situation. Here again, as in the case of reaction and causal sequences, the organic whole is the components in a specific relation.

Consider (i) concepts and (ii) entities such as relation, pattern, green, morally good, beautiful, etc. which, as such, are neither physical or mental, or concepts. Of course, these entities have membership in both organic wholes and aggregations without reference to space and time.

Two very important facts remain to be emphasized. Organic wholes frequently have very significant characteristics which their ingredient entities do not have. For example, a table may be beautiful but none of its components are so characterized. Awareness of pain is characterized by

30

value intrinsically[5] but neither awareness nor pain are so characterized. Also very significant is the fact that (for example) pleasure in morally good behaviour is characterized by value intrinsically but to a lesser degree than the sum of the value of its ingredients.[6]

In general some complex entities, which are organic wholes, are characterized by value-opposite intrinsically, others by value intrinsically. The constituent entities are in some cases characterized by either value or value-opposite intrinsically, or both (i.e., different entities), or neither. While these factors have a bearing on the intrinsic value, or value-opposite characteristics of the organic whole, the intrinsic value, or value-opposite of the organic whole is not constituted by the sum of, or "on balance", value or value-opposite characteristics of those constituent entities. In the causal situation "loud noise making a person jump"—the organic whole does not have either intrinsic value or value-opposite. The organic whole "chocolates giving nourishment" is a similar case.

The value of a mere group, that is aggregation, of entities, is the sum of the value characteristics of its ingredients, or in cases where value-opposite is present—the on-balance result.

II

We turn now to an examination of organic wholes of the reaction sort which are characterized by value intrinsically. There is a very large group of organic wholes, in that class which can be referred to simply as: "awareness of X". Hence quite literally X stands for any entity. It is here reported that "awareness of wood" is an organic whole which is valuable intrinsically. So likewise is "awareness of green" and "awareness of mud". Each of these organic wholes is a many-occurrence entity. Thus, for example, each par icular awareness of each particular occurrence of mud is intrinsically valuable.

It should be obvious that in discussing a complex entity of the "awareness of X" sort, we are concerned with cases of one sort of knowledge (in the broad sense) namely: the activity of knowing and the entity known. In brief, it is here reported that knowledge is intrinsically valuable. It must be stressed that only one sort of knowledge is here under discussion, namely so-called: immediate.

31

The preceding remarks require considerable clarificatory explanation. In general, it is being pointed out that "awareness of any ingredient of the world" is characterized by value intrinsically. Particular occurrences of organic wholes so described vary in amount of intrinsic value depending on the nature[7] and status of the entities of which one is aware and hence the level of achievement involved in being aware of them. The mere awareness of the entity mud has far less intrinsic value than awareness of the entity mud plus a number of propositions indicating the various uses of mud, its composition and so on. Likewise, the awareness of Einstein's Relativity Theory formula is an organic whole of far greater intrinsic value than the other organic wholes previously mentioned. A discussion of the value of all these entities will not be introduced here because it involves the later detailed discussion of value in the extrinsic mode. Neither mind, green, wood nor Einstein's formula are valuable intrinsically.

We turn now to cases of "X" which are intrinsically valuable.

Consider the following complex entities of the organic sort:

(i) Awareness of the entity: morally good[8]

(ii) Awareness of the entity: true[8]

(iii) Awareness of the entity: beautiful[8]

(These of course involve awareness of entities characterized by morally good, true, beautiful.)

Each of these intrinsically valuable complex entities has a lower degree of value intrinsically than morally good or true, or beautiful, as such. This may seem strange in view of the fact that, for example, morally good is an ingredient of the organic whole: awareness of morally good. However, being aware of morally good is not the same as being a particular occurrence of morally good. The basic issue here is the value of the reaction: awareness, with respect to the entity morally good. What is reported concerning awareness of morally good, beautiful, true is also so with reference to fitting, efficient, consistent, harmonious. The state of affairs is different in the case of awareness of pleasure, because pleasure only occurs in the context of awareness. The other entities are not thus "awareness linked" as such.

It is relevant to emphasize that awareness of the entities: morally evil, false, ugly, inappropriate, inefficient, inconsistent, discordant—in each case, is an intrinsically valuable organic whole. They are characterized by value intrinsically despite the intrinsic value-opposite characteristic of the object of awareness.

The amount of value intrinsically, of each of these organic wholes: awareness of morally good, awareness of pleasure, awareness of beautiful and so on, depends on the amount of value of the object of awareness. Hence "awareness of morally good" has a larger amount of value intrinsically than "awareness of true" or, in most cases, "awareness of beautiful" (see discussion Chapter 2 pp. 24-26). Involved here is the fact that, for example, in some cases intrinsically valuable simple entities differ in degree of (amount of) value. There are degrees of efficient, beautiful and of morally good. Hence particular occurrences of awareness of efficient or beautiful or morally good will differ in amounts of value. There are no degrees of differences in true, consistency, fitting, harmonious. As noted previously, the degree of difficulty in achieving awareness of an entity has a bearing on the value of the organic whole. It is, for example, more difficult to be aware of morally good than of some occurrences of beautiful.

In cases where the "object" of awareness is intrinsically value-opposite such organic wholes have less intrinsic value than any organic whole which has an intrinsically valuable entity as focus of awareness. Indeed this is the case when the object of awareness is characterized by value-opposite in modes other than intrinsic.

III

At this point it is advisable to consider a distinction between what may be termed "acceptable" and what may be termed "unacceptable" entities which are intrinsically valuable.

This has an important bearing on the forthcoming discussion of reaction sequence organic wholes. It also brings into focus factors which are relevant to subsequent discussion of other organic wholes. Further the acceptable-unacceptable characteristic is crucial in considering the position of extrinsic value and value-opposite. The point at issue is this: *The occurrence of* some simple entities, and the occurrence of some organic wholes—which are *intrinsically valuable —in certain specific contexts*, is characterized by value-opposite intrinsically.

Consider (a) the case of the reaction "pleasure" to an instance of human ugliness—in the context of the behaviour of a snobbish, beautiful, person. Likewise (b) examine the occurrence of honesty in replying to a request for information, concerning the location of the intended victim of a lynching party—and the resultant pain. Next (c) consider efficiency in "hatred of a fellow man" behaviour. In each of these cases, the *occurrence of* intrinsically valuable entities, namely pleasure, honesty, efficiency, is essentially linked with—is subordinate to—the occurrence of entities intrinsically value-opposite.[10] The *occurrence of* the intrinsically valuable entities in these contexts is characterized by value-opposite intrinsically. Therefore (i) these entities, in these particular occurrences, and (ii) their intrinsic value, in these cases, may be conveniently termed "unacceptable". Hence there are what may be termed (i) "unacceptable entities" and (ii) "unacceptable value".

The variety of contexts in which unacceptable entities occur is illustrated by the fact that (a) pleasure is an affective reaction component (ingredient) of an intrinsically value-opposite organic whole, (b) honesty is an instrument which is involved in a value-opposite effect and is likewise a component (ingredient) of an intrinsically value-opposite organic whole. (c) Efficiency is a characteristic of an intrinsically value-opposite entity which is an organic whole.

(d) Consider also the case of a ruthless, selfish, fame-seeking dictator who causes to be built a beautiful cathedral. Vast amounts of human misery are involved in its construction. In view of this misery, the occurrence of the entity beautiful is rendered unacceptable. So is its value. It is well to note that if a painter with the same motivation produces a beautiful landscape, but no great misery is involved in the process—the occurrence of the entity beautiful (and its value) in this case is not unacceptable.

The point at issue here is not the nature of the motive, but whether the "price to be paid" for the occurrence of a valuable entity, and hence its value—is open to decisive objection. Speaking technically, the occurrence of beautiful in the case of the cathedral, at the expense of so much misery, is characterized by value-opposite intrinsically, and hence is termed "unacceptable".[11]

It is well to realize that the price paid, in terms of painful drudgery, occurs not only during the building of the cathedral—as the result of forced labour. There may be a process of "payment" spread over several generations.[12] Consider also the misery resulting from the denial of opportunities for the enjoyment of a wide range of values, because all the resources of the community are directed to paying for the building. Indeed the price paid is not just physical and mental suffering. Other value-opposite forms of human behaviour may be part of the price—dishonesty, hatred of fellow men, and so on.

(e) There remains for examination another sort of unacceptable occurrence of an intrinsically valuable entity—hence unacceptable value. Consider the case of *pleasure* when confronted by the *unacceptable presence* of some intrinsically valuable entity. For example: a person feels pleasure when contemplating the unacceptable beauty of a cathedral. Or consider pleasure in the unacceptable honesty of a man who gives information in the lynching situation, or efficiency in a murder context. Such occurrences of pleasure are intrinsically value-opposite and hence unacceptable. So is the value of pleasure.

It may be the case that with the passage of time, the beauty of the cathedral may no longer involve misery, or any other decisive value-opposite factor. Beautiful in this case is no longer unacceptable.

In order to clear up possible misunderstandings, resulting from illustrations (a) and (b),[13] it is essential to stress that some intrinsically valuable ingredients of an intrinsically value-opposite organic whole do not have the status: unacceptable. Their *occurrence* in a specific context is not characterized by value-opposite intrinsically.[14] For example, consider a case of beautiful characterizing a sunset, or honesty involved in an ideal family relation—to which there is an affective reaction of pain. Both are organic wholes which are intrinsically value-opposite. However, the occurrences of both beautiful and honesty, in these contexts are not unacceptable. It will perhaps help to understand the point at issue if it is noted that there is no similarity between pleasure in illustration (a) and beautiful in the one just mentioned. Specifically, beautiful is not, like pleasure, an affective reaction—unacceptable in certain contexts. Likewise the entity honesty, in the family context, is not a positive behaviour reaction to an intrinsically valuable-opposite entity. Nor is it used as an instrument for value-opposite consequences. Hence beautiful and honesty, in these contexts, do not fall within the scope of: unacceptable. What is unacceptable is the reaction to them.

It must be re-emphasized that "unacceptable", in the preceding discussion, has been used to refer to the *occurrence*, in a specific context, of (i) an entity, and (ii) its *intrinsic* value. This *occurrence* is characterized by value-opposite intrinsically. This is unacceptable to a person who is concerned to have situations which are characterized by value—not those which are characterized by value-opposite, intrinsically.

There are of course many intrinsically valuable entities whose occurrence is not characterized by value-opposite intrinsically. In this sense these entities, and their values, are *acceptable*.

Subsequent discussion will make clear the fact that, in addition to their apparently paradoxical occurrence as ingredients of intrinsically value-opposite organic wholes, some acceptable entities, and their values, are ingredients in organic wholes which are intrinsically valuable, or characteristics of intrinsically valuable entities—. Consider for example pleasure in morally good, a beautiful sunset or efficiency in love of a fellow man. Further, some such valuable entities, and hence some occurrences of value are ingredients in organic wholes which are neither intrinsically valuable or value-opposite. Also in some instances they are ingredients in aggregations. Some intrinsically valuable entities are characteristics of entities which as such are neither valuable nor value-opposite intrinsically.[15]

To repeat: in the technical sense here used (and it is close to the ordinary use) *"acceptable" value or "acceptable" entity* means: any occurrence of value, or entity, which is free of the characteristic: unacceptable.

It is very important to realize that some entities which are characterized by value-opposite intrinsically—are acceptable, and so is the value-opposite. They may occur, for example, as essential ingredients, in behaviour which has beneficial results. Examine the case of "concern for the welfare of a fellow man" where essentially (i.e., necessarily) the physical exertion on behalf of a fellow man involves pain. Specifically, consider pain related to muscular strain involved in helping someone get his car out of a ditch. Here the occurrence of pain is not characterized by value-opposite intrinsically.

Another very significant case is that of the status of A's sympathetic pain when confronted by B's pain. A's pain is an essential ingredient in the organic whole termed: sympathy. A reaction of this sort, in this context, is acceptable.

So far, for the most part, attention has been focussed on the fact that some occurrences of intrinsically valuable entities are characterized by value-opposite intrinsically. In this sense the entities and their values, in such contexts, are unacceptable.

It is also the case that the same occurrences of some entities which are not intrinsically valuable—are also unacceptable. Consider the case of the cathedral discussed above. Its occurrence involved great misery. Hence the building was (as well as the characteristic beautiful) unacceptable.

Consider next a bomb used for the purpose of committing murder.[16] Because of the bomb's relation to the murder, its instrumental value in this case is unacceptable. That is: the occurrence of value of this sort, in this context, is intrinsically value-opposite.

Of course if instrumental value is a characteristic of an entity used to facilitate an ideal family life—the instrumental value is acceptable.

The preceding reference to the fact that some entities are valuable in extrinsic modes brings into focus a second sense of unacceptable, or acceptable. Entities which are neither intrinsically valuable or value-opposite frequently have some value characteristics and some value-opposite ones (though there are cases of uniformity). On balance such entities are valuable or value-opposite. In this sense entities are either acceptable (valuable on balance) or unacceptable (value-opposite on balance).

IV

Having dealt with the distinction between acceptable and unacceptable entities and values—with this as necessary background,—we now return to the consideration of various sorts of organic wholes.

There are numerous intrinsically valuable organic wholes which have the same general features: Internal Reaction to an entity—involving recognition, in each case, of its intrinsic and/or extrinsic value. Consider for example:

A

Consider: *Positive* internal reaction to an *acceptable* occurrence of beautiful; positive internal reaction to an acceptable valuable book. It must be realized that the entity: "positive internal[17] reaction" involves a large number of sorts—for example: interest in, concern for, approval of, pleasure in. In effect, for example, each of these "directed towards acceptable beautiful" constitutes an intrinsically valuable organic whole.

In addition to the amount of value in particular occurrences of beautiful and book, one must bear in mind the fact that there are different degrees of interest, concern, etc. These factors have an implicit bearing on the amount of intrinsic value of particular occurrences of an organic whole under consideration. Hence determinations of the amount of value of occurrences of positive reaction to beautiful, and positive reaction to book, must be handled on an individual basis. In all events, it will be noted that the amount of value of the organic whole is not the sum of value of the component ingredients, or determined by any sort of mathematical calculation.[18] Incidentally, many objects of positive internal reaction may either be "present before one" or be an object of thought or imagination.

In general, one can state: Positive internal reaction to acceptable valuable entities constitutes an organic whole which is intrinsically valuable. It should be realized that the phrase "positive internal reaction to acceptable entities characterized by value in any mode" does not name a specific organic whole of the sort under consideration. It is a general summary "covering label" referring to a number of entities which have something, as specified, in common.

B

Reaction to an entity may take the form of a negative internal reaction to an unacceptable value-opposite entity, which is recognized to be such. Organic wholes which are cases of this type are valuable intrinsically, despite the fact that some of the ingredients are characterized by value-opposite either intrinsically or extrinsically, on balance.

Consider the following: Dislike of unacceptable ugliness; aversion to unacceptable value-opposite book. Here we have organic wholes which have as ingredient something characterized by value-opposite. The other ingredient is neither characterized by value or value-opposite, as such. If there is, for example: pain in the presence of unacceptable ugliness, both ingredients are value-opposite intrinsically yet the organic whole is characterized by value intrinsically.

The same general set of comments made about determining amount of value of an organic whole concerning positive internal reaction, apply to negative internal reaction. Attention for the most part must be focussed on particular occurrences. Hence one must consider not only the amount of value-opposite of particular occurrences of the object (focus) of

38

reaction, but also degrees of strength of the negative reaction. For example, "intense aversion to unacceptable extreme ugliness is an organic whole which is characterized by a larger amount of value intrinsically than "slight aversion to unacceptable ugliness or "slight aversion to slight "ugliness".

It must be realized that the internal reactions, here under discussion, involve awareness of the presence of an intrinsically value-opposite entity. Hence there is a minor organic whole which is intrinsically valuable—within a major organic whole. Be that as it may, in all cases the intrinsic *value* of the major organic whole is greater in amount than the sum of the values of the ingredients. Indeed value is present "in the face" of: ingredients characterized by value-opposite.

(c) Some cases of intrinsically valuable organic wholes are positive reactions to acceptable entities which are characterized by value-opposite. Consider for example pleasure in the incongruous, i.e., inappropriate in the context of humour. (d) Also intrinsically valuable are negative reactions to unacceptable valuable entities. Consider aversion to *pleasure*, in the unjustified pain of others.

It must be pointed out that (e) when contemplating such simple entities (which are intrinsically valuable) as morally good, beautiful, etc. in complete abstraction from a particular context, a positive reaction to these entities is characterized by value intrinsically. Because the entities to which reaction occurs are intrinsically valuable and free of context, the distinction between acceptable and unacceptable does not arise.[19]

V

The preceding discussion of organic wholes of the "awareness of. . . ." or "positive internal reaction to . . ." sorts requires further clarification. There is a possibility of misunderstanding concerning the value status of these organic wholes.

It has been pointed out that this reaction sequence sort of organic whole has a lower degree of intrinsic value than the sum of the intrinsic value of its ingredients. Consider pleasure in morally good behaviour. It is of course the case that when there is a reaction of pleasure to morally good behaviour there has been an increase in the amount of value in the world.[20] In addition to the value of morally good behaviour there is now the value of pleasure. Pleasure and morally good are ingredients of the organic whole. It may seem plausible to suggest that the value of the organic whole (pleasure in morally good behaviour) should be at least equal to the sum of the value of pleasure and morally good behaviour. However, the organic which is in question is not the novel *result*[21] of its component relation. Rather it is a reaction sequence sort of organic whole. The point at issue is the value of a specific reaction to a specific entity. As a matter of fact it is found to be less than the sum of the value of its components. But to return to the total situation: When morally good is reacted to with pleasure, there is in the world an increase in value on two counts. In addition to the previous value of morally good behaviour, there is now present the value of pleasure and the value of the pleasure reaction to acceptable morally good behaviour. But to repeat the value of the organic whole pleasure reaction to morally good is much less than the value of morally good behaviour and pleasure together.

Incidentally it is interesting to note that the intrinsic value of a pleasure reaction to morally good behaviour is greater than the intrinsic value of pleasure alone.

At this point it is well to note the distinction between (i) intrinsically valuable, or value-opposite, ''as an organic whole'' and (ii) a situation valuable, or value-opposite, ''on the whole''. It has already been pointed out that the intrinsic value, or value-opposite, of an organic whole is not based on simple arithmetic concerning its parts. However, the topic must be put in broader perspective. Consider for example, dislike of unacceptable pain. As an organic whole of experience, this is characterized by intrinsic value. However, examine closely the value-opposite characteristics of pain. If the pain is actual, not just thought of,—in this case, ''on the whole,'' (everything considered)[22], the situation is such that it is a case of value-opposite. Namely the value-opposite characteristic of pain outweighs the value of: dislike of pain.

In the interests of comprehensiveness, it should be stressed that there remain, for discussion, many organic wholes of the novel result sort. These are not only intrinsically valuable. They are also characterized by morally good—which, of course, is intrinsically valuable. The importance of these entities is such that it seems appropriate to accord very extensive treatment to them. This is the content of the next chapter. It will also deal with organic wholes which are not only intrinsically value-opposite but also are characterized by: morally evil.

40

It is pointless here, or elsewhere in this one book, to attempt to go into detail concerning *all* the even more complex organic situations (entities) which are characterized by value intrinsically. However, some representative samples will be considered later in this volume. In any case, it is obvious that as a matter of fact the organic wholes mentioned above, frequently occur together in a highly complex situation.

VI

There remains for discussion at this point, a very complex organic whole which is intrinsically valuable. This is: the situation where each man achieves the highest level of acceptable value (and minimum of unacceptable value-opposite) attainable by him in this world. That is, each person develops his latent potentialities,[23] to the full and makes the best possible use of his abilities[24], in the context of what is available in the environment: physical, social, and cultural. Great care will be taken to ensure the maximum of attainable fruitful, unified and mutual support and balance in all personal, inter-personal and inanimate activities. Thus in this world-wide situation there is the largest attainable amount of intrinsic and extrinsic *acceptable* value (and relevant value-opposite) and a minimum of unacceptable value-opposite (and value), in the case of each entity present.

The qualifying entities "attainable" and "in this world" are crucial. There are in this world natural limitations as to environment and human potentialities and abilities. There are also occurrences of unacceptable value-opposite, and value.

The situation, outlined above,[25] constitutes an organic whole which, as such, is acceptably intrinsically valuable. Its value is greater than any other less inclusive organic whole, or indeed any other entity of this world. In brief, this organic whole is characterized by: the largest amount of acceptable value attainable in this world. The organic whole here under discussion may conveniently be termed: Long-range-ideal situation.

What is being thought about is admittedly a creation of imagination. However, it is based on facts of actual human experience in this world. What is imagined is a case of "more of the same"; for example, more

41

morally good behaviour, more extensive and skilled use of means, for example scientific agriculture. Past and present experience indicate that such developments are geniune possibilities—not mere unsupported flights of speculative fancy. It can not be legitimately denied that there are areas of experience which provide considerable information concerning details of individual human potentialities and abilities, and techniques for improvement. There is also sound information concerning some "measure" of the various natural resources available to men on this planet. Increased information can come from careful investigation. If one can not now specify, in exact detail, what the largest attainable amount of acceptable value in the context of this world would involve—one can certainly indicate, in at least general fashion, and indeed with considerable accuracy, approximately what it would "consist in"—that is, what entities must exist in order that such value be present. Obviously, in order to secure the presence of requisite intrinsically valuable entities—a full range and the largest attainable number of extrinsically valuable entities will be present.

It is important to note a distinction between (A) the complex entity which is characterized by: "the largest attainable amount of acceptable value in this world and (B) the complex entity which is characterized by: "the largest amount of acceptable value attainable in this world *now*." The latter involves the full use of present abilities and environmental resources, and an "all out" attempt to develop latent potentialities and to expand discovery and use of environmental resources of all sorts, including methods of discovery. Here again, controlled imagination is at work.

It has already been suggested that the complex organic whole here termed "A" may conveniently be referred to as "the long-range ideal situation". In this context, a convenient label for organic whole "B" is: "The immediate ideal-situation." Far more limitations in scope are involved in B than in A. For example, lack of suitable conditions[26] restricts range of techniques to be used in solving problems.

The sum of the acceptable value of ingredients of B is less than in the case of A. Also the intrinsic value of the organic whole B is less than that of the organic whole A. It is essential to stress that the organic wholes A and B do not now exist. But, in each case, some of the entities which if it did exist would be among its ingredients—now exist, i.e., particular occurrences do.[27] This is true to a greater extent concerning B.

In the interests of comprehensiveness, it is well to note that there is an entity (C) which is here termed "Best conceivable situation." It involves the largest *conceivable* amount of acceptable value. It, of course, is not restricted by the limitations of this world. As such it is impossible of attainment in this world. It has more value than any other entity. Further, it is important to note that the complex entity which involves the largest conceivable amount of acceptable value does not include holus bolus (in the case of each of its ingredients) the long-range ideal situation, though there are some common ingredients. The same comment applies to the immediate ideal situation.

VII

A

In order to "round out" the preceding discussion of complex entities which are valuable intrinsically, it is necessary to comment on a sort mentioned as (3) at the beginning of this chapter—namely, so called: "operational resultants". Among these are (a) Introduction of acceptable value, (b) removal of unacceptable value-opposite, (c) prevention of unacceptable value-opposite,—and others to be mentioned subsequently.

It is essential to stress that (a), (b), (c) are neither organic wholes nor aggregations. Since distinguishable elements are involved, each is a complex entity—a specific state of affairs which has resulted from a specific operation.

We turn now to a more detailed discussion of the preliminary comments.

(a) When acceptable value has been introduced, that state of affairs is characterized by value intrinsically. It must be stressed that the *process* of introducing an occurrence of value is not intrinsically valuable. What has this status is the *result* of this process. The process itself is valuable in the means mode of the causal sort and because of its consequences (to mention the obvious modes).

It is, of course, obvious that value is a characteristic of some entities, and is present in various modes. Hence the intrinsically valuable state of affairs "there has been introduction of acceptable value" has many occurrences in many contexts.

Consider for example the following cases: (i) to a specific situation an

43

occurrence of acceptable pleasure has been introduced. Pleasure is intrinsically valuable. Hence in this case there has been an introduction of acceptable value; (ii) into a specific situation a book is introduced. It is acceptably valuable, i.e., is valuable on balance—all relevant extrinsic modes having been considered. In this case acceptable value has been introduced into a situation.[28]

At this point, it is well to attempt to avoid possible misunderstanding. It may appear that there is no real difference between, for example (i) a particular occurrence of acceptable pleasure,—which is intrinsically valuable and (ii) a particular occurrence of the intrinsically valuable operational resultant: there has been an *introduction of a* particular occurrence of *acceptable value*, due to the presence (introduction of) acceptable pleasure. However, there is a very important distinction involved. It is the difference between (i) the fact that acceptable pleasure is intrinsically valuable—hence any particular occurrence of pleasure is valuable intrinsically and (ii) it is intrinsically valuable that a particular occurrence of acceptable value has been *introduced into a situation*.

A rather intriguing point must now be brought into focus. In dealing with the "introduction of", i.e., "there has been brought into a situation" state of affairs, it is essential to stress the "acceptable *value*" factor. Strictly speaking, for example, it is not "the fact that there has been an introduction of acceptable pleasure" which is intrinsically valuable. Rather it is the fact that a characteristic of acceptable pleasure, namely acceptable value, has been introduced—which is intrinsically valuable. After all, while value is a characteristic of pleasure—nevertheless pleasure is one entity and value is another. It is the value which is the essential factor in the operational resultant here under consideration.

It is important to realize that the term "introduction of", in both its verb and noun form, does not refer exclusively to a human process, or a human product or content. The case of human generation of pleasure and the human content result—pleasure—is not exclusively typical. Consider the non-human introduction of non-human results. By a purely physical process beautiful may be introduced into a non-human situation. Consider for example the beauty of an autumn hillside. On the other hand by a partly human process, a non-human content result may be introduced and be present. Take the case of a person planting a flower garden.

(b) Value-opposite is the characteristic of many entities in at least one of six modes. Hence the operational resultant entity: "unacceptable value-opposite has been removed" involves in its various occurrences, the removal of many different entities characterized by value-opposite. However, for the moment, one example will suffice. Consider the fact that an unacceptably ugly building has been torn down[29]. Hence the value-opposite character of ugly has disappeared from the scene, because the ugliness has been removed. Thus the intrinsically valuable resultant entity: removal of value-opposite—occurs in this context.

It is to be noted that it is not the *fact* that "the ugly" has been removed, that is intrinsically valuable. To repeat, it is the "no longer present status" of an occurrence of value-opposite which is the crucial factor. Of course the ugliness (of the building) is characterized by value-opposite.

This distinction is rather subtle and perhaps requires further discussion: It is not correct to suggest that the state of affairs "removal of the unacceptable ugly" is a "case of", or "sort of" "removal of value opposite" (a result) and hence is intrinsically valuable on that basis. It is true that the process of tearing down is a "sort of" removing. But the fact that there has been as a result; "the removal of ugly" does not fall into the case of a "sort of" state of affairs "there has been removal of value-opposite." One state of affairs *involves*, but is not a case of, or sort of, the other. The removal of ugly involves the removal of value-opposite. The latter state of affairs is valuable intrinsically. The former has value as means on the basis of its involvement. In brief, ugly is one entity. Value-opposite is another.

It is important to note that there may be removal—not only of actual value-opposite, but also of the possibility of value-opposite. Here, as before, this involves the context of entities of which value-opposite is a possible characteristic. For example, when a person spends a sum of money wisely he has removed the possibility of spending that money unwisely. Hence the possible value-opposite characteristic of possible spending has been removed.

(c) We turn now to the fact that the operational resultant state of affairs: "unacceptable value-opposite, which was about to be present was prevented"—is characterized by value intrinsically. As before, value-opposite is the characteristic of many entities in various modes. Further,—prevention is of various sorts. However, at this point one illustration will suffice: The refusal to allow the construction of an ugly building which is scheduled, and is being supported by strong forces in the

45

community, is a context in which the unacceptable *value-opposite* characteristics of ugliness is prevented from being present.

The same general *analysis* employed in the discussion of removal of value-opposite, applies in the case of prevention of value-opposite. Hence it need not be repeated.[30]

B

The question arises as to: amount of value found in the cases of the three states of affairs just under discussion. Each of (a) introduction of acceptable value, (b) removal of unacceptable value-opposite, (c) prevention of unacceptable value-opposite—is intrinsically valuable. Are all occurrences of (a) or (b) or (c) equal in amount of value? Further, what is the relation, if any, as to comparative amount of value with reference to (a), (b) and (c)? These matters are very complicated.

In most instances, each occurrence of each "many occurrence entity" has a different amount of value than another, despite the fact that each is valuable intrinsically. More specifically: as noted, such an entity occurs in the context of a specific situation. On this basis the amount of value differs. For example the "state of affairs" entity "introduction of acceptable value" occurs in the context of the introduction of acceptable pleasure and of acceptable book. In some cases, the pleasure context of occurrence has more value than the book context. In other cases it is the reverse. In any case, the value of the operational resultant is not identical with the value of what is introduced. It is considerably less.

In general, the amount of value of occurrences of removal of value-opposite is based on (is equal to) the amount of unacceptable value-opposite which is removed.[31] Consider the cases of the removal of pain and the removal of ugliness. For purposes of illustration: ugliness has more value-opposite than does pain in their occurrences in two particular cases. Hence there is a corresponding difference in value in the two occurrences of removal of value-opposite. However the situation may be different in other cases of pain and ugliness.[32]

In view of the preceding comments and illustrations it seems unnecessary to "spell out", in detail, the fact that an occurrence of (a) or (b) or (c) may be superior in value to occurrences of the other two.

C

The general pattern of analysis of (a) introduction of acceptable value, (b) removal of unacceptable value-opposite, (c) prevention of unacceptable value-opposite,—applies also to (d) introduction of acceptable value-opposite, (e) removal of unacceptable value, (f) prevention of unacceptable value. In addition, it is well to realize that the following operational resultant complex entities are intrinsically valuable, (g) the fact that: acceptable value has been continued in existence and (h) acceptable value-opposites have been continued in existence. In view of preceding discussion, it seems unnecessary to provide detailed analyses here.

Two other operational resultants remain for consideration. (i) It is important to note that the state of affairs: "there has been increase in the amount of acceptable value"—is intrinsically valuable. This resultant is not identical with "introduction of acceptable value." This latter complex entity does not necessarily involve literally an addition to the total amount of acceptable value in the world. In the normal course of events, some acceptable value may be "fading out", on balance the total may be less. For example, when there is the introduction of a slightly beautiful painting—a large amount of beauty may, at that time (a coincidence) vanish as a great cathedral collapses in ruin; or the beauty of summer replaces the beauty of winter.

It is to be further realized that the operational resultant state of affairs (j): "Progress toward the achievement of the largest attainable amount of acceptable value in this world"—is intrinsically valuable. This is not identical with: "the introduction of acceptable" or "increase in the amount of acceptable value in this world." In some cases the fact of introduction, or the fact of increase, of acceptable value is not computable with the so-called long-range ideal situation. Some entities which are characterized by acceptable value do not fit together in the best possible fashion with other entities, so as to constitute an organic whole which involves the largest attainable amount of acceptable value in the world.[33]

VIII

The following discussion of organic wholes which are intrinsically value-opposite will parallel the preceding examination of organic wholes which are valuable intrinsically. Hence less detail will be included—in the interests of avoiding useless repetition.

There are many organic wholes of this sort which involve internal reaction. They are either (a) negative or (b) positive.

(a) Consider negative internal reaction to acceptable beauty, for example: dislike. The value-opposite characteristic (which is intrinsically present) of this organic whole bears no mathematical relation to the fact that beautiful is intrinsically valuable and dislike is neither intrinsically valuable or value-opposite. In the case of "pain at acceptable beauty"— the amount of intrinsic value-opposite of the organic whole is greater than the intrinsic value-opposite of the pain. It is not alleviated by the intrinsic value of beautiful. In all such cases, the intrinsic value-opposite characteristics of the organic whole does not bear any mathematical relation[34] based on adding or subtraction of the amount of value or value-opposite of the ingredients.

(b) Turning to positive internal reaction—if they are directed to entities which are characterized by unacceptable value-opposite or by unacceptable values—such organic wholes are intrinsically value-opposite. Consider "pleasure in unacceptable ugliness" or "pleasure in unacceptable beauty". In the case of the former the organic whole has less intrinsic value-opposite than the ugliness. It is interesting to note that as the pleasure increases in profundity the value-opposite status of the organic whole also increases—just as it does if the degree of ugliness does. Obviously pleasure which is intrinsically valuable does not counteract the value-opposite character of ugliness as far as the organic whole is concerned. In the latter illustration both ingredients are intrinsically valuable but the organic whole is intrinsically value-opposite.

In the interests of comprehensiveness, and for devotees of horror movies, it should be noted that there are two other very complex organic wholes which are intrinsically value-opposite. They are: those characterized by: (i) the largest attainable amount of unacceptable value-opposite in this world[35] (a) now or (b) in the foreseeable future and (ii) the largest amount of unacceptable value-opposite, in any world which is conceivable. The difference between the two, of course, is due to the fact that in this world there are limits to the amount of unacceptable value and unacceptable value-opposite which can be present—while one can conceive a state of affairs where these limits are removed.

48

Paralleling the operational resultants: Introduction of acceptable value; Removal of unacceptable value-opposite; Prevention of unacceptable value-opposite (which are intrinsically valuable) are the following states of affairs which are intrinsically value-opposite: Introduction of unacceptable value-opposite, Removal of acceptable value; Prevention of acceptable value. In these cases, the *amount* of value-opposite of individual occurrences of these operational resultants depends on, and is equivalent to, the *amount* of acceptable value which has been removed or prevented. In the case of introduction of value-opposite, it is less than that of the entity introduced.

Consider further: Introduction of unacceptable value, removal of acceptable value-opposite, prevention of acceptable value-opposite, unacceptable value-opposite is continued in existence, unacceptable value is continued in existence.

Paralleling the previous discussion of "Increase of acceptable value (or acceptable value-opposite)" and "Progress toward "Long-range-ideal situation"", one might bring into focus: "Increase of unacceptable value-opposite, or unacceptable value"—or "Progress toward the largest amount of attainable unacceptable value-opposite in this world." However, the explanation of the details of these states of affairs seems unnecessary at this point.

CHAPTER 4

Morally Good—Morally Evil

In this chapter attention will be focussed on a specific group of complex entities which are organic wholes of the novel result sort.[1] Some are not only intrinsically valuable but are also characterized by morally good. Others are not only intrinsically value-opposite but are also characterized by morally evil. In the course of the discussion of these complex entities, comments on the entities[2] morally good and morally evil will be relevant. Thus the brief references to these entities in Chapter 2 (p. 24) will be supplemented.

In the interests of simplified presentation, attention, initially, will be focussed on entities characterized by morally good. Subsequently, morally evil ones will be dealt with.

I

It is essential to note, in general, that behaviour entities[3] which are characterized by morally good,[4] have as ingredients: specific sorts of motives, intentions and actions (or at least an attempt to act), in specific patterns of relations—with reference to specific entities. In some cases there are other sorts of mental entities, for example: choice and will.

Such ingredients are characterized, on occasion, by values and/or value-opposite in one or more of the following modes: intrinsically, when means, because of their characteristics, because of their consequences, as possible, as potential. (See later discussion.) At least some of these factors have a bearing on whether or not morally good characterizes a complex behaviour entity. Further, they have a bearing on whether or not the organic whole is intrinsically value, or value-opposite.

Before proceeding further, it is advisable to indicate the sense in which a number of key terms, used in this discussion—are employed.

The term "behaviour" is used to refer to each of the following: motive[5], intention, other mental states, action—directed toward some specific entity. Each of these is a case of: *simple* behaviour, i.e., one entity occurs with reference to another entity. For example, there is an emotion of love with reference to a fellow man, or an intention to help another person in solving a financial problem, or the action of so doing. When two or more of motive, intention, action, occur as ingredients of an organic whole, this is a case of: *complex* behaviour. Some people use the word "action" as a synonym for "behaviour", in its most complex inclusive sense. Also the term "behaviour" is employed (by some) in a far more restricted fashion, i.e., as a synonym for "physical activity". Be that as it may, the term "action", in the context of this discussion, is used to refer to (a) the doing of something physical or otherwise, or (b) the refraining from, or avoiding, something—usually but not always as the result of having a motive and/or an intention. The term "motive" is employed to refer to feeling (such as pleasure and pain), emotions (such as love and hate), desires,—when they function as internally initiated dynamic causes of human intentions and actions.[6] Concerning the item "desire", it is important to realize that it covers both (i) the activity of desiring and (ii) that on which activity of desiring focuses. The term "intention" covers (i) roughly speaking, the plan or goal which is envisaged and (ii) that activity of focussing on this plan. Further (iii) there is a tendency to implement the plan. It must be emphasized that the plan aspect may involve an *ultimate* goal of a behaviour entity, and means or *contributing* (supplementary) goals leading to the ultimate goal.

When there is a combination of *all* of: motive, intention (and in some cases other mental states) and action,[7] it is a case of "personal commitment" behaviour. When one of action, or motives or intentions is missing there is no personal commitment. Only personal commitment behaviour is capable of being characterized by morally good. Depending on its ingredients[8] sometimes such behaviour is so characterized— sometimes not.

51

At the beginning of this chapter it was noted that it is concerned with intrinsically valuable organic wholes of behaviour which are characterized by morally good. It was stated that such behaviour is of the "novel result" sort. Before proceeding to an examination of specific cases, it is well to emphasize that in discussing the ingredients of an organic whole of this sort, it will be kept constantly in mind that the organic whole is not just the togetherness of the ingredients. Rather because of their presence as components in specific relation—a new result is present. When, for example, the ingredients of love of a fellow man are present—as a result there is something new: an organic whole: love of a fellow man.

We turn now to consideration of specific complex behaviour entities which are characterized by morally good.

II

Love of another human being: What is here under consideration is a many-occurrence organic whole behaviour entity, of the personal commitment sort.[9] "Love of another human being" includes the following factors (i) an intense feeling of affection (emotion) directed toward another human being, (ii) a desire to (a) ensure that the loved one will have acceptable value characteristics, (which includes and involves experience of acceptable value) in the largest attainable amount, now and in the future; and (b) a desire to diminish and prevent unacceptable value-opposite (and value) characteristics (and experience) in an acceptable maximum fashion, (iii) an intention (in the sense of mental activity) to act in such a fashion as to achieve these results (intention in the sense of plan or goal) (in some cases choice and act of will are included), (iv) action along these lines, productive of the relevant results,—or an attempt to produce them. Desire, intention, action are "all out".[10] If "things go wrong", despite the presence of the factors just mentioned, this does not rule out the presence of: love of a fellow man. Also it must be emphasized that there is no "ulterior motive" in all this. There is no thought of, or desire for, unshared personal advantage in the form of valuable consequences as far as the lover is concerned. To put the matter positively: the object of desire is desired for the sake of the loved one.

Implicit in, and interfusing all phases of, love of another human being is a distinctive factor: the lover gladly *shares* with the loved one, to the maximum attainable extent, his own achievements in the field of acceptable value experience. The lover also joins with the loved one in the joint achievement of acceptable value, without reserve, in the attainment of the ideal situation. It is also essential to realize that if a person is to achieve the largest attainable amount of acceptable value (the ideal human situation), he must experience a wide range of valuable entities, in balance, and in accordance with their status in the realm of value.[11]

At this point it is appropriate to provide an illustration of the details of the preceding general analysis: Mr. A. loves Miss B. As he drives along a street he sees her walking rapidly. In the context of his love for her, in this situation he intends (i.e., has a plan and there is an inner tendency to implement it)[12] to share more effective transportation. This is a contributory (supplementary) goal involved with the ultimate goal in this sort of behaviour—namely: love of another human being. He stops his car and utters the invitation to ride.[13] She jumps in, is sped on her way and is pleased. Hence acceptable value is added to her experience. Mr. A. has behaved in the love of another human being fashion. It must be emphasized that this sort of behaviour does not necessarily involve a male/female association—nor does it necessarily have any sex implications or overtones. In the case of the example here under consideration, two males or two females may be involved.

In the situation described, the desire, the contributing intentions and actions are all completely appropriate. The desired and intended ultimate result occurs. The behaviour of course must involve value which contributes to the achievement of the largest attainable amount of acceptable value.

However, if, as the car stops the brakes squeal and the vehicle skids on a bit of ice which is covered by newly fallen snow—and the result is that Miss B jumps in fright and sprains her ankle—hence the ultimate goal is not achieved. But, Mr. A's behaviour is not removed from the love of another human being category. He could not have expected that the piece of ice was there, or that his brakes would squeal. Further, as the car started to skid, he made every effort to change its direction. In this situation Mr. A. did everything in his power to bring maximum acceptable value to Miss B.

If the behaviour entities present are: intense emotion, the desire to further the acceptable value characteristics of another, and the supplementary intention to take appropriate action—these, and nothing more—then this behaviour is *not* a case of love of another human being, characterized by morally good. Specifically, it is not a case of personal conventional behaviour because the relevant action is (actions are) not involved. Likewise if a person's action produces acceptable enhancement of value for another person, but is not prefaced by the relevant emotion, or desire, or intention—here again the behaviour is not the personal commitment sort. It is hence neither morally good, nor valuable intrinsically. More accurately, if a person's ultimate goal is merely narrowly personal benefit, his service to others is not a case of personal commitment to the greatest attainable good of another. Rather it is personal commitment to his own narrowly selfish benefit[14], and is characterized by morally evil.

Some further explanatory comments, concerning the preceding remarks, are now in order. Having outlined the general constitutive factors of: love of another human being,—it is advisable to stress the fact that this entity involves a number of different particular occurrences varying, as far as specific contributory intention and action ingredients are concerned, with reference to the situation in which the entity occurs. To put the matter as simply as possible: the deep affection and desire to develop acceptable value characteristics of the loved one to the highest attainable amount now and in the future, will issue in, be expressed by, different behaviour in different situations. In other words, the achievement of the ultimate goal involves a number of inter-related contributory intentional actions.

For example, in some cases: A in his love relation to B (specifically in order to achieve an increase of acceptable value for B), will refrain from discussing problems with him because he is firmly convinced that B has previously received all the help he needs.[15] B must now think things through to a final conclusion—by himself. On the other hand, if the situation requires it, A will spend almost an unlimited amount of time talking things over with B. In some cases the acceptable action may be to take the person to an art gallery. In another A will refuse to do so and instead pressure B to stay home and write a letter. Sometimes the appropriate behaviour involves offering a cup of coffee, in another a refusal to provide one. Of course, all the ways in which a person can express, or demonstrate, love of another human being are too numerous to be mentioned here. The point being made is that one should beware of concentrating on one particular intention and action, in all circumstances.

It will have been noted that in the general statement of the nature of any behaviour characterized by morally good, and in the preceding specific illustrations, it was indicated that choice and act of will are not necessary ingredients. Further, it was *not* claimed that the behaviour in question must be that of an informed adult, in good mental and physical health. Rather, the stress was placed on a pattern of certain sorts of motive (emotions and desires), intentions, actions (at least attempts to act). These are the essential core ingredients in behaviour characterized by morally good. The other factors (some or all) may also be present, but not necessarily so. These issues were discussed at length in *Experiential Realism*. It is sufficient now to point out that there are cases which support the point of view here expressed. Consider for example: a small child A motivated by strong affection for a play-mate B, desires to give him great beneficial pleasure, intends to share a large piece of chocolate and proceeds to do so. A, in this situation, does not engage in an act of choice nor does he exert his will. He merely proceeds in the fashion indicated, when confronted by B. He is not informed concerning moral principles. He is not adult. His physical and mental health leave much to be desired. Nor is his behaviour the result of habit based on knowledge of moral principles, or previous training in the application of them. Yet, in this case, morally good behaviour was performed by A. The question is sometimes raised as to the relation of freedom to morally good behaviour—is a very complex one. It is here reported that whether the chocolate sharing behaviour was caused or not, it is characterized by morally good.

At this point it is well to bear in mind that the ingredients of a complex behaviour entity, for example, love of another human being,[16] which is characterized by morally good—are not constituent ingredients of the entity: morally good. It, as such, is not just a result of arrangement of the entities considered above (and others to be discussed later). Rather, when complex behaviour entities (specific components, in particular cases, in specific patterns) are examined, they are found to be characterized by the entity: morally good. Further, moral goodness is not identical with any set of other entities. The question can always be raised: *are* these entities characterized by morally good or, on what grounds are they considered to be cases of morally good? In brief, morally good is one entity, what it characterizes is another entity. This is simply a fact of comprehensive experience. Likewise such entities do not jointly generate the entity morally good.

Further, it must be emphasized that when value characterizes the ingredients of a complex behaviour entity—their value does not bestow value on the entity: morally good. For example, the desire to facilitate the highest attainable level of value characteristics for a loved one, has value when it is a means leading to intentions and actions. Also, this ingredient in the behaviour has value because of its status as ingredient. However, these comments apply equally well to the ingredients of behaviour characterized by morally evil.[17] In any case, morally good is valuable intrinsically. Finally, since morally good is not identical with ingredients of the behaviour entity which it characterizes, therefore the value characteristics of the ingredients have no relation of identity with the value of morally good. This becomes even more obvious when cases of morally good behaviour are examined in which the ingredients are characterized by value-opposite.

IV

Sympathy is behaviour of the personal commitment sort. It involves: a feeling of intense pain when another person suffers misfortune, plus a sense of close personal relationship which results in a "sharing of" pain. There is also desire and intention (accompanied in some cases by choice and act of will) leading to an attempt (action) to improve the situation (ultimate goal). As in the case of love (above), what is contributory is intended and done (or not done, of a specific contributory nature)[18] depends on the situation which confronts a person. Here, as before, freedom from ulterior motives must be emphasized.

It is important to note that in the case of this complex behaviour, one of the main ingredients is characterized by value-opposite, intrinsically. Pain is a main ingredient in the sense that it gives rise to desire, intention, etc. to remove pain (i.e., entities which arouse pain) and add entities characterized by acceptable value. The desire, intention, etc. are as such not characterized by value intrinsically, yet the complex behaviour entity is characterized by value intrinsically. Further, it is characterized by morally good which in turn is characterized by value intrinsically. As in the case of the feeling of love without accompanying action, so likewise the mere feeling of sympathy alone—is not characterized by morally good. There is no personal commitment.[19]

V

It is now relevant to emphasize that there are degrees of the entity: morally good as it characterizes different many-occurrence entities. Consider *love of another human being* and *concern for another human being*. In the latter the emotional factor is different, and is less intense. More specifically: the term "concern" is here used to refer to a positive emotion directed to another person, coupled with an interest in his welfare, and intention to improve his lot, followed by relevant action. The term "concern" is sometimes regarded as a synonym for "worry". It is not here being employed in that sense. In the complex behaviour now under consideration the desires and intended results are less extensive in scope with reference to any one individual, than in the case of love of another human being. The goal is the improvement of a person's acceptable value characteristics and value experience. To put it simply: if a person is concerned for the welfare of another, he will, for example, contribute to a community service fund drive, desiring and intending to do so, in the context of desiring and intending to improve his lot. As in the case of love of another human being, this involves an acceptable increase in the amount of value which characterizes the beneficiary. If a person loves another human being, he is more deeply involved. He engages in more direct personal activity on behalf of the loved one, does more things for him (or tries to). There is a far stronger desire and emotional basis. Any occurrence of love of another human being involves an "all out" (complete) dedication in terms of intensity of desire, and full attainable use of personal and environmental objects, in formulating a perceptive intention and engaging in appropriate action—in accordance with the problem situation confronting one. No occurrence of concern for another human being reaches that level of dedication. There are varieties in degree of dedication within the range of occurrences of: "concern for". It is obvious that there is more moral goodness involved in the love of another human being than in concern for a fellow man[20]. Likewise the

57

amount of intrinsic value is greater in the case of the former than in that of the latter.

In order to avoid possible misunderstanding, it is essential to bear in mind that the "concern for another human being", frequently in ordinary discourse, is used in two senses: (a) reference is made to (i) a complex mental state including some or all of the following: emotions, desiring, being interested in, intending, and (ii) the entities to which these activities are directed. On the other hand (b) the terms may have reference covering not only (a) but also actions designed to achieve relevant goals. Briefly, one must distinguish between (a) the mental state sense of the term and (b) the complete behavioural sense of the terms, which refers to a case of personal commitment behaviour. As noted, only the entity referred to in the latter (b) sense is characterized by morally good.

In general, it is here contended that unless the emotions termed "love," "sympathy" or "concern" are linked with at least an attempt at appropriate action, what is present are not genuine cases of love of a fellow man, sympathy, or concern for a fellow man. Rather, these are shallow sentimental emotions unworthy of the terms commonly used to refer to them. Above all, there is no relevant action.

VI

In the case of personal commitment entities discussed above, obviously the name of the entity is derived from its motive ingredient. Let us now turn to a consideration of another group of behaviour entities. These derive their name on a different basis.

There is a complex behaviour entity which can perhaps be best referred to by the apparently cumbersome label: "*Personal commitment to justice*". Here "justice" means: fairness, i.e., sameness, of treatment, or situation, with reference to certain aspects of human life.[21] Specifically, (a) each person has an opportunity to develop his latent potentialities and use his abilities for acceptable value experience, to the highest attainable degree, (b) benefits or rewards and hardships or punishments accrue in an impartial fashion, on the basis of appropriateness. In general there are no special privileges of an artificial nature in a situation.

"Personal commitment to justice" involves, i.e., it has as ingredient factors (i) a desire to achieve justice, (ii) an intention with this focus and (iii) acting in accordance with justice in one's dealings with other human beings. That is, a person deals with his fellow men in such a fashion that they have equal opportunity to develop, and the same pattern of treatment "before the law", or in the matter of social benefits or the opposite. Hence his action is characterized by just.

If a person acts in accordance with justice, but is motivated by fear of punishment, or the pressure of public opinion,—or by the hope of future advantage at the expense of others, that is unjust future consequences,— he is not personally committed to justice. He does not really desire justice as such. As in the case of other sorts of behavior, mere action is not characterized by morally good. It is only when behaviour is of the personal commitment sort that it is so characterized.

Concerning personal commitment to justice, it is important to note that the specific contributory intention and action ingredient, involved in the general pattern of behaviour, will vary, due to individual and environmental differences. Nevertheless, there is a common core of treatment and concern for justice. Speaking technically, there are many different particular occurrences of a many-occurrence entity.

One set of factors, in all cases, is involved but there is not "identical" behaviour as far as *details* are concerned. Consider for example the attempt to ensure that all men in a community, not merely a few, receive adequate food, clothing, shelter and opportunity for education to the upper limits of their potentialities and abilities. Different people, depending on age and other factors will be given different amounts of food. An adult requires more than a child. Education will vary depending on IQ score, interests etc. There will also be variations on the basis of environmental characteristics.

It must be admitted that it is difficult, if not impossible, to find a human being who behaves in accordance with justice, either in the sense of mere action or personal commitment behaviour, with reference to all other human beings at all times. The fair treatment, even when it occurs, frequently is restricted to only a few entities of experience.

A further clarification is perhaps in order. It may be claimed that, for example, personal commitment to justice is found in "very strange places". Consider the case of a group of thieves who are "splitting the loot." Each thief "plays fair". However, he does so because it is to his own advantage. He knows very well if he does not act in a fair fashion he will be severely punished or "rubbed out" by his associates. He is not personally committed to justice as such.

As in the case of the other complex behaviour entities considered above, behaviour concerned with justice is characterized by morally good even if, despite a person's best efforts, justice is not obtained.[22] On the other hand, if his action somehow results in justice, but he does not desire or intend this result—then his behaviour is neither personally committed to justice nor characterized by morally good. Likewise, if he stops short at desires, or desires an intention, concerning just action, and makes no attempt to act—his behaviour is not characterized by morally good.

The admittedly cumbersome phrase (a) "Personal commitment to justice" has been used in discussing a specific complex behaviour entity in order to make as clear as possible its essential nature. It has as an ingredient an entity referred to by the phrase (b) "Action in accordance with justice."[23] Speaking technically, the former referent is a case of complex behaviour; the latter of simple behaviour. Two apparently convenient locutions "suggest themselves". Why not substitute for (a): "Just behaviour" and for (b): "Just action". There admittedly are several difficulties involved in this suggestion. In the first place, action is a sort of behaviour. However, if the suggested usages are kept carefully in mind, they are more convenient than the more cumbersome phrases. In subsequent discussion these suggestions will be implemented, at least on most occasions.

One very important point requires clarification. In using the phrases "just behaviour" and "just action" one is following a common precedent which may be misleading unless it is properly understood. In these cases, an entity is named on the basis of one of its characteristics or: characteristics of an ingredient. Specifically, when a person acts in accordance with justice, that action in comparison with what happens to, or is done by, others is in the comparative relation of: just. It is therefore characterized by that relation. In so far as a person desires and intends justice and acts in accordance with justice, his personal commitment behaviour is also characterized by just in the sense that one ingredient is so characterized. In either case, there is no reference to an essential ingredient as in the case of love of a fellow man, sympathy, or concern for a fellow man.

Another point requires clarificatory comment. The fact has been emphasized that a complex personal commitment behaviour entity, in the case of justice, involves a number of different specific occurrences— varying because of the differences in situations in which the basic factors are present. Each of the specific occurrences may be duplicated. In this sense reference has been made to many-occurrence entities. For example, if the situation is such that justice for "Little Willie" aged 5, involves 5 glasses of milk per day (a particular occurrence) then each one of other children of the same age, build and state of health, will require the same treatment, in the context of the appropriate motive and intention. This same general point should be noted concerning cases of love of a fellow man, etc., and with reference to other behaviour entities to be considered subsequently.

Finally it is well to appreciate the fact that a case of justice (a complex situation where the relation just is involved) is an organic whole characterized by value intrinsically. However, the relational characteristic just, i.e., same, is likewise intrinsically valuable since it is a case of consistency.

VII

We turn now to consider other cases of behaviour which are both intrinsically valuable and are also characterized by morally good.

Cooperation is a sort of complex behaviour which occurs when: (i) a person desires to work together with others in order to achieve a goal, (ii) intends to do so and (iii) at least attempts to engage in this sort of action. In some cases actual working together may be prevented by some factor. The motive must be unclouded by narrow self interest, or any other ulterior purpose.

In the strict sense, the mere activity of working together for the achievement of a goal is not a case of cooperation. Further it is not intrinsically valuable.[24]

It is to be noted that the phrase "cooperative behaviour" is frequently used as a synonym for "cooperation". This substitution of an adjective for a noun form is used also in reference to other complex behaviour entities which will be discussed subsequently.

VIII

So far illustrations of actions involved in morally good behaviour have commonly taken the form of reference to constructive physical activities.

It must be emphasized that in some cases the actions are essentially mental, and/or involve concepts. For example, one can work together with others in the realm of thought. Further, in some cases the action situation is one of elimination, or diminution, of entities. See later discussion of tolerance, forgiveness, mercy, self-control.

It is essential to realize that sympathetic, just, and cooperative sorts of behaviour entities frequently occur in the context of "love of" or "concern for"—another human being. However, the fact that they are ingredients in, "love of" or "concern for" a fellow man, does not deny the distinctive nature of sympathetic, or just or cooperative behaviour. Nor does it deny their intrinsic value. Further, it doesn't imply that love or concern are the motives of sympathetic, just or cooperative behaviour, as such.

It is well to take note of the place of *knowledge* in behaviour characterized by morally good. When, for example, a person is motivated by love and desires to facilitate the highest attainable acceptable value achievements of another person, it is obvious that in formulating contributory plans of action and implementing them, knowledge, both theoretical and practical is required. Further, as noted previously, when a person has love for another human being, he will make the best attainable use of his own potentialities and abilities and environmental facilities in order to achieve his goal with reference to his loved one.[25] This involves the fullest possible attainment of knowledge and its full use in specific problems and situations. Of course, the level of attainment and use varies from person to person (including environmental facilities). Even more fundamental is the fact that if a person does not have knowledge relevant to a specific situation, he can not manifest love of another human being in that situation.

What has been pointed out concerning love of another human being applies as well to other sorts of morally good behaviour—with an important exception. While love of another human being involves the achievement of the largest attainable amount of knowledge, and its fullest possible use with reference to the loved one in general, and specific problem situations in particular,—this is not the case with reference to concern for another human being, sympathy, justice and so on.

A person, for example, can manifest genuine concern for another human being, in a specific situation, by achieving and/or using an amount of knowledge which does not "come up to" his attainable level. In any case, the range of knowledge required is much more limited than that involved in love of another human being, since the range of intention and relevant action is much more limited. Likewise the range of sympathy and justice is much more limited than both love of and concern for another human being. Of course, in all cases there is a minimum amount of knowledge required in order that there can be contributing intentions and relevant action such that cases of concern, sympathy and justice occur in a specific situation. To repeat: the achievement and use of knowledge is involved, otherwise love, concern, sympathy and justice do not occur. It is obvious that concerning cooperation, the same general comments apply. One can not cooperate with others in a specific situation unless he has relevant knowledge of it. At least a minimum level must be present and used in formulating subsidiary intentions and/or figuring out appropriate actions.[26]

The relevant knowledge concerning some contributary goals is at the disposal of almost everyone. For example, at least some of the things which one can do in showing concern for another person are "common knowledge".

In brief: if a person motivated by concern for another human being, intends to improve his lot,—has in mind, because of ignorance of what is relevant in the situation, subsidiary intentions which will, if implemented, defeat his ultimate purpose—and proceeds to implement these intentions—such behaviour is not a case of concern for another human being. This is clearly so if the person can't be bothered to seek relevant information. It is also so even if he is not capable of obtaining it. These comments can be generalized to apply to the love of another human being, sympathy and cooperation in so far as specific situations are involved.

C

The emphasis on three distinguishable factors: motive, intention, action, should not be misunderstood. It does not imply that each item appears in clear awareness, one after the other—in all cases of experience. A person who has, for example, behaved justly on a number of occasions will, in all probability, not, on a later particular occasion have in "centre-stage" of awareness a desire or an intention—as the basis of the action which he is performing. However, the person who habitually behaves in a just fashion does so only because the habit is based initially on desire, intention, action, clearly present to awareness—while the habit is being established. The factor of gradual transition from desire to intention to action is much more noticeable in first occurrences of behaviour.

D

The preceding discussion of entities which are characterized by morally good has involved a number of recurrent themes either explicitly stated or implied. In addition to the basic one: the fundamental ingredients of such behaviour are motive, intention and action—of specific sorts, in a specific pattern of relationship—there are others: (a) motive and intention are not enough. There must be action, or at least an attempt at action. (b) If motive, intention and action are appropriate—value-opposite consequences do not reduce or eliminate the morally good characteristic of behaviour. (c) In view of variation in situations and hence problems, many different subsidiary intentions and actions are involved in each sort of behaviour characterized by morally good. Each of these specific intentions and actions, and related motive, occurs on a number of occasions. Hence each sort of behaviour is, technically speaking: "many-occurrence". (d) There are differences in degrees of morally good. (e) It is well to bear in mind that almost all behaviour entities characterized by morally good, on occasion, occur within the context of love of, or concern for, another human being. (f) Apparent cases of morally good behaviour on the part of persons regarded as morally evil, turn out, in most instances, to be behaviour which is not morally good. This is so because the action is motivated by some ulterior concern, for example, hope of narrow unjust personal advantage, or fear of punishment. (g) It must be reiterated that each motive involves a desire for what is intended and its relevant action—for its own sake. No narrowly selfish or ulterior "purpose" is appropriate.

IX

Now that these recurrent themes have been brought clearly into focus, it is no longer necessary to reiterate them in discussing additional "many-occurrence" complex behaviour entities which are characterized by morally good. It will be sufficient to concentrate on what is *distinctive* about these various complex entities, rather than on what they have in common with other intrinsically valuable entities which are also morally good. The distinctive nature of behaviour entities next to be considered, generally speaking, is occurrence of a specific sort of action. The same general pattern of analysis as in the case of cooperation, for the most part, applies. However, in some cases there is a distinctive mental state as well (in the context of desire for its own sake, and relevant intention). As we proceed with the examination of the remaining group of behaviour entities, it will become obvious that the motive factor is not primarily a matter of some distinctive specific emotion or, strictly speaking, the presence of a desire. Rather it is a case of a strong positive, or favourable, attitude with reference to the distinctive sort of action involved in the behaviour entity. A *detailed* discussion, with illustrations, of these factors is omitted at this stage. A perceptive reader will have little difficulty in providing suitable illustrations along the lines of preceding treatment of such issues. However, occasionally illustrations will occur.

It must be borne in mind that sometimes a term, such as "cooperative", is loosely used (*not only* in ordinary discourse) to refer to an action alone rather than, more accurately, to the complex entity in which the action is an ingredient. This general comment applies for example, to the entities to be discussed forthwith.

X

The term "*honesty*" is applied to two sorts of complex behaviour. One may conveniently be termed "truthful", the other "trustworthy". Truthful behaviour involves (at least) an attempt to report facts (entities) as they are. Trustworthy behaviour has as distinctive ingredient: the keeping of promises, and in general honoring agreements and discharging responsibilities.

Reciprocation of benefits does not involve, necessarily, an exact repayment in kind and amount. A person may genuinely reciprocate, within the limits of narrow resources, even if the literal amount of benefit in return is not equal to that received, nor of the same sort.

Generosity is a sort of complex behaviour in which a person gives to another more value than is required in the context of justice or reciprocity. In some cases of generosity there is the factor of, at least a degree of, self-sacrifice.

Tolerance has as its major ingredient a willingness to accept the presence, or occurrence, of differences in ideas, emotions, feelings, intentions and action in and by others, insofar as this does not involve major threats of destruction of other values.

Forgiveness involves the overlooking of harm done by another person, and a willingness to "start over again" in personal relations. Usually emotions such as anger and hatred are replaced by a positive feeling.

Merciful behaviour occurs when a person is in a position to harm someone who has done harm to him, or to "society"; and refrains from doing so, or introduces "restriction" instead of harm, to a lesser degree than required by justice,—and for purposes of reform.

The term "*self-control*"[27] is applied to a number of organic wholes, each of which can be described in summary fashion as: complex behaviour in which a person controls a specific tendency. The specific tendencies under consideration are (a) those which if expressed in an *excessive* fashion, the expressions are characterized by unacceptable value-opposite or (b) those which *if expressed at all*, the expression is characterized by unacceptable value-opposite. Hence self-control involves either (a) a restriction of expression within appropriate limits, or (b) the complete prevention of expression of such tendencies. *Ideally*, as far as self-control is concerned, tendencies for which all expressions are value-opposite—will be eliminated. Of course, self-control also involves a desire and an intention focussed on these results. For example, a person "exerts himself" so as to avoid eating and drinking to a degree which results in pain. Also, he avoids talking in a situation where, due to ignorance and courtesy, it would be appropriate for him to listen. These results are based on his own initiative, i.e., his desires and intentions, choices, etc. Without these inner controls, his avoidance of value-opposite extremes are merely a case of accident, or bowing to threat of pressure by external authorities—hence not morally good *self*-control. It

66

is well, at this point, to notice the relation between self-control and other morally good behaviour.

Consider, for example, courage: *Courage* is, in part, self-control of the emotion of fear[28], on the basis of an understanding of the situation which gives rise to fear. This involves the avoidance of two extremes: (a) so much fear that one is paralyzed by it, (b) so little (or none) that one is not reacting to a situation in a suitable fashion, that is, shows a silly lack of concern for danger. Coupled with the factor "self-control of fear" is appropriate action in the face of danger—that is, doing what is required for purposes of obtaining acceptable value, despite the danger. It is to be noted that there are different degrees of courage, in different occurrences of it, depending on the amount of danger, and hence tendency to excessive fear, involved in situations in which a person finds himself. For example, when a person rushes into a relatively sparse traffic flow to rescue a dog, his behaviour is an occurrence of courage,—given the motive and intention factors mentioned above. But there is a higher degree of courage present in the case where a man goes out on a field of battle in the face of intense enemy fire, to rescue a person who has been wounded. There is a higher degree of morally good characterizing a higher degree of courage.

The examination of courage makes it clear that self-control is involved as an *ingredient*. This state of affairs is not the case with reference to the relation of self-control to other behaviour entities characterized by morally good.

Generally speaking, self-control is a *condition* for the presence of other behaviour entities which are characterized by morally good. For example unless a person has exercised control over tendencies to, expressions of, narrow selfishness or extreme emotions such as fear or anger, he is not going to engage in such behaviour as love of fellow man,[29] sympathy, concern for fellow men,[29] justice, honesty, tolerance, cooperation and so on. It must be emphasized that the relation of self-control to these entities is not that of ingredient, or a case, or characteristic. To repeat, it is that of condition. It should be obvious that the relation is not that of identity.

Incidentally, one of the major areas in which self-control is operative is with reference to tendencies to, and expressions of, for example, hatred of fellow man—injustice, intolerance, etc. These, when they occur, may be the result of lack of self-control of certain tendencies and other

67

expressions. For example, because of lack of control of anger, a person may proceed to engage in unjust or intolerant behaviour.

Technically speaking, the illustrations of self-control used above do not constitute 'sorts' of self-control. These are differentiated as to what is controlled rather than in terms of distinctive acts of controlling.

Since all the entities characterized by morally good are "free of" selfishness,[30] they may be termed: "unselfish" behaviour. However, this is not to be regarded as an inclusive entity of which love of fellow man—honesty—are sorts. Rather, each of these has in common the lack of narrow selfishness. The term therefore may refer to the fact of a common factor. It should be remembered that the term "unselfish" is sometimes used as a synonym for concern for the welfare of others, or indeed willingness to sacrifice oneself[31] for the welfare of others.

XI

The preceding discussion has not covered all the basic *issues* involved in behaviour entities which are not only valuable intrinsically, but are also characterized by: morally good.

The fact that there are degrees (varying amounts) of morally good, and intrinsic value, characterizing various behaviour entities has been briefly noted. It is now in order to deal with this topic in a more detailed fashion.

To begin with, it should be stressed that the degree (amount) of value which an entity has intrinsically, and its degree of morally good, depends on the nature of the entity. It is essential to realize that the amount of morally good parallels the amount of intrinsic value. For example, if the degree of morally good is high so is the degree of intrinsic value. Further, it is well to bear in mind that the amount of intrinsic value of an occurrence of morally good depends on the amount of morally good.

It may seem that there is something very strange in respect that, for example "concern for a fellow man" is intrinsically valuable and is characterized by morally good which itself is intrinsically valuable. To some people it appears that there is here an excessive reference to intrinsic value. May it not be that the only intrinsic value in this situation is that of the behaviour characteristic: morally good, and not of the behaviour as such?

68

In reply it can only be stated that, in the context of comprehensive experience, it is found that behaviour which is characterized by morally good is also intrinsically valuable. Indeed in many cases behaviour which is intrinsically valuable is not only characterized by morally good but also by other intrinsically valuable entities, for example beautiful, efficient, consistent, harmonious. But this is another story!

We turn now to a more detailed discussion of the fact that there are various degrees (amounts) of intrinsic value and morally good which characterize some behaviour entities. As background it will be recalled that emotions, attitudes and desires differ in intensity. Also persons intend to do something with varying degrees of determination (i.e., commitment). It must be further borne in mind that persons *make use of* their abilities and available facilities, and develop potentialities, in varying degrees of "fulness"—in the course of their behaviour.[32]

On the basis of the above factors,[33] one can distinguish the *comparative degrees* of morally good, and of intrinsic value, which characterize particular occurrences of the behaviour entities which have been discussed in the preceding paragraphs—with the exception of: love of a fellow man.

The matter is complicated by the fact that each major behaviour entity has a number of specific occurrences and each of these *specific*[34] occurrences has a number of *particular*[34] occurrences. For example, concern for a fellow man has as specific occurrences (which may be termed "specific cases") (i) contribution to the Red Cross, (ii) a friendly greeting. There are, however, a number of particular occurrences of *contribution* or *greeting*. These are, of course, particular occurrences of concern for a fellow man.[35]

Let us consider initially (a) differences in degrees of morally good, and intrinsic value, present in different particular occurrences of the same specific occurrence of a major behaviour entity; then (b) an attempt will be made to consider the relative status of different specific occurrences of a major behaviour entity.

First, however, a related issue requires comment. It has already been noted that in one very important aspect the situation is different concerning love of a fellow man, than with reference to all the other major behaviour entities here under consideration. Unless the emotion of love and the relevant desire have maximum intensity, likewise determination in implementation of the best available plan—love of a fellow man is not present. A person must also make full attainable use of his abilities and available facilities (and developed his latent potentialities) in action.

Under these conditions, every particular occurrence of helping with an essay (specific case) will have the same degree of value intrinsically and the same degree of morally good. This comment applies also to every occurrence of "take to an art gallery", in the context of love of a fellow man.[36] Further, (b) each particular occurrence, be it of the "essay" or "art gallery" sort, will be of the same degree of morally good and of intrinsic value, *if this is what is required in a specific situation*.[37] Persons differ in their degree of ability.[38] Some are able to give more detailed help in the essay situation than others. Nevertheless, as long as a person makes full use of his abilities in action, and his emotion of love and determination to implement his plan, are at maximum intensity, his behaviour is equal in intrinsic value and moral excellence to that of any other man in the same situation. Specifically, the wisdom of a professor is greater than that of a student, but under maximum conditions their behaviour is equal in moral goodness and intrinsic value. It is, of course, true that the consequences of their behaviour will differ in value on the basis of superior consequences in some respects. One behaviour entity also may be superior to another because of some characteristic other than morally good.

The crucial difference between love of a fellow man and other morally good behaviour entities can now be brought into focus: As has been pointed out these entities—with the exception of some occurrences of self-control—do not involve, in a specific situation—the maximum intensity of desire (positive attitude), emotion, or determination with reference to a specific goal. Particular occurrences vary in degree of intensity of emotion, desire, determination. They may involve, but usually do not, the maximum attainable use of abilities and facilities in formulating the details of subsidiary (contributary) intentions (plans), and in the action of reaching the ultimate goal, via the specific end of the behaviour process. Hence there are in the context varying degrees of occurrence of these entities. Specifically for example, in the context of "concern for a fellow man"[39] (a) there are particular occurrences, for example, of support for the Red Cross, which vary in degree of intensity of desire for, and determination to implement the plan, to support a Red Cross campaign for funds. Also persons make varying degrees of use of their abilities in formulating procedural details and translating the intention into action. On these bases there will be varying degrees of morally good and intrinsic value,—and of course varying degrees of concern for a fellow man. The same general comments apply to another specific case of that entity: concern for a fellow man. Consider for example: desire for, intention to provide, a Free Library,—and relevant action. It is important to note (b) that particular occurrences of support for the Red Cross and a particular occurrence of support for a Free Library are equal in moral goodness and value intrinsically (if they are equally required in a specific situation) if the same intensity of desire and determination are present, and a person makes the same proportionate use of his abilities and available facilities. Lacking the sort of sameness under discussion, they are evaluated in accordance with their pattern of difference. As before, the actual differences in human abilities are not crucial here. It is the degree of approximation to fullness of personal commitment which is fundamental.[40]

The question arises as to the comparative degree of morally good, or intrinsic value, in cases where particular occurrences of an entity, either of the same specific case or of two different specific cases, do not, as in the occurrences considered above, have a uniform pattern, high or low, of degree of intensity of desire, etc. Rather, some of the relevant factors are such that some are high and some are low in degree. At this point it is perhaps sufficient to indicate only in rough fashion the general nature of a suitable approach. Consider (i) a situation where desire and determination are on a high level of intensity but degree of use of abilities is only minimal, and (ii) desire and determination are medium in intensity but use of abilities approximates the status of: full. (ii) has a higher degree of morally good and intrinsic value than (i).

The foregoing general analysis of concern for another human being applies also to the following behaviour entities: sympathy, personal commitment to justice, co-operation, generosity, reciprocation.

It will have been noted that the following remain for comment: self-control (courage), honesty, tolerance, mercifulness, forgiveness. All have, in their particular occurrences, degrees of intensity of attitude and of determination to implement intentions. However, the factor of proportionate use of differing abilities and facilities is not crucial, in the sense in which it is concerning other entities. A person either has the ability and facilities to behave in these fashions or he doesn't. The question of

71

variation in details of performance in formulating details of subsidiary intentions and implementing them does not arise, as it does, for example, in the case of concern for a fellow man, justice, cooperation and so on. A person in the context of honesty, for example, conveys the truth. Whether or not he uses his specific individual abilities to the full is not fundamental as far as degrees of moral goodness and intrinsic value of honesty are concerned.[41]

Mercifulness is a hybrid sort of behaviour. As far as the "refraining from doing harm" factor is concerned, it is like honesty, etc. However, with reference to the "restriction instead of harm" factor, the issue of degree of use of ability and facilities does arise.

There is a further basis for comparison of the amounts of morally good, and also of intrinsic value, of different occurrences of the same entity. This frequently serves to differentiate entities which otherwise have the same status.

It was noted in the earlier discussion of courage that occurrences of courage differ in amount of moral goodness and intrinsic value, depending on the amount of danger confronting one, and hence the *difficulty* in dealing with emotional reactions which are common to all human beings. Thus, it must now be pointed out that various factors, other than the ones just discussed (i.e., motive, intention, use of ability and facilities) are relevant to the amount of morally good and intrinsic value present with reference to all behaviour entities considered above.

Consider generosity: If A gives "more-valuable" and personally prized entities to B than C does[42] (in the context of equality of relevant desire and intention), A's behaviour is more generous than C's and hence is characterized by a higher degree of morally good and intrinsic value. If A overlooks "very harmful" behaviour of B, and C only will overlook "mildly harmful" behaviour A's behaviour is more forgiving than C's. If A withholds "punishment" for "seriously evil" behaviour by B, and C withholds punishment only for "slightly evil" behaviour, A's behaviour is more merciful than C's.

In brief, given ordinary human nature A's behaviour involves greater difficulties in overcoming temptation to do otherwise than in the cases of C's behaviour entities.

One very important topic remains for consideration, namely that of the ranking with reference to intrinsic value, and amount of the characteristic morally good, of the various sorts of major behaviour entities which have been under consideration. Brief reference has already been made to love of a fellow man, sympathy and concern for a fellow man.[43]

A careful consideration of the data of comprehensive experience leads to the conclusion that in the case of any particular occurrence, the ranking is as follows:

I Love of a fellow man
II Sympathetic behaviour
III Generosity, tolerance, mercy, forgiveness—equal
IV Concern for a fellow man
V Justice, honesty—equal
VI Reciprocation

Implicit in this ranking hierarchy is a recognition of the significance of varying degrees of positive commitment to the value achievement of others and/or the freedom from devotion to one's own narrowly selfish interests. Degree of difficulty in behaving in these various ways also has a bearing on their rank order. It is to be noted that the degree of difficulty depends on the common nature of human beings and the ingredients of the behaviour entity in question. For example, it is harder for human beings to engage in love of another human being than to reciprocate a benefit.

The problem of assigning a ranking to *self-control* is very complex. This is so because the extent of the range of (amount of) intrinsic value, and the degree of morally good, varies depending on context. There are occurrences of self-control which are just as intrinsically valuable, and morally good, as occasions of love of another human being. Consider the following case: A member of A's family has been killed in an automobile accident because of the insolent carelessness of B. However, A controls his very strong tendency to hate and harm B. On the other hand, self-control in the matter of wanting to eat a chocolate bar on Friday after a good lunch, and before a long meeting, does not rank as high as just behaviour in the provision of educational opportunities for others.

The ranking of cooperative behaviour presents problems. Insofar as it involves a profound respect for others and mutual value achievement on a very high level, it comes just below sympathy. If, however, it is merely a case of working together in, for example, a job or sport situation it appears in the lowest position along with reciprocation of benefits.

73

Implicit in the preceding comments about self-control and cooperation is a fundamental point concerning the ranking of major behaviour entities on the basis of being morally good and valuable intrinsically. It is the simple fact that each of them has a range of degrees of morally good and intrinsic value[44] such that each can be appropriately ranked as indicated. The freedom from narrow self-interest in all cases and varying degrees of a positive commitment to value achievement of others, in some cases,— are characteristics of entities which are intrinsically valuable and morally good. The difficulty factor, in varying degrees, is involved in all cases. But these characteristics do not constitute the nature of morally good or intrinsic value. Rather morally good and value intrinsically characterize in varying degrees entities which have in varying degrees primary commitment to the value achievement of others, and/or avoidance of narrow self interest—the difficulty factor being relevant.

At this point, it is advisable to note that (a) there are other entities which are intrinsically valuable and characterized by morally good. Further (b) there are entities which may appear to have this status, but actually do not. For example, (a) when a person experiences strong negative reaction, e.g., pain[45] when confronted by morally evil behaviour in self or others, and proceeds to try to eliminate it, intending to do so—this complex entity is characterized by morally good. However, (b) the mere fact of internal negative reaction to the entity morally evil, contemplated in abstraction from any presence as characteristic of behaviour—does not constitute an organic whole characterized by morally good. The case is the same when there is merely an internal negative reaction to behaviour characterized by morally evil. In both situations relevant intentions and action are lacking. The experiencing of approval and/or pleasure when confronted by morally good behaviour in others, or pleasure in one's own morally good behavior,—and a concerted effort to continue and extend this sort of behaviour,—are complex entities characterized by morally good. Of course, the positive internal reaction alone in these cases is not characterized by morally good. The case is the same when there is merely an internal positive reaction to the entity morally good contemplated in abstraction—and nothing else is involved.

Finally, among the entities which may appear to be characterized by morally good but actually are not, consider: *gratitude*. The feeling of gratitude and the "plus intention," and action involving expression of gratitude—are cases characterized by *fitting*.

It is further appropriate to emphasize that at least some of the morally good behaviour discussed above can be present apart from an individual's relation to others. For example, a man can be honest in dealing with himself. He can achieve just behaviour in handling the various ingredients of his personality.

It will have been observed that in discussing behaviour characterized by morally good (which is also intrinsically valuable) attention has been focussed on the sample situations involving only 2 persons. It remains to point out that a complex situation in which one person behaves in any of these fashions with reference to more than one other human being,—involves a greater amount of intrinsic value and more morally good, than when only two are present. Obviously, a man who, for example, manifests love for, or concern for, or sympathy for another human being with reference to five persons is characterized by more morally good than a person who reacts in these fashions to only one person (see later discussion). Strictly speaking, in the one-to-five relation, five items of behaviour occur. It is not a case of one behaviour entity which is five times more morally good than the other case. In a few very exceptional cases there may be love of an entire social group as such. But, in implementing it, attention must be paid to individual differences of persons composing it.

Where a person consistently engages in one of the sorts of morally good behaviour discussed above (i.e., love of fellow man, sympathy etc.) he has a *virtue* of that sort, and the same name is used. Thus a person who regularly or habitually, behaves in a sympathe ic fashion is said to have the virtue: sympathy.

XII

The question of the comparative value of various behaviour entities, each of which is intrinsically valuable, becomes very complex as one widens the range of observation from various sorts of morally good behaviour entities,—to include entities of other types. Consider a comparison (dealing *only with the intrinsic* mode) of (a) courageous behaviour in which a person rescues a terrified dog in the midst of medium traffic and (b) the activity of understanding Einstein's relativity formula.

It was pointed out (Chapter 2, pp. 24-26) that the entity morally good has more intrinsic value than pleasure, true and so on —a few cases of beautiful being an exception. It has been noted in this chapter that the relative degree of intrinsic value and of morally good—characterizing an entity—parallels each other. If one is high so also is the other. Does this relation, between morally good and intrinsic value, lead to the conclusion that because morally good has a higher level of intrinsic value than true— that therefore illustration (a) involving courage has a higher degree of intrinsic value than (b), i.e., the grasping of Einstein's formula? The answer is: No. As a matter of fact (b) has greater intrinsic value than (a).

While morally good is a characteristic of courageous behaviour, true is not a characteristic of the activity of grasping knowledge. It is the knowledge which is true not the process of understanding. Hence the line of argument is not sound (because of confusion and neglect of basic differences).[46]

At issue is the problem of comparing achievements in the area of human behaviour—as far as their intrinsic value is concerned.

In general, it is found that the degree of intrinsic value varies with variations in a number of related factors: (a) degree of personal commitment, i.e., intensity of desire, intention etc. and use of abilities and facilities, (b) degree of difficulty involved in dealing with the ingredients of the situation (c) the nature and value of ingredients such as reaction entity and focal entity (in reaction sequence), (d) degree of concern for other creatures and avoidance of narrow personal interest (in the case of behaviour characterized by morally good).

A word of further explanation is perhaps in order concerning the *difficulty* factor. The nature of the entity which is focal in behaviour (i.e., what is the end to be achieved, or entity reacted to) is sometimes such that difficulties arise in reaching it, or dealing with it. Relevant here also, as a source of difficulty, are the common characteristics of human beings and, in some cases, environmental factors. This general topic has already been noted with reference to the value of morally good behaviour.[47]

With this in mind, it becomes clear that the case of courage considered above is less valuable intrinsically than the understanding of Einstein's formula, since more effort and difficulty are involved in the latter than in the former. Basically, the amount of value (when all modes are considered) of understanding Einstein's formula is greater than the value of controlling one's emotion of fear in the traffic situation.

The complex behaviour of formulating an adequate and acceptable philosophic system is more valuable intrinsically than the enjoyment of an acceptable beautiful cathedral—considering the amount of energy and difficulty as well as the value of the focal entity. The enjoyment of the cathedral is superior in intrinsic value[48] to the rescuing of the dog. Also the understanding of $2+2 = 4$ is inferior in value to both the enjoyment of the cathedral and any case of love of a fellow man. The enjoyment of the cathedral is inferior to love of a fellow man. This is so even if the occurrence in question is merely that of giving the loved one a cup of coffee, if this is what is required in a specific situation. The point at issue here is that the achievement of love of a fellow man is supremely difficult and involves great personal commitment, and exertion. The fact that the value of a cup of coffee is apparently slight in comparison with the beauty of the cathedral (and the pleasure it arouses) does not serve to reduce love of a fellow man to a lower level of intrinsic value than the enjoyment of the cathedral. Here the cup of coffee is in this context of the achievement of the largest attainable amount of acceptable value. All cases of deep sympathy, just behaviour, honesty, are superior in intrinsic value to awareness of a sports activity, enjoyment of a TV commercial, the efficiency of a social ''personality''—and so on through most of the behaviour which most people consider valuable during the course of their daily lives.

The fact that all cases of love of a fellow man are superior to all cases of enjoyment of beautiful or awareness of truth, and are superior to behaviour characterized by pleasure, efficiency, fitting, harmonious, consistent—should not be interpreted to mean that this sort of morally good behaviour is superior in intrinsic value to all other sorts of human behaviour. The exception is: ''Complete devotion to the project of achieving what is involved in the largest attainable amount of acceptable value.'' As will become increasingly obvious as discussion proceeds, this organic whole has as particular occurrences a vast range of inter-related and balanced behaviour characterized by or involving: morally good, beautiful, true, pleasure, efficient, fitting, harmonious, consistent. In particular it will be emphasized that this behaviour entity involves not only value achievement in interpersonal relations but also what a person achieves on his own.

The problem of the comparative value of various entities will be dealt with much more thoroughly in Section 4—after the extrinsic mode of presence of value has been examined in Chapters 5 and 6.

XIII

The entity *morally evil* is found to be characterized by value-opposite, intrinsically. It is simple, not complex. It is a characteristic of various sorts of complex entities[49] which are also intrinsically value-opposite. Let us now consider some representative samples of such entities.

Hatred[50] *of a fellow man*, of *minimum* scope, is a complex entity which has as ingredients: the emotion hate and "direction toward" another human being. To this may be added the desire and/or intention to harm.

An even more complex entity is also appropriately termed "hatred of a fellow man". In this, which may be termed "*maximum* scope", the ingredients are, in addition to the emotion hatred which is directed toward a fellow man—desire and an intention to harm in some way, indeed to increase the amount of unacceptable value-opposite (in some cases choice and act of will are involved), leading to at least an attempt to implement the intention[51] in action. Both of these complex entities, in addition to being intrinsically value-opposite, are characterized by morally evil. It will be noted that the state of affairs here is not the same as that concerning morally good. In the latter case "stopping short" of action removes behaviour from the status of: characterized by morally good. A man who hates a fellow man is morally evil even if "he does nothing about it". There is a higher degree of morally evil (and of value-opposite) in the second than in the first "scope" of hatred behaviour considered above.

If there is a beneficial result for others, despite the agent's desire, and intention, to harm them—and the resultant action—this fortunate result does not prevent the agent's behaviour from being morally evil. Consider, for example, an unscrupulous promoter who sells stock in "Pie in the Sky Gold Mine Co." to a naive citizen—intending to rob him of his savings. Unexpectedly the stock turns out to be valuable. The "moose pasture", as a matter of fact, covers a rich vein of gold.

The maximum aspect of hatred of a fellow man requires further comment. There are, of course, many particular occurrences of this entity. Depending on differences in situation, there are striking differences in the specific subsidiary (contributory) intentions and actions used as techniques for bringing about the ultimate goal. Consider, for example: knock a person down, withdraw financial support, poke fun at. Each specific case involving one of these sorts of action, is a many-occurrence entity.[52]

Indeed, hatred of a fellow man, of the *minimum* scope, may involve intentions, i.e., plans of a specific means to harm relevant to a specific situation. But there is no relevant action.

With the preceding remarks as background, it is now necessary to be reminded, paralleling the discussion of concern for a fellow man,[53] that there are varying degrees of morally evil and value-opposite in different cases of hatred of a fellow man of the maximum sort. The factors to be examined are (a) intensity of hatred, (b) intensity of desire and intention, to harm, (c) degree to which a person makes use of available facilities[54] in formulating plans relevant to a specific situation, (d) the degree to which a person makes use of available facilities in implementing a plan. The minimum sort of hatred of a fellow man does not involve item (d).

Obviously these factors introduce considerable difficulties in reaching decisions on the relative value-opposite, of morally evil characteristics, of particular occurrences of the behaviour entity: hatred of a fellow man. It is not necessary here to attempt to spell out a large number of detailed illustrations (see the discussions of: concern for a fellow man, and other behaviour entities which are morally good). However, it is probably advisable to indicate, in a couple of instances, some of what is involved.

Dealing first with a simple minimum scope situation: very intense hatred of a fellow man is characterized by more morally evil, and intrinsic value-opposite, than less intense hatred. Turning now to maximum scope: When two persons A and B hate with equal intensity and make equal use of their abilities and facilities to plan harm,—but A is more dedicated (i.e., makes fuller use of abilities and facilities) in implementing the plan than B—than A is more morally evil than B. It must be emphasized that if a person makes full use of his ability to do harm, regardless of the *extent* of his ability, he is equally morally evil as another person who has greater ability to do harm, and also makes full use of his ability. Of course the value-opposite characteristics of consequences would likely be different.

The factor of difficulty also, of course, is relevant here. A person who spends much time and effort in *manifesting* hatred, other factors being equal, is worse than a person who experiences only slight difficulty. It will be noted that here the discussion has been couched in terms of the morally evil characteristics of A and B. This is, of course, a way of referring to their behaviour.

As in the case of behaviour characterized by morally good, so with behaviour characterized by morally evil, the basic ingredients are initially in clear focus of awareness. Later when habits are established, these elements may fade into the background, although still vaguely present to consciousness. The speed-up factor of sequence from desire to intention to action is here also present. The comments concerning will, knowledge, health, adulthood, made in connection with morally good behaviour apply here.[55]

XIV

Let us now return to an outline[56] consideration of other cases of morally evil behaviour.[57] *Envy* with reference to valuable characteristics of another person's behaviour, or possessions, is so characterized. When this feeling issues in desire, intention (and in some cases choice and acts of will) together with an attempt to act in a harmful way, this complex entity (maximum scope) has a higher degree of morally evil than the limited case of merely feeling envy (minimum scope).

The minimum scope sort of envy might include also a desire and an intention factor—as noted with reference to hatred of a fellow man. However, in the interests of simplified presentation in some cases, only the emotion or attitude factor will be mentioned in cases of the minimum sort of a behaviour entity which is both morally evil and intrinsically value-opposite. Further, in dealing with maximum scope cases here and subsequently, in the interests of simplified presentation, no reference will be made to the factors of (i) degree of use of available abilities and facilities or (ii) a difficulty overcome.

XV

Excess[58] There are a number of complex behaviour entities (involving motives, intentions and relevant actions) which if kept within limits are characterized by value in various modes. However, if these motives, intentions and actions are pushed beyond appropriate limits the behaviour entities are characterized by value-opposite intrinsically and by morally evil. For practical purposes, the appropriate limits for strength of motive, range of intention, range of action—are exceeded when their presence involves harm to oneself and, in some cases, to others.

Consider the following simplified examples of maximum scope: *gluttony*, which is excessive concern for food involving the undermining of a person's health and efficiency; *avarice*: desire for money involving a distortion concerning what is important in life; *lust*: concern for sex involving deterioration of personality harmony and interference with the welfare[59] of others; *sloth*: desire for relaxation such that there is interference with one's own welfare and that of others. Another instance of "excess behaviour" characterized by morally evil is *false pride* (arrogance or insolence) that is, over-emphasis on one's own achievements or status, and resultant danger to the welfare of self and others. *Wrath*[60] is present when a person indulges in excessive anger, intends and implements harm. *Cowardice* is excessive fear issuing in value-opposite consequences to self and frequently to others.

All these sorts of excess behaviour have a maximum aspect (preceding illustrations)[61]. There is also a minimum aspect, as in the case of the behaviour entities previously discussed. Consider a person who has, for example, an intense interest in food and intends to gorge himself—but actually doesn't do so. Nevertheless, if the desire for food and/or intention to eat a great deal, disturb the balance of his mental health or efficiency, since he is being harmed, this behaviour entity is intrinsically value-opposite and also morally evil. The maximum form of this behaviour of course has a higher degree of intrinsic value-opposite and morally evil.

XVI

Dishonesty, like honesty, takes two forms. This involves either (a) falsehood (incorrect report) or (b) unreliability in undertakings. If behaviour is merely a matter of desiring and/or intending to provide an inaccurate report, or desiring and/or intending to act in an unreliable fashion—and "nothing else"—this behaviour is characterized by morally evil (and is intrinsically value-opposite)[62]. A higher degree of morally evil characterizes the more complex behaviour (maximum scope) which involves not only the motive and intention but also its implementation in action, or at least an attempt at implementation.

Selfish behaviour occurs when a person (i) desires, (ii) intends that top priority be given to his own private interests, at the expense of the welfare of others, and (iii) acts accordingly,—resulting in interference with the achievement of acceptable value in this world. In all such cases his behaviour is characterized by morally evil. As one proceeds from (i) to (iii) the degree of morally evil increases.[63]

Unjust behaviour involves unwarranted "differences in" treatment with reference to opportunities, possessions, status before the law, and in general in interpersonal relations. Morally evil characterizes (i) the mere desire for unfair treatment, (ii) the intention to obtain it, (iii) the complex behaviour in which (i) and (ii) issue in relevant action. As one proceeds from (i) to (iii) the degree of morally evil increases.

Indifference ("can't be bothered with") is the opposite of: concern for another human being. More specifically, there is a negative approach to any, or all, aspects of concern for another human being. Hence there is the activity of refraining from any attempt to help others and indeed to have relevant desires or intentions to do so. As in the other cases, the degree of morally evil increases as behaviour becomes more complex.

The same general pattern of discussion, emphasizing the negative, or "refraining from", approach, applies appropriately to *unsympathetic*, *non-cooperative*, and *non-reciprocation of benefits*—behaviour. The same is the case with reference to: *intolerant*, *unmerciful*, *unforgiving*. It is essential to stress that in the case of these sorts of behaviour, there is a knowing and deliberate refusal to permit the presence of any ingredient of sympathy, cooperation, tolerance, reciprocation, mercy, forgiveness. Indeed, the concern is to indulge in their opposites. For example, instead of sympathy, there is a hard, cool, unfeeling approach to the suffering of others. Instead of cooperation a man's behaviour is a case of being strictly on one's own ("I'll look after things myself"). Tolerance is replaced by a rigorous adherence to one point of view and a refusal to consider others—and so on.

XVII

It is important to realize that *actions* which are involved in behaviour characterized by morally evil have as characteristics entities which are characterized by value-opposite intrinsically.[64] Specifically, unjust action is characterized by inconsistency. The actions involved in selfishness, dishonesty, excess, uncooperative, unreciprocating, intolerant, unforgiving and merciless are characterized by unharmonious (discordant).

"Hatred of a fellow man", in the maximum scope sense, frequently has as an ingredient some behaviour entity (also in the maximum sense), which is characterized by morally evil. Consider, for example, injustice, dishonesty, non-cooperative, non-reciprocating.

Let us next consider: *Selfishness.* Other morally evil behaviour entities are frequently involved, as ingredients, functioning as means in selfishness, in the maximum sense. Consider for example, the complex behaviour entities (maximum sense); dishonesty, injustice, intolerance, unmerciful, unforgiving, non-cooperation, non-reciprocation.

In view of the close relation of (a) hatred of a fellow man or (b) "selfishness",—to the other morally evil behaviour entities, it is important to emphasize their distinctions. Being an ingredient, or being an effect, (in the case of maximum scope selfishness) is not the same as being identical. Thus, for example, while unjust behaviour may be an ingredient in either hatred of a fellow man or in selfishness—unjust behaviour is a distinct entity. The nature of unjust behaviour is concern for a "not the same treatment for all" state of affairs. It does not share the component ingredients of hatred or selfish as such.

It may seem that, when a person desires an unjust state of affairs, in all cases it is because he selfishly hopes to profit from it. As a matter of fact, this is the case only in some instances. A selfish motive may lead to unjust behaviour as a result—or unjust behaviour may become an ingredient in selfish behaviour in the maximum sense. But strictly speaking the motive, i.e., immediate motive, for unjust behaviour is the desire for it. Be that as it may, it must be realized that even the "background" motive for unjust behaviour is not necessarily selfishness (or hatred). A person may have been so conditioned that he desires an unjust state of affairs even if it does not involve his own advantage.

The preceding pattern of analysis applies to other behaviour entities (characterized by morally evil) discussed above. For example: excess may include as means ingredients dishonesty and injustice. However, despite this relation these are distinct entities.

The problem of ranking different major behaviour entities[65] in order of amount of intrinsic value-opposite and morally evil, is complicated by the distinction between minimum and maximum scope.[66] A careful examination of the various behaviour entities leads to the conclusion that from the maximum point of view, they may be "arranged" as follows:

I Hatred of a fellow man; selfish behaviour (equal)
II Unjust behaviour; excess (equal)
III Envy, intolerance (equal)
IV Indifference, unsympathetic, unmerciful, unforgiving (equal)
V Dishonesty
VI Non-reciprocation

Non-cooperation has the same variable status as cooperation (see p. 73). The same ranking is in effect when minimum cases are considered. A very difficult question arises: Is any case of a minimum sort worse than any case of a maximum sort? Here one must concentrate on particular occurrences. It seems, for example, that a minimum sort of hatred is worse than a maximum sort of non-reciprocation.

Several related possible misunderstandings remain to be "faced" and removed.

An internal positive reaction to the entity morally evil, contemplated in abstraction for any entity which it characterizes,—is not a case of morally evil behaviour, though it is intrinsically value-opposite. The situation is the same concerning an internal negative reaction to the entity morally good contemplated in isolation.

An organic whole which is a positive internal reaction to morally evil behaviour is characterized by less morally evil than the morally evil behaviour to which it reacts. An organic whole which involves negative reaction to morally good behaviour has a degree of morally evil corresponding to[67] the amount of morally good to which the negative reaction is directed.

As in the discussion of morally good behaviour, it must be realized that as one extends, for example, hatred from one person to more than one, the amount of morally evil of the person's character is increased.

It was noted earlier that some apparent cases of morally good behaviour actually are not such. Similarly some behaviour which seems to be morally evil actually is not so characterized. Consider the following contrasting cases: When a person does not reciprocate a favour, desires and intends not to do so, this is a case of behaviour characterized by morally evil. If a person is ungrateful for favours rendered, the behaviour is intrinsically value-opposite but it is not morally evil.

There are cases of morally good behaviour which are less valuable intrinsically than some behaviour entities which involve beautiful, true and pleasure. It is likewise essential to bear in mind the fact that some cases of morally evil behaviour are "not as bad" (have less intrinsic value-opposite) as some behaviour involving ugly, false and pain. For example pain when contemplating an acceptably beautiful cathedral or pleasure when contemplating an ugly slum are worse than some cases of non-cooperation, or non-reciprocation, in dealing with one's enemies.

SECTION THREE

EXTRINSICALLY; RELATED ISSUES

CHAPTER 5

Extrinsic Modes of Value and Value-Opposite

On the basis of the outline in Chapter I of the nature of value and value-opposite, and their various *modes of presence*, it is now appropriate to undertake a more detailed examination of modes other than intrinsic. Thus this chapter will deal with modes in which entities are characterized by value and value-opposite: extrinsically.

I

Consider first the mode (2)[1]: *valuable when means*. An entity has the characteristic means when it so functions as to contribute to the attainment of an entity which, with reference to it, has the characteristic: end (result, consequence, effect). Entities which have as characteristic: instrument, or cause, or operational condition,[2] or ingredient—also have the characteristic: means. In less technical, though more common locution—entities are designated in terms of their prominent characteristics. Thus entities which have the characteristic instrument or cause, or operational condition, or ingredient are termed: "instruments", or "causes", or "operational conditions", or "ingredients". Instruments, causes, operational conditions, ingredients, are termed: "means".[3]

It must be emphasized that the means-end relation is specialized in the sense that a specific entity is a means to a specific end result (consequence). This involves the presence of suitable prerequisite factors. In other words: an entity is able to function as a means because of the total situation. The phrase "total situation" refers to (i) the nature and characteristics of the entity which functions as means, (ii) the nature and characteristics of the result (consequence). (iii) Also relevant is the fact that for an entity to function as cause or instrument there must be present a state of affairs which can function as operational condition. The term "situation" is frequently employed as an abbreviation for "total situation". It is also used to cover (ii) and (iii) only.[4]

In general, it is important to realize that an entity is a means only when it is functioning so as to bring about an actual end (result). Hence it is only valuable in this mode *when* it is, i.e., is functioning as, a means.

Consider the following illustrations:

A

A pen is an instrument, and has value as an *instrument*, for example *when* it is being *used* to write something on a suitable surface.[5] A pen does not have this status, or mode of value, when a person tries to use it as a life-raft when he is drowning. A person's finger is not of such a nature that he can use it to write on paper, if no ink is available. Hence it does not have instrumental value in such a situation. Yet if a person writes on sand, then his finger does have instrumental value. However, a person's finger does not have instrumental value when he tries to use it as a lever to move a large block of marble.

It must be stressed that, in the context of this discussion, any entity has instrumental value when it is being used to produce a result, regardless of whether the result is characterized by value, or value-opposite. Indeed, what is valuable when an instrument, may have as result: entities which are characterized by extreme value-opposites.

B

An entity has value as *cause*[6] when it exercises any sort of causal function and is producing[7] an effect. Causal functions are: (i) pressure, (ii) generative, (iii) stimulus, (iv) lure.

Consider the following: (i) A gasoline engine is the source of motion of a motor car. It functions by exerting pressure on the drive mechanism. (ii) A mind produces memory images. Here the causal function is generative.

(iii) A beautiful picture causes a person to gasp in amazement. In this case the causal function is stimulation. Likewise the presence of food in the body stimulates activity which results in the satisfaction of a desire for food.[8] (iv) The activities of a person who manifests morally good behaviour, inspire others who follow his example—specifically, the morally good behaviour functions as a lure.

C

The preceding references to ''total situations''[9] bring into focus the factor: *operational condition*. An entity which has a specific nature and a cluster of characteristics such that it is capable of functioning as a cause or an instrument, with reference to a specific end—requires as context, a facilitating state of affairs. Otherwise it does not function as cause or instrument. When present in a means-end sequence such a state of affairs has the means status: operational condition.

In some cases, the operational condition is a characteristic of a person who functions as a cause. In other instances the operational condition is, or is a characteristic of, some entity external to the cause or the user of an instrument. For example: a gasoline engine cannot be a cause of the drive reaction unless the engine, and the rest of the car are on a sufficiently smooth surface. A mind cannot generate memory images unless health is present as an operational condition, and there are no excessive environmental distractions.

Entities have value when they are operational conditions, regardless of the value or value-opposite of their consequences.

Further explanatory comments are in order: Some effects produced by a cause, involve a relatively simple operational condition,—while other consequences depend on the joint presence of many factors. Contrast the movement of a ball by a cue—with the achievement of a civilized society. In the case of the former the operational condition is a smooth surface. The latter requires a favourable physical and social environment—a very complex state of affairs indeed.

Other issues come into focus when one considers the following situations: The extensive use of heroin will produce extreme physical and mental deterioration, or death, in a human being, regardless of (a) the particular personality traits of the person taking the drug, or (b) special environmental factors. Of course the effects of the drug depend on the nature and general characteristics of human beings. On the other hand,

91

the production of positive effects by using rational explanation, or analysis, in dealing with other persons, depends on: age, training, the specific personality traits of a person, and frequently on specific factors in the environment. Thus it is well to distinguish between *minimum and maximum dependence* on the total situation, specifically the nature and characteristics of the entities effected by causes, and the operational conditions of all sorts. A related distinction is relevant,—that between *standard* and *variable* (or *relative*) reaction to a cause. Almost every human being reacts to heroin in the fashion described above. Hence there is a standard reaction. On the other hand, different people react to rational explanation and analysis in a variety of ways, depending on the topic under discussion hence variable reactions.

Operational condition may *seem* to be a case of instrument. But, there is a basic distinction between being an entity actively used by another entity with which to reach a goal, or produce a result—and a permissive context, entity. Also it may appear that operational condition and cause are indistinguishable, in the sense that both are required if an effect is to occur. But, there is a difference between permissive factors and causes which as such actively produce effects.

It was noted previously that the nature and characteristics of means entities and their effects have a bearing on the fact that these entities are able to function as means or be effect. In some contexts it seems convenient to term such natures and characteristics: "conditions". However, in the "derivation of value" context it is clear that the status: *natures and characteristics* is not the same as: *operational conditions*. Natures and characteristics (though in a broad sense conditions) are means in the sense that they are *ingredients* of the entities to which they belong. They derive value on that basis. It seems appropriate in the context of the discussion of value derivation to use "condition" as a convenient abbreviation for "operational condition". This procedure will be followed for the most part in subsequent discussion.

D

An operative gasoline engine, on occasion, is an *ingredient* (that is, a component part) and hence a means for achieving a result—for example an automobile. In this sense it has value. The car would not be what it is without the engine! Obviously a chicken sitting under the engine hood would not be an ingredient in this case. However, the chicken under the hood is an ingredient in one situation, namely the comic one. It is well to realize that for example, a pen, on occasion, has value both as an ingredient in a writing situation and because of its instrument status.

It is essential to note that in the means-end situation, entities which are means do differ in amount of value because of a factor which is now to be discussed, namely: *importance*.[10]

In general terms: when an entity is functioning as cause it makes a greater contribution as means, and hence is more valuable as means, than an entity which, *in that situation*, functions as an instrument or one which has the status: condition. The amount of importance is in descending order. The cause is more important in the sense that it is the dominant factor, i.e., it uses the instrument in the context of the environment (condition). Some entities which function as essential ingredients[11] have a higher degree of value, on the basis of importance, than instruments or conditions. Roughly speaking, they are on the same level, on that basis, as an entity which functions as a cause.

Turning from an examination of a particular situation to a more general basis of comparison of entities which are valuable in the various means senses,—one finds a somewhat complex state of affairs: (i) an instrument in one situation is not equal in value to one in another situation as far as their means function is concerned. This is so because instruments differ in impor ance. For example, a stick is an instrument used by a bean plant in climbing upward. The stick is passive in this situation. On the other hand, consider a knife used as an instrument by a man. The knife has a causal function, i.e., in its instrumental use it causes pain. Thus it has a more important instrumental function than the stick in the growing illustration. There is, of course, a vast range of difference in value when consequences are taken into consideration. (ii) Some causes are more valuable as means than other causes because of their greater relative importance in a complex situation (see later discussion of initial and decision-stimulus and generative causes, this chapter pp. 104-10). (iii) Some ingredients are more basic, i.e., essential than others (see above), in view of the situations in which they occur. Hence there is variation in value when means. Some conditions are more extensive than others, i.e., function as condition for more entities than others. For example, life is more extensive than property and equality as a base for value achievement. However, all satisfactory environmental conditions are equal in value as means.

II

A

The mode of presence of value (3): *because of the value* of characteristics, requires very careful examination. Specifically, this mode "operates" within the limits of fundamental general qualifications. (a) The entity if it is a characteristic of a *person*, must be acceptable.[12] This is not the case with reference to *some* characteristics of *inanimate* objects. (b) An intrinsically value-opposite entity does not have value because its characteristic has value. There is a further particular qualification concerning pleasure.

By way of background, it is important to note two sorts of the relation: being "a characteristic of an entity": (a simple (direct), (c) complex (mediated). In the case of the simple sort, an entity is a characteristic of an entity without depending on another characteristic. Consider for example, a specific shade of green which is characterized by beautiful. Likewise the entity beautiful is characterized by value.

On the other hand in some cases (b) an entity has characteristics in a complex fashion, namely, its characteristics are characteristic-dependent. Specifically, entity A has as a characteristic an entity which, strictly speaking, is a characteristic of one of A's characteristics. In this sense the relation is that of being characteristic-dependent. For example, a pen is characterized by oval. Oval is characterized by beautiful. On this basis the pen is characterized by beautiful. In like, but more complex fashion, a person has as characteristics: emotions, intentions and overt activities,— which constitute a case of courage. This behaviour entity, which is a characteristic of the person, is characterized by morally good. Thus morally good is a characteristic-dependent (mediated) characteristic of the person.

It is important to note that not all characteristics of characteristics of an entity, are characteristic-dependent characteristics of that entity. For example, a random memory image of autumn leaves is a characteristic of a mind. The memory image is characterized by yellow. However, the

94

mind is not characterized by yellow, on this basis. Likewise, consider a dress which is characterized by yellow and yellow is characterized by beautiful. In some cases at least, a dress is not characterized by beautiful on this basis.

Having examined briefly the relation: characteristic of, we are now in a position to consider the mode: value because of value of characteristics.

Returning to the yellow image: This yellow is characterized by beautiful. Value characterizes beautiful intrinsically. The image is thus characterized by value in the mode: because of the value of its characteristic. More specifically, it is valuable because of the value of its characteristic-dependent characteristic: beautiful. In like fashion the beautiful oval pen, discussed above, is characterized by value.

An important, complicating, fact must be stressed. The mind which is characterized by the beautiful yellow memory image, is valuable. It is valuable because one of its characteristics, the memory image, is valuable. This is so even though the characteristic of the memory image, namely its yellow colour which is a basis of its beauty and hence its value, is not a characteristic of the mind. Further, the entity beautiful is not a characteristic of the mind even though beautiful is a characteristic of the memory image.

It is to be noted that when an entity is valuable because of the value of its characteristics, the amount of its value is the same as the amount of value of its characteristics.

It is essential to realize that in the case of: valuable because of the value of characteristics—if the characteristics are valuable intrinsically it does not follow that the entities which have these characteristics are likewise valuable intrinsically.

B

The report that a person is, on occasion, characterized by morally good, and valuable on that basis requires clarification. It has been pointed out that morally good behaviour has the following ingredients: specific sorts of (a) motive, (b) intention, (c) action, all of which are characteristics of a person.

It will be realized that motives, intentions and actions are *consequences* of the causal initiative of a human mind. Hence we have before

95

us as characteristics of a person—entities which are consequences of that person's causal activity. (It must be remembered that behaviour characterized by morally good is, as a matter of fact, also intrinsically valuable as such.)

That an entity is both characteristic and consequence seems to involve difficulties. However, what is reported is simply a matter of fact. More specifically, motives and intentions are mental contents and hence characteristics. Sometimes the action ingredient of morally good beahviour is mental—hence again a case of mental content. If it is overt physical activity, it is a characteristic of a body—still a characteristic of a person.

An apparent problem also occurs with reference to the report that a person is characterized by knowledge, for example (to consider one sort of knowledge): awareness of true propositions. The problem seems to arise in view of the fact that propositions are not characteristics of minds, nor are true. How then can knowledge be a characteristic of a mind—and the mind be valuable on that basis? The reply is that a mind in knowing, is aware, and the occurrence is focussed on true propositions. To this extent a mind is characterized by knowledge.

So far attention has concentrated on the fact that an entity which is characterized by true, or beautiful, or morally good, is valuable because these entities are valuable. These ''characteristics'' are valuable intrinsically. However, the total situation is far more complex. Entities also are valuable because their characteristics have value in other, extrinsic, modes.[13]

In order to avoid possible error, care must be taken to count an entity only once in the: valuable because of the value of characteristics mode. For example, consider the case of a man who is characterized by courage. Courage is valuable because of its characteristic morally good. This particular occurrence of courage is also valuable because of its consequences. It will not do to assign value to the person because of the total value of his courage characteristic and also, in addition, assign value because of the value of morally good which is basically a characteristic of courage. If, however, attention is concentrated exclusively on the morally good characteristic (a characteristic dependent one) of the man (omitting the other value aspects of courage), then the procedure of course avoids objectionable duplication in assigning value.

C.

It is now advisable to examine, in some detail, the basic qualifications concerning the mode: valuable because of the value of characteristics. Consider first (a): In the case of a person, the entity which is a characteristic, must be acceptable.[14]

C.1

Take, for example, a person who is efficient in burglary. He does not have value because of the value of efficiency since the presence of efficiency in this context is characterized by value-opposite intrinsically, and hence is unacceptable.[15]

Similarly, it is well to realize that a person who is honest does not necessarily have value because of the value of this characteristic. Honesty is unacceptable, and its value likewise, if it occurs when dealing with a lynching party which inquires concerning the location of an intended victim. Here an entity characterized by morally good is a means to value-opposite behaviour. On this basis its presence is intrinsically value-opposite and hence unacceptable.[16]

It is relevant here to examine a somewhat similar but more complex case. Consider a person who generates a beautiful imagination image for the purpose of arousing a morally evil reaction. Hence beautiful is an instrument used to produce something which is intrinsically value-opposite—such an occurrence of beautiful is unacceptable. The person does not derive value from its intrinsic value. However, it is well to emphasize, as pointed out previously—beautiful here is not a characteristic of the person. Rather technically speaking, it is a consequence.

Consider now cases where value *is* derived by a person because of the value of characteristics. A parent who is honest in dealing with his children in the context of love—is a case in point. His efficiency in manifesting his love is a further illustration.

It has been noted earlier that pleasure is an intrinsically valuable entity of which the occurrence in some situations is unacceptable.[17] In addition, as pointed out earlier, there is a special particular qualification to be made concerning pleasure.

The state of affairs concerning pleasure is not the same as that involving efficient and honesty. If these two are acceptable, they are the basis of value derivation by the person who has them. However, there are cases of

97

pleasure, though acceptable, from which no value accrues to a person on that basis: Specifically, in the case when a person is not the decisive initiating cause of pleasure, the pleasure derived from eating a sandwich does not bestow value on the eater.[18]

There are some complex behaviour entities, with pleasure as an ingredient, which are intrinsically valuable and acceptable.[19] Such characteristics (i.e., complex behaviour entities) of a person are the basis of value derivation. Here strictly speaking it is not the value of pleasure, as such, which is of concern. True, in some cases of complex wholes of behaviour, which have pleasure as an ingredient, pleasure has the status: acceptable. But to repeat, it is the value of the behaviour which is important: not pleasure alone, but pleasure in reaction to a specific entity.

This emphasis on the value of an organic whole of behaviour, rather than on one ingredient—as the basis of value derivation by a person, is very relevant when one notes some apparently paradoxical facts about pain.

In some cases the presence of pain is involved in value derivation by a person. Specifically when a person feels pain sympathetically with reference to the pain of others and proceeds to ''do something about it,''—this complex behaviour entity is the basis of value derivation by the person who is characterized by this behaviour. It is to be emphasized that it is not a case of deriving value from acceptable (value-opposite) pain as such. Rather, the valuable organic whole of behaviour has as an essential factor: pain. In this sense acceptable pain is involved in a: valuable because of value of characteristic, situation.

C.2

The preceding discussion has concentrated on the characteristics of *persons*. The situation is different with reference to *inanimate objects*. Consider the case of a beautiful cathedral. It has been built by a selfish dictator. Much human misery is involved in the construction of the building. The presence of beauty under these conditions is intrinsically value-opposite. The beauty is unacceptable. However, in this situation, the building does derive value from the value of its characteristic.

On the other hand, consider a toadstool which is mistaken for a mushroom, and so is eaten. This inanimate entity is efficient in causing pain. The presence of efficiency in this context is characterized by value-opposite. Hence its value is unacceptable. In this case the inanimate object does not derive value from its unacceptable characteristic. The difference seems to lie in the fact that the toadstool is the cause of the unacceptable valuable characteristic. The building is not. It should be realized that the comments concerning efficiency with reference to the burglar and the toadstool, and to the building concerning beautiful,— would apply also if the characteristics under consideration were: appropriate, harmonious, and in the case of persons—consistent.

It must be emphasized that efficient and other such entities occur in a context analogous to that of beautiful in the illustration above. That is, efficient etc. are characteristics of entities which are not causes of (involved in) value-opposite consequences. When, for example, efficient is a characteristic of knife (i.e., it is sharp) or consistent of a story—in some cases efficient and consistent are the bases of derivation of value by the entities so characterized.

D.

Let us examine briefly qualification (b): An intrinsically value-opposite entity does not have value because a characteristic has value. Consider for example unjust behaviour which is characterized by efficiency. The value of efficiency does not form a basis for claiming that unjust behaviour is valuable.[20] A *"like to like"* pattern is relevant as far as derivation of value from a characteristic is concerned. Specifically what is intrinsically *value-opposite* does *not* become valuable because of an intrinsically *valuable* characteristic. Value-opposite and value are not "like" entities. On the other hand, under certain conditions, an intrinsically valuable entity has additional value because of the value of its characteristics. As will be pointed out later, an intrinsically value-opposite entity has additional value-opposite under certain conditions, because of the value-opposite of its characteristics. But if the members of the pair of entities under consideration are in different categories, i.e., one is valuable, the other value-opposite—the mode of presence of value (or value-opposite) is not in effect.

E.

A rather technical question remains for consideration: It is obvious that some entities which have valuable characteristics also *lack* unacceptable value-opposite characteristics. Under certain conditions[21] they derive value because of the value of their characteristics. Do they also derive value from the absence of unacceptable value-opposite *possible* characteristics? The answer is: yes.

In general, the absence of unacceptable value-opposite characteristics from a situation where they can be, and sometimes are, present—is characterized by value intrinsically. On the basis of this complex entity being a characteristic in the case of some entities—they have value because of the absence of unacceptable value-opposite characteristics. Consider the case of an inanimate object: a chair. It is acceptably beautiful. It could have been unacceptably ugly. It is characterized by value because of its beauty. It is also characterized by value because of the absence of ugliness. It is obvious that we have here a case of a pair of entities—such that if one is present as a characteristic the other is not. In such cases the "absence factor" basis of value can be termed "a standard supplementary factor". It adds value to what is already valuable on the basis of the presence of the other member of the pair—which is characterized by value. In the interests of simplification in evaluating an entity it is usually sufficient to note only the value of what is present.

In dealing with the absence of entities which, in some cases, are characteristics of *persons*—a complexity arises. For example the absence of cowardice from the behaviour of a person may not be the basis of value as a characteristic of this person. Instead of being courageous he may be insensitive to danger, or unaware of all threats, or under overwhelming presence of fear of punishment if he is cowardly! His avoidance of cowardice is not on the basis of personal commitment to courage. On the other hand, if a man has overcome the temptation to be cowardly and has achieved courage[22]—then he not only is characterized by value because of the value of his courage, but also because of the absence of cowardice. Further, since his behaviour in overcoming a tendency to cowardice is a case of preventing the presence of an entity characterized by value-opposite—this preventive behaviour is characterized by value. Since this is one of his characteristics, he is valuable on this basis.

Incidentally, even if the overcoming of a tendency to, i.e., preventing of, cowardice does not result in achievement of courage—the process of (acceptably) preventing a value-opposite is characterized by value. Further, if the behaviour is based on personal commitment the person is characterized by value on this basis, to an amount equal to the amount of value-opposite prevented.

III

(4) An entity, on the basis of its means function, *in some cases*[23] has value because its *external* consequences are characterized by value. Thus value may be said to "accrue" to it.

A

The fact that mode (4) stresses consequences and some cases of mode (3) involve consequences (see pp. 95-96) may seem to cast doubt on the advisability of claiming a distinction between mode (4) and at least some occurrences of mode (3). However, it must be realized that the derivation of value from characteristics (which in some cases are consequences) is different in degree from cases of derivation from *external* consequences. Also many complexities arise in the latter case which do not occur in the former. However, the most fundamental point, to be made here, is that it is essential to realize that the consequences considered in mode (4) are not characteristics of the entity of which they are consequences. In this sense they are external. In brief, value is present in different ways in mode (3) and (4). It is the difference between value present because of the characteristics of an entity on the one hand and because of something other than the entity and its characteristics, on the other. The fact that some characteristics are consequences of the entity which is so characterized is an interesting fact, but does not blur the distinction between modes (3) and (4).

In all this discussion of derivation, or accrual,[24] of value because of the value of consequences, it must be noted that, strictly speaking, it is not a taking of value from the consequences, i.e., syphoning it off. Rather it is a case of entities becoming valuable because they are causes, instruments etc. with reference to entities which are consequences and are characterized by value.

In the interests of simplified presentation, unless otherwise specified—the term "consequences" will refer to *external* conse-

101

quences.[25] Consequences which are characteristics will be termed "characteristics."

It is important to realize that the term "consequence" is used in a rather broad sense. For example, if pain is involved in the process of the construction of a cathedral, the pain is a consequence of the cathedral, at any time during its construction, though strictly speaking the cathedral does not exist in completed form. A more usual sense of "consequence" is the case where the completed cathedral, because it is cold and draughty, has as a consequence the pain of its uncomfortable users.

B

The phrase "in some cases" (introductory statement) brings into focus the two important qualifications mentioned in connection with the mode: valuable because of the value of characteristics. Adjusted to the consequences mode, it is essential to bear in mind that (a) the entity which is a consequence, if intrinsically valuable, must be an acceptable entity[26] and (b) an intrinsically value-opposite entity[26] does not derive value from the value of its consequences (which may be valuable in any mode).

C.1

The exact nature of the situation whereby an entity acquires[27] value because of the acceptable value of its external consequences, requires considerable elaboration. In the first place, it must be borne clearly in mind that one is here concerned only with actual consequences, i.e., consequences which have occurred or are occurring. Any discussion of future consequences falls into other modes, namely the possible or potential (5 or 6). It is essential to stress that accrued values are not identical in amount with the value of the consequences, nor do entities to which value accrues always have value in the same mode as their consequences. The fundamental point is, to repeat: external consequences are not characteristics of an entity. Nevertheless the amount of accrued value depends on the amount of value of the consequences.

A book[28], money, air, each of which in a specific situation is a means to someone's acceptable pleasure, will have thereby accrued value in some amount. But the book, money, air, are not characterized by pleasure, hence do not derive the value of the pleasure in the fashion in which those who have the pleasure as a characteristic do. Likewise, a stool may have as a characteristic the intrinsically valuable entity, beautiful—its

102

ingredients (the stool being a result) do not thereby acquire the beautiful characteristic in simple transfer fashion, and thereby its amount of value. In any case, they would not be valuable in the same mode as beautiful, i.e., intrinsically.

It was pointed out in discussing mode (3) that in many instances an entity does not have the characteristics of its characteristics, for example, the yellow dress illustration. This is a further basis for the report that even if external consequences were characteristics, it would not follow that an entity would have the value of its consequences by simple transfer.

C.2

In the case of an entity deriving value because of value[29] of its external consequences, the situation is very complex indeed. Specifically, the question as to the proportional amount of value of the consequences,[30] which accrues to the entity which has consequences, cannot be answered in simple fashion. It must be kept clearly in mind that in a situation where an entity has consequences, the entity is functioning as a means. This brings into focus the various sorts of means which are involved, namely: instrument, cause, operational condition, ingredient. This four-fold distinction has a significant bearing on our question as will now be elaborated.[31]

Consider a particular situation:[32] A skillful surgeon (cause) uses a knife (instrument) and saves the life of a high-grade human being—that is a person characterized by value in various modes. Thus a very valuable consequence takes place.[33] A greater proportion of the value of the consequences accrues to the surgeon as cause, than to the knife as instrument. In neither case does the total amount of the value of the consequence accrue[34] o the entities functioning as means. Consider next the table used in the course of the operation. It has the status of: operational condition. Here again the accrued value is only a fraction of the value of the consequences, with reference to which the table is a condition. Further, the proportion of value accruing to the table is smaller than that which accrues to the surgeon or to the knife. In general, this is typical.

Consider next the *ingredient* sort of means with reference to organic wholes. By way of background it must be remembered that *organic wholes* have characteristics, and/or consequences, which are not possessed by any of their ingredients. Many of these are characterized by

103

value; for example, a committee characterized by a balanced wisdom which is not found in any member. The consequences of implementing the decision of the committee are different from, and superior to, what would have been produced on the basis of individual action. It must be realized that some ingredients have the status: major or essential, and others that of minor or "mere." This has an important bearing on the question as to the proportion of value of the consequences, i.e., the committee, which accrues to an entity which is functioning as a means (ingredient). For example, in the case of a man who is one of five equally important members of a committee, one fifth of most of the amount of value of the committee accrues to each of the equally important members. On the other hand, the committee's recording secretary has the status of minor ingredient. Hence he derives less than the value obtained by each essential member of the committee. Still less is derived by mere members of the committee who contribute little to its deliberations.

Consider again the *knife* used by the surgeon in performing a beneficial operation, intending to do so, motivated by concern for fellow men. The knife has accrued value not only because of its consequences due to its instrumental function. It also has value since it is an ingredient in a complex organic whole of behaviour (its consequent) which is intrinsically valuable, and also characterized by morally good. It is to be noted that the amount of value accruing to the knife because of its ingredient status in an organic whole, is relatively small in comparison to the value accruing to the motive in the same organic whole situation.[35]

It should be further noted that an entity[36] which functions as instrument, or cause, in one situation does not have the *same proportion* of the value of the consequences, accruing to it as any other entity which is an instrument or cause in another situation. However all occurrences of conditions are the same in this respect (see pp. 92-94). As has been pointed out there is a variation among occurrences of ingredients. But ingredients which have the same status have the same relative proportion of value.[37]

In any case, it should be obvious that an entity which is an ingredient in a complex organic whole—does not have the characteristic ingredient only. In most cases it is characterized by at least one of the following: cause, instrument, condition. For example, the surgeon's knife is not only an ingredient in the operation behaviour. It is also an instrument, or a cause, of the removal of tissue.

The preceding remarks constitute a general survey of mode 4. Further clarification of this complex mode is now in order.

D

So far discussion of causes, instruments, conditions, ingredients and their consequences has proceeded on a very simplified level—many crucial issues have been avoided in order to get main points in focus. Some of the more complicated matters must now be examined. Attention will first be directed to cause-effect relations.

D.1

Consider the case of an apple. Mr. A. had the apple for lunch. In this context the apple caused pleasure. Subsequently Mr. A., being in a "good mood", performed an act of concern for the welfare of a fellow man. Is this morally good behaviour a "consequence" of the apple? Does the apple derive value because of the value of this behaviour? The answer is: No. The morally good behaviour is not even a so-called "indirect consequence". It certainly occurred subsequently to the eating of the apple. But, strictly speaking, it is not a consequence of the apple. The apple is not a cause, instrument, condition, or ingredient of the morally good behaviour. The pleasure, which is a consequence of the apple, is in this context a condition for the morally good behaviour. One of the main causes of the morally good behaviour is the impressive example set by others.

It is well to note the sense in which the apple has as consequences pleasure. In the context of eating, it produces changes in the stomach, which produce brain states, which result in the experience of pleasure.[38] Thus, "linking" the apple and pleasure, there is a series of entities each of which, in turn, is both consequence (effect) and cause. The apple's efficacy with reference to pleasure obviously is mediated through a series of other entities which have causal function. Thus, in a sense, both the apple and stomach changes, in the eating situation, causes pleasure involving other things, for example brain changes. In the complex behaviour unit sequence, the apple is both *decisive*, and *initial*, cause.[39] The pleasure is the *terminal* consequence. In between are entities which have the status of *mediating* causes, and consequences. However, for ordinary purposes, it is a convenient locution to refer to the initial cause

105

as "the cause" and the terminal, i.e., full, effect in a cause effect series—as "the effect."

The question may arise: Surely the apple has a cause—specifically a seed. Is not the seed the decisive initial cause leading to the terminal effect (consequence): pleasure? The reply is: no. After all, the seed, as such, does not arouse bodily reaction and so on. Its consequence is the apple. The apple is the decisive initial cause of pleasure. It should be obvious that we have before us examples of a specific *causal unit of entities*[40], each with a definite beginning and a definite end, i.e., a definite decisive initial cause and a definite terminal consequence. One unit is: seed as cause—apple as effect, the other is: apple as cause—pleasure as effect. An essential point is that some entities with the relative status, cause and consequence are within one such unit of entities. We must bear all this in mind in order to avoid mistakes in identifying causes and consequences. *Only thus can one avoid errors in assigning value to entities on the basis of a mistaken claim that they are causes of certain valuable consequences.*

Concerning the relative value (because of value of consequences) of decisive initial cause and mediating causes—the greater proportion of value derived because of pleasure, goes to the initiating (i.e., decisive) cause. Incidentally with reference to consequences within the series (which are not terminal), all preceding cause entities derive value because of the value of the consequences in question. For example, the apple and the stomach states derive value from whatever value brain changes have. The apple deriving more than the stomach states.

D.2

Consider again the case of the surgeon A who performs an operation and so saves the life of an outstanding human being: B.

It is, of course, the case that "A performing the operation and thus, as a consequence, the life of an excellent man was saved" is a complicated series of entities. It involves A's decision to save B's life, which results in physiological changes in A, which result in him using the knife[41] in such a fashion as to remove diseased tissue from B. As a consequence of this B's life is saved.

It is essential to note that this case is different from that of the apple causing pleasure. In the latter, one and the same entity is both the initial and the decisive cause. The surgeon is the decisive cause in the case of saving a life. But the initial cause is the illness of B. A is the decisive cause in the sense that the operation would not have occurred, despite the presence of B's illness, without A's decisive decision to operate, and subsequent activity. The final terminal effect is the saving of a life.

The valuable consequences of surgeon A's decisive causal initiative are the bases of the accrual of a very considerable amount of value to him. In similar fashion, as in the case of the decisive causal apple and the effect of pleasure,—various intermediate entities in the series from A's decision to the actual saving of B's life—derive lesser amounts of value than A derives. As far as the initial cause, i.e., B's illness, is concerned, no value is derived from its valuable consequences. This is so because essentially the basis of B's illness causal status is the pain it involves. The *like to like* pattern is not in effect, i.e., no value accrues to what is intrinsically value-opposite, namely pain.[42]

It may be suggested that, in a geniune sense A is not the decisive cause of saving B's life. Specifically: a complex causal series begins before the appearance of A. In fact, he is one of its mediate effects. After all, it may be argued, A's activity of proceeding to save B's life is caused by the influence of A's teachers at medical school. Therefore his teachers are the decisive initial cause of B's continued existence. Indeed, it may be claimed that the teachers of A's teachers, and so on *ad infinitum*, are the decisive cause—and each generation of teachers derives value from the fact that B continues to ''enjoy life''.

The reply to these ingenious suggestions is that A's teachers are not the decisive initial cause of A's activity of saving B's life. The decision and activity were A's. None of his teachers made the decision and performed the operation on B.

It is true that without his teachers A could not have performed the operation. Specifically, without his teachers A would not have been trained in medicine. But it was A who benefitted from the training, and later exercised the decisive causal initiative and proceeded to perform the operation on B.

Speaking technically, one unit of entities is: A's teachers aiding in the professional development of A. Another unit of entities is: A proceeding to perform the operation and so saving B's life. Indeed there is a series of other units of entities describable thus: the teachers of A's teachers training them, and so on. Of course A's teachers derive value from the fact that they helped to make A ''what he is''. A, their effect, has value because of the operation on B. A's teachers derive value because of the value of their consequence A.—but not (immediately) from the operation, because they did not perform it. It is very important to realize that in the process of causing A to be a skillful and dedicated surgeon, the causal initiative did not rest exclusively with his teachers. He also took initiative in making use of their assistance. Hence a plurality of cooperating causes was involved. Both the teachers and A derive value from their valuable consequence, namely: the efficient surgeon A. An outstanding teacher derives more value than a "run of the mill" student. In some cases the derivation is roughly equal in amount. In most cases the student's initiative is more important.

It may be objected that A's teachers, by their example, inspired him to save lives. Hence his long period of study and his saving of B's life were a consequence of his teachers' example. Thus the decisive initial cause does lie with his teachers. However, it is surely the case that the student had this goal before he came to medical school. How a medical student comes to have such a goal will be discussed subsequently.

D.3

Reference to another illustration will serve to bring into focus several very important factors involved in dealing with decisive and initial cause, and terminal consequences, in a causal unit of entities. Consider the case of a man Z who uses a knife to stab X, thus causing pain. It appears obvious that, in terms of the preceding discussion, Z causes pain for X. Of course, the knife is a mediating cause (as well as an instrument).

At this point it is appropriate to re-emphasize the fact that a unit of entities may involve a very considerable number of ingredients. Consider the situation where Z, under pressure from a group, of which X is a member, feels frustration, reacts with an emotion of anger, desires to stab X, and proceeds to do so. Pain results. In this complex unit of entities, the group which exerts the restricting pressure is the initial cause, and X's pain is the terminal consequence. Which entity is the decisive cause? At first sight it may appear that the group, by exerting pressure on Z, is not only the initial but is also the decisive cause of his feeling of frustration and hence of subsequent reactions, including the infliction of pain on X. Is the situation analogous to: the apple causing pleasure for Mr. A?

It is relevant to observe that: any human being, under normal condi-

108

tions, derives pleasure from eating an apple. But there are at least some people who under group pressure do not feel frustration; or if they do they are not angry; or if they are angry they do not desire to stab a person; or if desiring do not implement the desire. More specifically, an apple automatically produces pleasure for a human being. Given the stimulus, the organism "passively" responds by generating pleasure. The effected person does not exert decisive initiative, or control, in determining whether or not he feels pleasure. However, it seems to be the case that whether or not a particular person feels frustration under group pressure etc., depends on him. In other words, in some cases a person's reactions are decisively controlled by an initial or prior cause—in other cases the decisive initiative, i.e., control, is vested in the reacting organism.[43] The human person gives every indication of being an entity which is capable of a vast range of development of creative initiative—as well as possessing a considerable number of standard[44] patterns of reaction which are decisively controlled by initial causes. The details of even these patterns of behaviour may be c langed by a process of conditioning. Here again is a basis of novelty and creative initiative on the part of persons. There can be a replacement of dependence on initial stimulus by a location of decisive initiative in the reacting entity, i.e., the person.

D.4

Before returning to a consideration of whether or not Z exercised decisive causal intuitive in stabbing X, it is appropriate to look briefly at the process of *conditioning* which *in part* explains why people react as they do in specific situations.

One standard pattern of reaction is that of pleasure, or favourable attitude, to what satisfies a basic desire. For example, a group which satisfies a person's desire for social approval functions as a decisive initial cause which arouses pleasure. Almost anything which is associated with the group takes on its status: initial decisive cause of pleasure, or of a favourable attitude. For example, the headquarters building of the stimulus group may become an object of pleasure. More important, almost any pattern of behaviour of the stimulus group, be it morally good or morally evil, may serve to arouse pleasure in the persons who receive social approval. Thus the conditioned person comes to feel pleasure in, and approve, either unjust behaviour or tolerant behaviour;

109

or indeed, a way of life characterized by self initiated search for entities of great value, or a robot like reaction to a given stimulus—because he finds these traits in a group which satisfies his desire for social approval.

Likewise relevant is the standard pattern of behaviour such that a person likes and approves those who help him, in any matter.[45] It is to be noted that what one strongly approves is likely to become a part of one's own behaviour.

In brief, as the result of such a conditioning process a person may become a decisive initiating cause of behaviour characterized by value or of behaviour characterized by value-opposite. He may also be so conditioned that when confronted by a specific situation he reacts to it in a complex pattern of behaviour in a passive fashion. Here the initial cause is decisive. His reaction involves no decisive initiative on his part.

The process of conditioning discussed above is based on the presence of a decisive initial stimulus, which involves certain basic human desires which are conditions.[46] Another conditioning situation involves the extension of the range of desire. When what a person desires is associated with almost any other entity, the other entity becomes the focus of desire as well. The usual illustration, in the realm of advertising, is the following: there is in most people the desire for the presence of a sex object. When a beautiful young lady is portrayed sitting in a car, there is a desire for the car. In this fashion, particular ways of dealing with particular problems, or more general attitudes either passive acceptance of stimuli—or active individual decisive initiate—can be established in a person. The point being made here is that individual differences in behaviour can be understood, *at least in part*, by reference to presence of conditioning.

In summary: the sort of person a man is depends not only on his standard pattern of automatic reaction to specific initial causes. His personality is shaped by the conditioning process to which he is exposed (thus individual differences emerge). As a result of this he, in many cases, with reference to specific problems, is not reacting passively to stimuli but actively, and indeed, creatively.

On the basis of the preceding discussion, we return now to the problem of the derivation of value from the value of consequences.

As noted, in many cases, what a man is, in part, is the result of the influence of other persons. They derive value from what the man is, i.e., their consequence. But the influenced man, insofar as he is the controller

110

of his activities, is the one who derives value from these activities. Those who have helped to shape him do not derive value directly from his activities. He performed them—not those who influenced him.[47]

On the other hand, if the influencer (shaper) functions as a decisive initial cause in the conditioning situation and the person influenced subsequently reacts in a purely passive fashion to certain specific stimuli—the person influenced derives no value from value consequences which may result as far as *causal* function is concerned. However the influenced person may derive some value if as the result of the conditioning he is used as an *instrument* by his shaper.

Consider now a case of *inspiration*. C inspires D if D is actively seeking the solution to some "way of life",[48] problem, and C provides, by precept or example, a solution, in such a fashion that D, on his own initiative, is willing to accept it and proceeds to implement the suggestion. In such a situation, the initial cause is D's problem. The decisive initiative is found in both C and D jointly. It is not a case of the inspirer conditioning the inspired in such a fashion that the inspired subsequently becomes a decisive initiator.[49] In the inspiration situation C and D both derive value from the sort of person D becomes. The relative amount of value accruing to C or to D depends on the amount of effort, initiative (in the detailed activity) and such factors. In some cases C derives more value than D. In other cases the reverse is the case.

It should be obvious from all the preceding discussion, that though C has a decisive part in helping D to adopt a way of life, C does not perform D's acts. Hence C does not derive value directly from D's behaviour.

In any case, one must not place undue emphasis on conditioning or suggest that men are ultimately under its complete control. When others are attempting to condition persons for some selfish advantage (of the conditioner), in at least some cases, the intended victims become aware of the fact—admittedly sometimes belatedly—and react negatively. When things go wrong the results of conditioning are rejected. More fundamentally, the human organism, at least initially, is very energetic and active in its reaction to its environment. Considerable creative initiative is manifest. Even after a great deal of conditioning has occurred, almost all human beings retain decisive critical initiative in examining the world around them, and adopting techniques which satisfy them. There is a strong and continuing tendency to resist control by others, no matter how subtle it may be.

The immediately preceding reports may seem unduly optimistic—indeed downright inaccurate. It is true that some men and women are the victims of skillful conditioning. However, the record of history serves to substantiate the statement that a large number of persons, given time, see through the process of their victimization and attempt, in varying ways, to escape from it.

Most people are concerned to achieve valuable entities of many different sorts. However, it must be admitted that in the absence of certain stimuli—in general certain sorts of environmental facilities, a person has great difficulty in exercising decisive initiative with reference to certain goals. For example, if a child is never confronted by an adult who manifests control of, or absence of, anger in a problem situation—he is not likely to develop such behaviour. However, on the basis of enlightened observation he may note the inefficiency of anger.

D.5

With all this by way of background, let us return to the situation involving Z and X's pain. A survey of various sorts of human behaviour, in such a situation, indicates that what has been reported may be the result of several different causal factors. It may be the case (a) that Z did not function as the decisive cause when he felt frustration and anger. They were an automatic reaction resulting from the decisive initial cause: group pressure. But his desire to inflict specific harm and resultant activity were decisively initiated by him. It may be true that he became the sort of person who acts that way as the result of conditioning. But when performed these activities were decisively initiated by Z.

In this case since the decisive initiative is vested in Z, a considerable amount of value-opposite accrues to Z because of X's pain. Group pressure is this situation has the status of initial but not decisive cause. It derives a relatively small (in comparison with Z) amount of value-opposite in the consequence mode.

However (b) it may be the case that in the situation as described, Z had been so conditioned that when group pressure impinges on him, he automatically (i.e., without any internal initiative) proceeds to feel frustration, anger, desires to stab a member of the group and proceeds to stab X (conveniently within range) and so causes pain. Hence the initial and decisive cause is group pressure. It derives a considerable amount of value-opposite from the consequence pain experienced by X. Hence Z

112

derives a relatively small amount of value-opposite. In effect he is merely an instrument (with causal function).

There is (c) a third possible state of affairs. The feeling of frustration and emotion of anger manifested by Z in the group pressure situation, instead of being an automatic response to a decisive initial stimulus—might have been rather part of a pattern of life activity, decisively initiated by Z. Specifically, it might be that Z is the sort of person[50] who sets himself to be angry and feel frustrated when group pressure occurs. The reaction is thus decisively initiated by the person Z, not the group.

The same is the case with reference to the remaining items in the sequence of entities under discussion, leading up to X's pain. In this case Z exercises decisive initiative and derives considerable value-opposite. Group pressure as initial cause derives a relatively small amount of value-opposite.

Which of these three alternate possibilities, as a matter of fact, is the case must be determined by careful investigation. Only after this is settled can one correctly decide the amount of value-opposite which accrues to group pressure and to Z, in the situation under consideration.

D.6

On the basis of the preceding discussion, consider the case of: a person reacts with pleasure to acceptable morally good behaviour. The behaviour derives value thereby. The person derives value only if he exerts actual decisive initiative in reacting with pleasure to acceptable morally good behaviour.[51]

The point at issue is that the mere presence of pleasure as experienced by a person is not the basis of value derivation by that person. He must be the decisive cause. Thus pleasure aroused by eating an apple does not serve as basis of value derivation by the eater.

Returning briefly to the person who reacts as decisive cause with pleasure when confronted by morally good behaviour. Here obviously the morally good behaviour as initial cause derives relatively less value than does the person—from the resultant pleasure.

D.7

The preceding discussion of illustrations involving the apple, the surgeon, and Mr. Z have brought into focus a number of critical issues involved in the distinction between initial and decisive, as far as causes are concerned with reference to derivation of value (or value-opposite). A

113

number of more general problems remain for clarificatory discussion.

A word about natural and conventional *units of entities* (which are organic wholes) is in order here.

The unit sequence or entities: "apple—pleasure" is natural in the sense that this happens without decisive arrangement, or external contribution, by human beings. The surgeon—saved life sequence is a conventional professional procedure. However, it involves a natural sequence, i.e., given certain operational techniques, a life is saved. A more clear case of a conventional unit is that of the sequence involved in playing a game from start to finish.

It is easy to overlook distinctions between units of entities and components of units—particularly when instruments are mistaken for causes.[52] The importance of such distinctions, with reference to derivation of value, or value-opposite, from consequences, is brought into focus in the following illustration: Consider a telephone in a "terminal illness" hospital. It is used as an instrument to provide information, that is: true propositions. Pain results from this "bad news". Does the telephone have as a consequence: pain? Does value-opposite accrue to the telephone on this basis? The answer is: No. There are two units of entities here. The telephone is an instrument not a cause. Specifically (a) the cause of the pain is the information. (b) The presence of information is a consequence of the use of the telephone. In any case, value-opposite does not accrue to information. This is because information is a case of: true proposition. The truth of the statement is characterized by value intrinsically. True is the decisive factor in producing the pain experience. The pain arising from information does not result in value-opposite accruing to the true information.[53] There is no derivation from like to unlike, in the case of intrinsic value and value-opposite. The telephone, strictly speaking, is valuable because of the value status of its consequences, namely presence of information. The subsequent pain has no bearing on the value (or value-opposite) characteristic of the telephone. It has no means relation to pain.

D.8

A further complexity arises concerning cause-effect (consequence) relations. In some instances an entity has several cooperating causes.[54] Each derives value from the consequence, on the basis of its relative importance in the causal process. Consider, for example, a house. It is the consequence of the activity of a number of different men—using different skills. To make the case more specific: if the terminal end is protection from the weather in comfort—carpenters are more important and hence derive more value than interior decorators. In terms of structural stability, cement pourers and carpenters are of equal importance and hence have equal value.

It is essential to stress that many particular entities which function as causes, instruments, conditions, have consequences which are "one-time occurrences" and are of brief duration. Consider for example an apple. The apple in the process of being eaten causes pleasure once.

On the other hand, some entities remain as continuing sources of consequences. Consider for example a surgeon who continues to perform beneficial operations; or a physical object, such as a building, is a continuing source of protection. Further, because of a continuing memory of a great man, he continues to have a causal influence. He produces consequences for centuries. In this sense, an entity continues to derive value as consequences continue to occur. In many other cases only a few consequences are produced, over a brief period, and in a restricted area.

It may well be objected that in some cases there is a practical problem —that of determining what the (actual) consequences of an entity are, also what value characterize these consequences. It is of course true that in many instances there are grave difficulties, in view of the complexities of human life. However, there are general patterns of human behaviour which are known. For example, it is possible to find out, at least get a general picture of, the medical results to date of the discovery by Banting and Best of insulin as a method to treat diabetics. Knowledge of the number of people in a group where insulin has been used, is available. At least a "fair notion" of consequences and their value can be obtained.

At this point it may be wise to re-emphasize what was stressed at the beginning: the mode "valuable because of the value of consequences" is concerned with *actual* consequences. Hence it does not involve a discussion of so-called "future consequences". It is confined to a consideration of what has happened from the time a particular occurrence of an entity began its means function until the present, or until it stopped its means function—if that event has already occurred.

D.9

It is now appropriate to examine in more detail the fact that entities which are intrinsically characterized by value-opposite do not derive value because of the value of their consequences. For example, when the entity morally evil produces pleasure for some people—morally evil is not thereby characterized by value.[55] The same is the case with reference to the entities: false, ugly, pain, inefficient, inappropriate, inconsistent, discordant. The like to like principle is relevant here.

Further, organic wholes which are intrinsically value-opposite do not derive value from the value of their consequences. For example, cowardice, when it produces pleasure for some observers, does not thereby derive value.

Turning to a related issue: A false proposition, or an ugly face or a person "filled" with pain—when pleasure is aroused in others—does not derive value thereby.

False, ugly, pain are the essential (i.e., decisive) factors in promoting the pleasure reaction to the proposition, face, persons. Hence it is a case of a value reaction to a value-opposite entity.[56]

It is important to stress the distinction between *essential* and *incidental*. Consider, for example, an ugly pen. When used to write an important letter it derives value from the value of its consequences. The value-opposite ugly factor is incidental. It has no essential bearing on its instrumental function and the resultant consequences.

Thus, in brief: In the means-end situation the "assigning" of value, because of value of consequences, to an entity which is intrinsically value-opposite, or to an entity which is essentially characterized by intrinsic value-opposite, does not legitimately occur. In other words, the appropriate pattern of derivation is from "like to like".

D.10

This point, however, must be set in the context of the other main qualification—of the general statement of the mode: valuable because of the value of external consequences. Careful attention must be paid to the issue: acceptability or unacceptability of consequence entities—and hence their value.

Consider, for example, the now familiar case of a person who is honest in answering a question concerning the location of the intended victim of a lynching party. Pleasure is experienced by the lynch mob—with reference to this occurrence of honesty. However, value does not accrue to the honest behaviour from its consequent pleasure. Nor does the informer

116

derive value thereby. The *occurrence of pleasure* in the presence of a means (honesty) to what is intrinsically value-opposite behaviour (hatred of a fellow man) is intrinsically value-opposite. Hence, it (pleasure) is unacceptable. In general, an entity derives value from a valuable entity only if it (the consequence) is acceptable.

In other words, there are cases where the *"like to like"* pattern is not decisive. Honesty is intrinsically valuable and so is pleasure, but honesty does not derive value because of the value of pleasure. Such pleasure is unacceptable in the context under discussion.

It is well to note further that in some cases non-derivation of value involves both the "like to like" pattern *and* the unacceptability factor. Consider pleasure when contemplating cowardice. Pleasure is not the basis of accrual of value to cowardice because cowardice is intrinsically value-opposite. The like to like pattern is not in effect. Also pleasure in this case is unacceptable.

Despite all the preceding negative conclusions, and implied warn-ings—in many cases value accrues because of the value of conse-quences,—specifically when the value is acceptable. This is true of many entities characterized by value intrinsically, or entities which have characteristics which are intrinsically valuable (or have no status in this mode).

Consider reaction of pleasure to the entity morally good. Value accrues to morally good because of the value of pleasure. Likewise when a beautiful face arouses pleasure in an acceptable context, the face derives value from the value of the pleasure. The case is the same with reference, for example, to acceptable courage arousing pleasure. Courage is an organic whole which is intrinsically valuable.

The preceding discussion of the derivation of value has concentrated on consequences which are characterized by value intrinsically—for example, pleasure. It is now appropriate to emphasize the fact that value also accrues because of consequences which, as such, are not intrinsical-ly valuable. They are characterized by value in several extrinsic modes. However, one must consider the fact that many such external conse-quences involve the presence of intrinsically valuable entities which have the status of characteristics or consequences—with reference to these consequences.[57]

Examine the case of a bishop who "builds" a beautiful, acoustically efficient cathedral (consequence). If the building is acceptable, he derives value from the fact that he is the cause of the extrinsically valuable building.

However, the building is unacceptable if the process of its construction involves a vast amount of misery on the part of an "exploited" group of persons. If this is the case, the bishop derives no value. It must be emphasized that the cathedral is characterized by value on the basis of its beauty and efficiency—despite the fact that it is unacceptable and so are its values.[58]

A clarificatory comment concerning pleasure which results from the unacceptable cathedral is in order. If the pleasure results from contemplation of the beauty of the building, this is a case of a pleasure reaction to an unacceptable occurrence of beautiful. Hence the pleasure is unacceptable and the beauty and the building it characterizes, derive no value from the value of the pleasure. On the other hand, persons who take shelter in the building from a winter storm experience pleasure as a result. Such pleasure is acceptable. The building does derive value therefrom.[59]

The cathedral loses its status of unacceptable—so do its valuable entities, if in due course the misery accompanying its construction[60] is no longer present. However, even if the cathedral becomes acceptable at a later date, this does not change the fact that the bishop does not derive value from it—if in the context of building it he caused great misery. As far as his relation is concerned, it is an unacceptable building. Its values are unacceptable.

If a cathedral which once had the status unacceptable subsequently becomes acceptable, in the fashion noted above—pleasure in, for example its beauty, now becomes acceptable. It derives value on that basis and so does a person who feels (decisively initiates) the pleasure in this context—though he didn't in the former context. Further, while previously the building on balance was characterized by value-opposite, with the passage of time and change of situation, it may well become on balance: valuable. This, however, does not eliminate the earlier value-opposite characteristics. It is merely a case of overbalancing of value-opposite by value.

It is very important to realize a fundamental difference between the valuable because of the value of consequences and valuable because of the value of characteristics, modes. In the case of the latter as has been noted, some inanimate objects derive value from unacceptable characteristics. However, in no case does an entity derive value from unacceptable value consequences.

E

The preceding discussion has tended to concentrate on the derivation of value on the basis of having as consequences *specific* concrete acceptable valuable entities. It is to be noted that in some cases there is a derivation of value from more abstract, general, states of affairs. Consider, for example, consequences such as: preservation of acceptable value, introduction of acceptable value, instances where there is increase of acceptable value, progress toward the immediate ideal situation. Since each of these operational resultants is intrinsically valuable, a means entity derives value because of the value of the abstract entity to which it is a means.

In many cases an entity is a means to operational resultants through the medium of a specific intrinsically valuable consequence. Hence, for example, a person derives value on the basis of consequences (a) increase of acceptable value, which results from the presence of consequence, (b) acceptable case of beautiful. The person derives value on both bases.

Further, there are many entities (which function as causes, instruments or conditions) which derive value from the fact that they are involved in the consequence: removal, or prevention, of unacceptable value-opposite. Consider the case of a person who causes the removal of an ugly building. Likewise a machine used in the process. It is essential to realize that removal, or prevention, situation is different from the introduction, or increase, situation. In the latter, a cause derives value from a specific consequence entity which is the means to the introduction, or increase, of acceptable value, i.e., another consequence entity. There is a dual derivation of value in the consequence mode as noted. Such is not the case when concerned with the removal, or prevention, of something which is value-opposite. Specifically, here there is only one intrinsically valuable consequence, namely *removal*, etc. of unacceptable intrinsically value-opposite.

Incidentally, the consequence "removal of ugliness" is not characterized by value intrinsically. It is a means to what is intrinsically valuable, namely: removal or unacceptable value-opposite.[61]

An entity which functions so as to produce the consequence "removal of an entity which interferes with, or prevents, the occurrence of accept-

119

able value'' acquires value in the same fashion as the cases considered above.

An entity which has a consequence: "makes good" a deficiency which stands in the way of the attainment of acceptable value—thereby acquires value, in a somewhat more complex fashion than the preceding cases. As a matter of fact, it is not only a case of removal of a concrete value-opposite entity, it also involves introduction of a valuable one. Such a result could be obtained, for example, by a process of instruction which removes the defect of ignorance in a child by providing knowledge and enables the child to solve a problem resulting in pleasure.

IV

A

(5) We turn now to consideration of value in the mode: *possible*. An entity is valuable in this mode if it is capable of being valuable, in one of the following modes: (2) when means, (3) because of the value of characteristics, (4) because of the value of external consequences[62]—in the same fashion as other members of the same class, which are actually valuable in some or all of these modes.

The amount of value in the possible mode depends on the amount of value the entity would have if its capacities are fully actualized. However, the amount is not equivalent to the amount in an actual mode (2-4). It is proportional to the degree of probability that the values it is capable of having—will characterize it in the future.

For example: an oil field has the capacity for producing billions of barrels. But suitable conditions are not present. Specifically, extraction and transportation procedures are not now available. Hence probability of actualization is minimal. Therefore the proportional amount of value in the possible mode is slight. If, on the other hand, almost immediately the possibility of full use has a high degree of probability of actualization,—the proportion of value is very high. It is almost equal in amount to the value of an actualized state of affairs.

B

Calculation concerning the mode: value as possible involves practical questions such as: How many times can the entity have specified valuable

120

consequences? In the case of a pen this can be determined by examining the nature of its components and the environment. Hence, if it has an expectation of "1000 hours[63] of use" and the environment is normal for writing, and it has been used 200 hours, its possible use as a means to write is "clear enough". Consider a human being who has been behaving in a "love of fellow man" fashion (characteristic)—on an average of five times a day. This provides the basis for figuring the future probability of a similar number of such behaviour entities. This, of course, assumes that his standard pattern of behaviour will continue in the future. This can be supported by noting that the situation does not seem to be on the point of changing. The amount of value of characteristics and consequences is also determined on the basis of the standard pattern.

In brief, because of the nature of the entity under consideration, and the environment in which it is—possible occurrences of entities are implied, and in at least some cases they can be known. In many cases, as above, possible means, consequences and characteristics and their respective values, are indicated by actual past and present occurrences.

In a few instances, it is appropriate to claim that an entity which has not yet been used as a means, hence not yet had consequences, not yet has manifested certain characteristics—nevertheless is capable of having them. For example, a newly discovered metal has possible means status with reference to airplane strength and possible "appearance characteristics" when polished. Here, of course, the new discovery is in the context of a generally familiar situation concerning sorts of metals. Otherwise possibilities in this sense are not known.

It must be emphasized that there are varying degrees of definiteness in the possible mode. For example, if a man has a well established pattern of courageous behaviour his possible future courageous behaviour is fairly reliable, given continuing environmental conditions, internal and external. In the matter of specific consequences involved in the use of a particular pen, difficulties arise. There are some common elements in the actual use of a pen by most human beings. But the details of additional use hence, consequences, vary greatly. In addition to the common writing use, some men use a pen to tap, bite, scratch, throw, etc. Thus in specifying the possible use of a pen one can obviously refer, with confidence, only to common elements in use. However, if one is discussing the possible use and consequences of the use of a pen by a particular person whose personality traits are well known, additional possible uses

121

and consequences are determined and can be discussed. It is obvious that all possible uses can not be known.

V

A

(6) An entity is valuable in the *potential* mode if it is capable of becoming something else; or contributing as an ingredient to the genesis of a different entity, or developing a different characteristic—which is characterized by value in one, or more, of the modes 1—6.

The amount of value which an entity has in the potential mode depends on the amount of value possessed by the new entities it is capable of becoming, contributing to, or having. However, the amount of value in the potential mode is less than that of the value of what it is capable of "becoming". For example, a child who is potentially a high-grade human being is characterized by less value in this mode than the actual adult under consideration (different characteristic). Likewise sand (ingredient) which is potentially valuable with reference to glass is characterized by less value than the actual glass. Similarly water has less value than ice (something else)—in some situations. This is so because of the difficulties involved in transition from potential to actual.

The proportionate amount of value in this mode depends on the probability of realization and the temporal nearness of the occurrence. As in the case of the possible mode, so with the potential, even if a specific entity has not yet been "changed", nevertheless as long as it is of a specific sort, the entity has value in the potential mode.[64]

B

The problem of knowing potential value is handled in the same fashion as that concerning value in the possible mode. Specifically, some potentialities are known on the basis of a well-established and well-known linkage of entities—as in the case of illustrations used above.

It will have been noted that in discussing value in the *possible* mode, attention was focussed on three other modes, namely: valuable when means, valuable because of value of characteristics, valuable because of value of consequences. This was done because, while an entity which is

122

not now functioning as a means, does not now have certain characteristics or consequences which if present would be valuable—this may be the case. However, concerning entities such as courage, and just behaviour—they are always valuable. They are valuable as such, that is intrinsically. Therefore the issue of possible intrinsic value does not arise. However, some entities are potentially other entities which *are* intrinsically valuable.

It is essential to realize that the possible mode of value is literally: valuable because of the possibility that an entity which does not now have value in modes 2—4, that is actually have it—may have it. It is not the case that in this context there can be a possibility of value in the possible or the potential mode. However, an entity can be valuable in the potential mode in the sense that it is capable, for example, of becoming, or being involved in or with, some other entity which is characterized by value in all six modes.

VI

A digression at this point is perhaps relevant in order to clear up a possible misunderstanding. It may appear that the characteristics *possible* and *potential* both are *means*. More specifically, it may appear that an entity which is a possible with reference to some characteristic or a potential for the development of something new and different, in both cases is, as a matter of fact, a means to that something else. Hence it may appear that possible and potential are not modes of value destined from: valuable when means. However, in the context of this discussion—in the interests of care in noting geniune distinctions—it has been pointed out that an entity has the characteristic (is a) means only when it is actually functioning as a means to some end. Hence, for example, a pen when it is not being used to write is, strictly speaking, not a means for writing. The pen in this situation is only "a possible" with reference to that means function. In fact, there is a distinction between possible and actual; means being in the actual category. The same distinction "holds" between entities which are potentially means and those which have the characteristic: (actual) means.

In discussing simple entities valuable in the intrinsic mode and complex ones characterized by morally good (Chapter 4), it has been noted that such entities can be compared as to amount of value. Further some general patterns of relative amounts of value become evident.

It is now appropriate to "look into" the matter with reference to entities which are valuable in various extrinsic modes (2—6).

In the first place it is to be observed that any entity which is valuable in the intrinsic mode has a higher degree of value than any entity which is valuable in the mode: when means. A comparison of the value of entities involving other pairs of modes of value cannot be made in this sort of general fashion. This fact will become obvious from the subsequent discussion of specific entities (Section 4).

VII

It is now appropriate to turn to a brief consideration of the various sorts of extrinsic value-opposite modes. In view of the extended discussion of modes of value, what is offered here is a "bare outline".

A

(2) Any entity when it is functioning so as to prevent, interfere with, or stop (remove) the presence or occurrence of any entity—is thereby characterized by value-opposite as far as that entity is concerned. The "preventing etc." entity may be functioning as an instrument, cause, condition. It is characterized by value-opposite when "preventing etc." regardless of the value or value-opposite, characteristics and/or conse-quences[65] of what it prevents, etc.

As was noted, the differences in amounts of means value of cause, instrument, condition, depends on the factor: importance. This state of affairs is paralleled by differences in amounts of value-opposite on the same basis, that is, relative importance of cause, instrument, condi-tion.

It was pointed out in Chapter 1 (p. 13) that cases of value-opposite when entities prevent etc. occurrences of entities, from one perspective, i.e., with reference to one end—are cases of positive means function. They are means to a specific goal. Hence it is actually a case of valuable when means. For example, the tapping pen (of the previous illustrations) prevents concentration on fruitful thoughts. In this sense it is characterized by value-opposite. But on the other hand, it functions as a means in order to achieve this result. Hence it is characterized by value when means.

A more clear-cut case of opposite to means function would be the complete absence of entities which normally function as instrument, cause, condition and ingredient. For example the absence of a pen would be a clear case of value-opposite in the writing context.

B

(3) An entity which is characterized by any one of: morally evil, ugly, false, inefficient, or inappropriate, inconsistent, discordant, is characterized by value-opposite because of the value-opposite characteristics of its characteristics—and in the same amount,—unless the characteristics and their value-opposite are acceptable. Pain has the same status if it is decisively initiated by the person experiencing it.[66]

As was pointed out earlier, acceptable value-opposites are cases where an intrinsically value-opposite entity is involved as means, or essential accompaniment, with reference to value (a valuable entity), or is in a reaction sequence which is intrinsically valuable in a specific context.[67] In dealing with an enemy in time of national emergency (if the nation is characterized by value on balance) dishonesty, inefficiency, inconsistency and so on, though intrinsically value-opposite, are acceptable since they involve the achievement of valuable consequences—the retention of valuable national life. Hence a person who is dishonest, inefficient and inconsistent in this context is not characterized by value-opposite on that basis.

The same comments apply to characteristics which are characterized by value-opposite in modes other than the intrinsic.

If an entity is lacking in a characteristic which if present (and on occasion is present) would be characterized by value,—because of this defect, the entity is characterized by value-opposite proportional to the value of the entity if it had been present.

It must not be overlooked that the "like to like" pattern applies here as elsewhere. For example, inefficiency in doing what is appropriate is not the basis of derivation of value-opposite by the entity: appropriate. It does, however, cast aspersion on the person who so acts.

C

(4) Let us consider next the mode: value-opposite because of value-opposite external consequences. As in the parallel case of valuable because of the value of consequences—two important general qualifications must be borne in mind. (a) the "like to like" pattern applies. That is, an entity which is characterized by value intrinsically does not derive value-opposite from value-opposite consequences. (b) Value-opposite is not derived if the value-opposite of the consequence is acceptable.[68]

In general means entities of various sorts (cause, instrument, etc.) derive value-opposite from their consequences proportionately in the same pattern as in the case of derivation of value from valuable consequences.

The preceding summary statements require particular clarificatory illustrations concerning mode 4: (i) In the case of entities which are not intrinsically valuable or value-opposite—value-opposite is derived from the unacceptable value-opposite characteristics of consequences. For example, a knife used in viciously slashing a person and hence causing unacceptable pain, derives value-opposite thereby. Likewise a pen maliciously used in tapping and hence in interfering with valuable thought, derives value-opposite.[69] Further, the knife and the pen each derive additional value-opposite because of their status as ingredients in an organic whole of behaviour which is intrinsically value-opposite.

A slum, which by its ugliness arouses pain, derives additional value-opposite from the value-opposite characteristics of pain in this situation.

Acceptable value-opposites have already been mentioned.[70] For example, when exercise has as a consequence pain, the exercise does not derive value-opposite thereby if the pain is acceptable. That is, it is naturally involved in the achievement of health.

(ii) We turn now to supplementary comments on entities which are intrinsically valuable or value-opposite, or have such characteristics.

In some cases an entity which is intrinsically value-opposite, and has intrinsically value-opposite consequences,—nevertheless does not derive value-opposite thereby. Consider a case of human misery (pain). When a person reacts with sympathetic pain, this consequence does not add to the value-opposite characteristics of the pain of human misery. The sympathetic pain is a case of acceptable value-opposite. The "pain reaction to pain" pattern of behaviour, is characterized by value intrinsically.

No intrinsically valuable entities, simple or complex, when causing value-opposite consequences derives value-opposite thereby. (Here the "like to like" pattern is relevant.) Consider any one of the eight entities: morally good—harmonious, when causing pain. The case is the same with reference to all the intrinsically valuable organic wholes of behaviour which are characterized by morally good.[71]

So far the discussion of non-accrual of value-opposite to intrinsically valuable entities has occurred in the context of cause-effect relations. This topic must now be expended to cover entities which are ingredients in organic wholes which are intrinsically value-opposite. Consider the case of a pain reaction to just behaviour. Just behaviour does not derive value-opposite because it is an ingredient in an intrinsically value-opposite organic whole. Here the "like to like" pattern is relevant. On the other hand (unacceptable) pain does. Its amount of value-opposite is increased. What has been remarked concerning just behaviour applies equally to pleasure in the case of pleasure in morally evil behaviour.

We turn now to examine entities which though not themselves intrinsically valuable or value-opposite—have as characteristics simple entities which are intrinsically valuable. These are entities characterized by true, pleasure, etc. which arouse pain or any other value-opposite consequence. For example, a true proposition, a beautiful face, or pleasant experience is not contaminated by an accrual of value-opposite from pain. This is so even if the entities in question are unacceptable.

The preceding comment (report) requires some clarification. It applies only if the value-opposite consequences are decisively dependent on the intrinsically valuable characteristic, as in the case of a beautiful face arousing pain. However, if the characteristic beautiful is not a decisive factor in producing the consequence, the entity does derive value-opposite from the value-opposite consequences. A beautiful pen, used in tapping and productive of disturbance of valuable thought processes, definitely derives value-opposite. But here the beautiful characteristic has no bearing on the consequences. Likewise entities characterized by efficient, appropriate, consistent, harmonious, on occasion, derive value-opposite from consequences. For example an efficient insult derives value-opposite from the pain caused by it.

In order to avoid confusion, it is well to note the distinction between what may be termed (a) a negative feeling produced by a characteristic of an entity and (b) a negative reaction to an entity which is on balance characterized by value. For example (a) an uncomfortable chair produces a feeling of pain if one sits in it for a time. On this basis the chair is characterized by value-opposite. However, if it is beautiful and of great historic significance, it is on balance valuable, despite the fact of its uncomfortableness. If a person reacts to the entity beautiful, or to the valuable chair, with pain—value opposite does not accrue to the chair. The reaction of pain to value is characterized by value-opposite and hence unacceptable.

As in the case of the discussion of value consequences, it is well here to be reminded of the complexity of some value-opposite consequences. When an entity functions in such a fashion that its consequence is for example: "prevent, or remove the presence or occurrences of entities characterized by acceptable value"[72]—value-opposite accrues to the entity on the basis that its consequences are unacceptable intrinsically value-opposite. Here again the preceding discussion of the mode valuable because of consequences, is in general relevant.

D

(5) An entity may be characterized by value-opposite in the *possible* mode with respect to its possible means function, characteristics, consequences.

E

(6) An entity may be characterized by value-opposite in the *potential* mode with reference to: the value-opposite of another entity (with reference to which it is potential) in the following modes: intrinsic, means, because of characteristics, because of consequences, possible, potential.[73]

CHAPTER 6

Problems Concerning: The Value- and Value-Opposite Characteristics of an Entity

The preceding chapters (1—5) have provided an exposition of the nature of each of six modes of the presence of value and six modes of the presence of value-opposite. In the interests of simplified presentation, each of these modes has been accorded separate treatment. The illustrations used were discussed in the context of a specific mode—the main concern being to clarify the nature of the mode of presence then under consideration.

As discussions proceeded, it became obvious that (i) there are relations between various modes of presence of value and/or value-opposite, and (ii) that an entity, on occasion, is characterized by value, and/or value-opposite in more than one mode.[1] In addition, (iii) there are other complexities in the value or value-opposite situation. Namely in some cases there are differences between particular occurrences of one many-occurrence entity.

At this point discussion will shift from an examination of the *nature* of modes of value and value-opposite, to a consideration of the value and/or the value- value-opposite characteristic,—of *entities*. This chapter will provide a general outline of the complexity of this situation.

Some entities, for example, morally good, beautiful, true, pleasure, efficient, fitting, consistent, harmonious,—are valuable as such, that is, intrinsically. Therefore all occurrences of them are characterized by value in this mode. However, this is not the case concerning other entities. Many entities are valuable only on the basis of their relations to other entities. Hence, their value characteristics are extrinsic. This is true of modes of value numbered 2 to 6^2 inclusive.

It is essential to realize, concerning extrinsic modes that some occurrences of an entity are valuable because of the value of their characteristics, but some are not. They do not have the appropriate characteristics.[3] The situation is the same with reference to consequences. Further, obviously some occurrences of an entity function as means, others do not. Hence some occurrences are valuable on this basis, others are not. This is so because in some cases the situation is such that occurrences of an entity can not function as a means, e.g., as instrument, cause, etc.

Hence, in general, and in the sense noted above, an entity (many occurrence one) both *has* and *does not have* (depending on which particular occurrence is under consideration) the value, "in question", in the case of each of the modes of (presence of) value types 2—4. There is a further complication. Some particular occurrence of an entity has value under certain circumstances and not under others. So even a particular occurrence both has and does not have a specific mode of value. These general comments will now be clarified by means of illustrations and supplementary specific comments. In the interests of simplified presentation, reference will be made to different entities, each in a different mode of value.

The entity pen is not, as such, valuable as an instrument. A pen (particular occurrence of the entity pen) when functioning as instrument is valuable in the means mode. Other pens when not being used, for example, to write a note, are not functioning as instrument and hence do not have means value. The case is the same with reference to the entity cue. This entity, that is a particular occurrence of it, has value when functioning as a cause. However, not all cues function as cause at any one time. Hence as in the case of pen, so also for cue, the entity both has and does not have value in the means mode.

It is important to realize that a particular pen, or a particular cue, which at one time functions as a means and hence is valuable in that mode—when laid aside and hence is not functioning,—no longer has the means value which it once had. These comments concerning the entities pen and cue, in other words entities valuable as instrument and as cause, when functioning as such—can be paralleled by comments which apply to other sorts of entities in means-end situations. In brief, an entity has value in the means mode only when it is functioning as a means.[4]

In dealing with the mode of value (3): because of the value of its characteristics, here again one must, in most instances, concentrate on particular occurrences of an entity. One cannot in this context deal with a many-occurrence entity as such. For example one man is characterized by value because his behaviour is just and is characterized by morally good. Both, such behaviour and morally good, are intrinsically valuable and the value is acceptable[5] in the case under consideration. On the other hand, another man (a particular occurrence of the entity man) is not characterized by just behaviour. Thus this man is not characterized by value on this basis. The matter is further complicated by the fact that a man who at one time is valuable because of his just behaviour,—at another time is lacking this mode of value because he is not behaving in a just fashion. Thus, while the entity man as such is a living organism, it does not, as such, have the characteristic just or morally good (in an acceptable fashion) and hence does not as such have value on this basis.

It will have been observed that in introducing this topic, the phrase "in most instances" was employed. Consider the "exception case" of a specific shade of blue. It is characterized by beautiful which in turn is characterized by value. Any occurrence of blue has the characteristic value on this basis.

In considering the mode of value (4): because of the value of consequences, the same general point must be made. A particular occurrence of an entity which has valuable consequences is not completely typical. For example, one book[6] has value accrued to it because of the beneficial consequences which follow from the reading of it. Another book has the opposite effect. Hence, the entity does not, as such, have value because of its consequences. This depends on the situation in which the entity occurs. Likewise one particular book in one situation has value consequences, in another it does not.

However, there is one difference between the presence of value in this mode and in the previously considered extrinsic ones. For any particular entity, once value has accrued to it because of its consequences, that value remains even if, at a particular time, it is not having valuable consequences. For example, a book which has produced beneficial results is valuable for that reason, even though it is no longer, or is not at the moment, productive of those results.

It must be realized that the general state of affairs concerning modes of value 2—4 is not "in effect" with reference to modes 5 and 6.

In dealing with value in the possible mode (5), it is the case that, given specific nature and characteristics, *any* occurrence of an entity has value as possible. In this sense, one does not need to "single out" and accord different "treatment" to particular occurrences. One can refer to the "value as possible" characteristic of an entity *as such*. For example, the entity pen has value as possible, with reference to *means*, that is, it[7] *can be* used for writing. This is the case even if the environment is such that writing is impossible. This applies to a pen even when it is, at the moment being used in writing a note. It applies in the sense that the pen is also now available for that purpose in the future. In like fashion, the entity pen has value in the possible mode with reference to the value of the possible consequences which are involved in the possible use of a pen.

In the case of valuable as *potential* (6) the total situation is complicated, in some instances, by the "associated" problem of obtaining knowledge of the entities under discussion.[8] However, an entity such as a specific sort of sand has value as potential with reference to the means mode concerning the production of glass. It is also valuable on the basis of the acceptable valuable consequences and characteristics of the glass to which it stands in the relation of potential. More specifically, it is valuable because it is potentially a means in producing beautiful, useful and pleasurable—glass.

No qualification is necessary concerning any particular occurrence of the entity: sand. Likewise consider the case of a child with excellent heredity being brought up in a suitable environment. Given these specified conditions for development, the child will become, in due course, a mature superior adult. In other words, the child is potentially such a person and is valuable in the potential mode with reference to the valuable characteristics and consequences (etc.) of the excellent adult. Indications are that if sufficient care is taken in "selecting" the child, and the environment, one can identify potentiality,—and value on that basis. However, there are geniune difficulties in the obtaining of knowledge of this sort, which do not arise with reference to entities such as sand.

I (B)

Turning from a consideration of value, to *value-opposite*, it should be obvious that the same general comments apply as those concerning modes of value. Some entities, that is, all occurrences of them, are characterized by value-opposite, intrinsically, for example: morally evil, ugly, false, pain, inefficient, inappropriate, inconsistent, discordant. However, when one examines the extrinsic modes, the situation is different in cases 2—4. Consider value-opposite in the means[9] mode. In terms of the illustrations used in Chapter 1[10], it is the case that the entity finger, as such, is not characterized by value-opposite, even if one or more occurrences of finger are used as instruments to distract attention and hence are characterized by value-opposite. It is not the case that other fingers are so used, and hence are so characterized. Further, even a particular finger which at one time is being used as an instrument and is characterized by value-opposite,—later on is not being so used and will not be so characterized. Therefore, to repeat, in discussing value-opposite characteristics in this mode one cannot refer, legitimately, to an entity without extensive qualification. It is necessary to specify, with great care, that one is concerned with particular occurrences, at a particular time, in a particular situation. To refer to another example: A stick which is used to jab a person in the stomach, and hence prevent his forward motion, is characterized by value-opposite when so used, as a cause. Later on the same stick, lying on the ground, is not characterized by this value-opposite. Many other occurrences of the entity stick do not have this causal function at all, and hence are not characterized by value-opposite on this particular basis. The same comments apply to the entity uneven table, and to a particular occurrence of it with reference to the condition sort of means mode, for example when playing billiards.

It seems pointless to engage in repetition of obvious comments concerning value-opposite characteristics in modes 3—6. The same general points are relevant as in the case of value characteristics.

133

Consider next the fact that a particular occurrence of an entity may be, and frequently is, characterized by *both* value and by value-opposite in *the same extrinsic mode*. A man may be characterized by morally good and by ugliness. Hence on that basis he is characterized by both value[11] and value-opposite in mode 3.[13] This obviously raises a problem as to the *balance* of one over the other.

The same state of affairs is found with reference to mode 4, namely: a particular entity has both value and value-opposite because of value and value-opposite characteristics of its consequences. For example, a finger tapping on a table may annoy, and cause pain for one person and hence value-opposite accrues to the finger. But the tapping may also acceptably relieve tension and so produce pleasure on the part of the person doing the tapping. So in this situation, value accrues to the finger. Here again the question of balance of value versus value-opposite arises. Similar comments can be made concerning the other illustrations of entities which were given in discussing the various sorts of cause etc. function. The finger that interferes with attention and hence is value-opposite, is a means to interference, hence valuable. A further related point is that any entity is valuable as an ingredient in the sense that as an ingredient in that situation, and indeed in the universe, it has value. In other words, the situation and the universe would be different if it were not for this particular entity.

So far in this section, attention has been focussed on the fact that particular occurrences of an entity may be characterized by both value and value-opposite in each of various extrinsic modes 2—4. It of course follows that the same comment applies to a many-occurrence entity since what has been under discussion are particular occurrences of a many-occurrence entity.

Consider next the mode: as possible (5). After all, it is possible that an entity will have various characteristics or consequences (or means functions). Hence one entity will have both value and value-opposite in the possible mode, in view of the complexities discussed above. For example, it is possible for a lady to be in the future,—ugly and also morally good. A stick, when not in use, has the possibility of being a means which can be used to jab someone, producing pain for the person jabbed and pleasure for the person doing the jabbing.

In dealing with inanimate objects such as a hunting knife, it is important to note a significant qualification. In the possible mode in a general sense the characterization may be both value and value-opposite. However, when the knife has been purchased by a person, if the owner is a benevolent wood carver, one set of consequences can be expected to follow. If on the other hand, he is a member of a street gang, there will be other possible consequences. Thus one should appreciate the distinction between the general use of the knife, to produce value and value-opposite consequences, and the probability that it will be used in one fashion rather than another. The possibility of value and value-opposite is based primarily on the nature and characteristics of the knife. The probability of one sort of consequences, rather than another, is based on the personality of the owner.

The same *general* comments made above concerning modes 2—5 apply to value and value-opposite in the potential mode (6). It should be obvious, for example, that sand is valuable because it is potentially glass, and glass is valuable in several modes. In like fashion, sand is characterized by value-opposite in the potential sense in view of the value-opposite characteristics and consequences related to glass. A piece of glass is, on occasion, used to commit murder.

As noted previously, since some particular occurrences of a many-occurrence entity are characterized by both value and value-opposite—in this sense such many-occurrence entities have the same status. The question arises as to the on-balance value or value-opposite characteristic of many-occurrence entities, in modes 2—6.

The complexities discussed in the two main topics above are indeed awesome. The *summary* conclusion is that (i) in many instances, one cannot assign value or value-opposite to many-occurrence entities as such. One must specify the mode under consideration. In the case of some modes one must further concentrate on particular occurrences of an entity. Some occurrences are characterized by value, others are not; also a particular occurrence in one situation is characterized by value, in another it is not. The case is the same with reference to value-opposite. (ii) It is important to stress the fact that in some cases a particular occurrence of an entity is characterized by both value and value-opposite in a specific mode. The same comment applies obviously to the many-occurrence entity which is involved. The issue arises as to whether there is a balance in a specific mode on one side or the other, that is: does the value outweigh the value-opposite or vice-versa. This must not be allowed to blind a person to the fact that the entity *is* characterized by value-opposite or value, though on balance the weight is on the side of value or value-opposite.

III

So far in this Chapter, examination of the complexities of the value and value-opposite characteristics of entities, many-occurrence and particular, has tended to concentrate on *separate* discussions of each of the six modes. In the interests of simplicity in presentation, in each mode, usually a different entity has been considered.

However, it was noted earlier and, in connection with the present discussion, that the value/value-opposite situation is more complex than the simplified presentation of entities in the different modes in this chapter and in Chapter 5 seems, for the most part, to imply. The point at issue is this: in evaluating and comparing entities, it must be realized that (a) an entity in some cases has value in several modes, (b) an entity in some cases has value-opposite in several modes, (c) an entity in some cases has both value and value-opposite characteristics, and several modes of each are involved. (d) In situation (c) there is an "on balance" result.[13]

The preceding summary requires examples: (a) an occurrence of beautiful (i) is intrinsically valuable. It is (ii) valuable when it functions as means, namely, is instrument or cause and is (iii) valuable in the mode of possible when not functioning as means. (iv) It has several consequences.[14] On this basis value accrues to beautiful. Likewise a pen may be valuable: (i) because it has the characteristic: beautiful, (ii) when used to write a letter, (ii) as possible when it is not being used, (iv) because of consequences: a letter. Next consider a pile of shining white sand. It is characterized by value (i) because it is characterized by beautiful, (ii) when it is an ingredient of glass (that is, means), (iii) because of its potentiality of becoming glass (because of value of glass).

As an example of (b) consider: an occurrence of ugliness. It as means stops the enjoyment of pleasure. It has unacceptable pain as a consequence. It continues to have these possibilities.

(c) A pen in addition to being beautiful and hence on occasion a source of pleasure—because it is used to tap on a table, also causes value-opposite consequences such as anger at, hatred of some person, or other forms of immoral behaviour. Hence it has means, characteristics, consequences, value and value as possible with reference to some entities. It also has value-opposite characteristics in the means, consequence and possible modes.

(d) Obviously the problem of determining the balance, on the side of either value or value-opposite of an entity,—in many cases is very difficult. However, the fact remains that in some cases the determination is achieved.[15] Before proceeding to comment further on the problems involved in evaluation,[16] a brief digression is in order.

IV

A further complication must now be faced. The fact that many entities are valuable and/or value-opposite in several modes involves more complexities than might initially be apparent. In the interests of simplified presentation attention will be focussed on value. The same general comments apply to value-opposite. Specifically the point at issue is this: Entities which are characteristics may be valuable in several modes. Likewise entities which are consequences may be valuable in several modes. The matter is further complicated by the fact that frequently a specific consequence has consequences and these in turn have consequences and so on for at least a considerable period of time. These facts obviously complicate the process of ascertaining the value of an entity in the modes (3) because of the value of its characteristics and (4) because of the value of its consequences.

Consider the case of a building which has the characteristic (*acceptable*) beautiful. The entity beautiful is valuable intrinsically. It also has value in the means mode because it is the initial cause of the presence of another occurrence of beautiful. It is thus valuable in the consequence mode. Further the characteristic beautiful (of the building) is valuable in the possible mode. Strictly speaking, it (the beauty of the building) is not valuable because of the value of its characteristics,—it is intrinsically valuable.

The value which the beauty (A) of the building derives from its consequences, i.e., another occurrence of beauty (B) involves the fact that this consequence, since it is an occurrence of beautiful, is valuable in the same several modes as the beauty of the building. In its turn, it has value in the intrinsic, means, possible, and *consequence* modes. Hence there is a third occurrence of beauty (C) and so on. Concentrating on A, B and C: A derives value from the value of B; B derives value because of the value of C (A does not directly derive value from C).[17] When B appears, A's value is increased. When C appears B's value increases. Hence with the passage of time, A's value derived from B increases and so does the value which the building has because of its characteristic beautiful. These comments are set in the context of the preceding discussion of the proportionate amount of value an entity derives from its characteristic and what an entity derives from its consequences.

We turn now to consider a building which, because of its shelter function, has as a consequence: (acceptable) pleasure A. It derives value from the value of this consequence. Here again the same sort of complication is involved as discussed above. The consequent pleasure (A) is valuable in the intrinsic, means, consequence and possible modes. Further the pleasure (B) which is the consequence of pleasure A in its (B's) turn is valuable in several modes. Likewise the (C) consequence of the consequences of the consequence and so on. The preceding comments about gradual increase of value accruing to the building because of the increase in value of A apply in this case as well.

It is of course difficult to determine how long the consequence series extends. However, for practical purposes in some cases it can be approximately determined on the basis of a careful examination of available facts.

It must be re-emphasized that as far as intrinsically valuable entities are concerned, no infusion of value-opposite intrudes to change the fact of value accrual if a value-opposite factor is involved (because of the pattern of "like to like"). For example, if beautiful has as a consequence ugly or pleasure has as a reaction (consequence) pain, these value-opposite entities do not undermine the value of beautiful and pleasure. Hence, for practical purposes, in most cases of evaluation of an entity, for example a building, a simplified treatment is employed. For example, reference is made to the fact that a characteristic or consequence is intrinsically valuable. In such a situation a reference to value-opposite reactions to such characteristics and consequences is not necessary.

At this point it is perhaps relevant to stress that some intrinsically valuable entities may be characterized by value-opposite in the means mode, i.e., they function to prevent the achievement of value.[18] In all such cases the amount of intrinsic value is enough to overbalance the amount of value-opposite. Similarly all intrinsically value-opposite entities have value as ingredients and some have value as instrumental to the achievement of an end. However, here the amount of value is not enough to overbalance the amount of value-opposite.

A more detailed discussion of some aspects of these related complexities will be undertaken in the context of following chapters where an attempt will be made to examine the value and value-opposite states of various familiar entities.

At this stage in the discussion of value, the problem of *change* needs to be faced: Returning to the pen illustration: a pen may remain beautiful (and hence is valuable) during its entire existence. But in one situation it is valuable because of its instrumental character; it is being used in writing—while on another occasion, when it is not being so used, it does not have value in the means mode. It is of course the case that a pen may lose its beauty, and hence value, in the characteristic mode, with the passage of time. For example, its colour and shape may be marred by constant use, or by emersion in water. Hence one cannot, without qualification, attribute extrinsic value to an entity, as such, on the grounds that it is at any particular time possessing characteristics which have value. However, as noted, "value because of consequences" does not suffer this sort of "fade out". The same sort of comments are relevant with reference to value-opposite modes.

It is well to note the basis on which one can discuss the *possible* and *potential* modes of value and value-opposite. It may appear that there is a serious problem here since reference is being made to what is "not yet", indeed to what is not present to awareness. The future is notoriously hard to predict because of the complexity of the situation in which entities are found and on which extrinsic modes of value and value-opposite depend.

However, such comments miss the point. What is at issue is this: In the past, it has been found that a specific entity in a specific situation has been characterized by value or value-opposite in various modes. It is not now in that situation. However, if it is in that situation again it will have these value or value-opposite characteristics.

In the case of the potential mode,—In the past, in a specific situation, particular occurrences of an entity became, or were ingredients in, something else which had value or value-opposite characteristics. If the situation is the same in the future, the same transitions will occur for other particular occurrences of the entity in question.

Before turning, in the next chapters, to an examination of the value, or value-opposite, status of specific entities it is well to bear in mind a number of fundamental factors.

V

In considering the amount of value or value-opposite which characterizes an entity, it is important to note that "amount" has two mean factors: (i) degree, (ii) number of occurrences. For example (i) some occurrences of beautiful or pleasure have a higher degree of value than others.[19] Likewise some occurrences of pain or ugliness have a greater degree of value-opposite than others. On the other hand (ii) three occurrences of pleasure (or beautiful) involve more value than one occurrence—if the degree of pleasure (or beautiful) is the same in each case; likewise concerning value-opposite involved in occurrences of pain (or ugliness). The "number of occurrences" factor is particularly significant with reference to consequences of an entity, or more specifically value or value-opposite which accrues because of values, or value-opposite, characteristics of consequences.

It is very important to understand the significance of the *temporal duration* of intrinsically valuable, and intrinsically value-opposite, simple or complex entities which are characteristics or consequences of other entities. For example, variations in temporal duration of *occurrences* of morally good, beautiful, true, pleasure, efficient, appropriate, consistent, harmonious, do not have a bearing on the amount of value they possess. Likewise, when an entity is characterized by (or has as consequence) any of these entities except pleasure, the duration of presence of the characteristic is not relevant in determining the amount of value derived by an entity because of the value of characteristic (or consequence). For example, because one occurrence of beautiful lasts longer than another, intensity being equal, the former is not more valuable than the latter. Also a beautiful building which lasts a long time is no more valuable, on the basis of its beauty, than a building which lasts a short time. (The situation is the same concerning value-opposites and the

140

entities they characterize or with such consequences.) The case of pleasure is a special one when it is a consequence of an entity. The longer the pleasure consequence lasts the more value the means entity derives (the pleasure being acceptable). However, as noted, the duration factor does not add value to the occurrence of pleasure as such.

It is of course the case that, for example, an object which is beautiful and lasts a long time, may well derive a larger amount of value from pleasure consequences of its beauty than a beautiful object of brief duration. In other words, because of longer duration of existence *more occurrences of* pleasure, of equal intensity, may well occur.

In the case (a) where an entity is valuable in several modes, in order to reach a sound conclusion concerning its value, obviously one must consider all its modes of value. Having examined the amount of value in each mode, one can then proceed to note the total amount of value characterizing that entity. This process of assessment does not involve the assigning of exact units of measurement. Rather it is a case of recording a position on a scale running from low to high amount of value.[20]

A similar procedure should be followed in the case (b) where one is dealing with entities characterized by value-opposite in several modes.

When one is confronted by a situation (c) where an entity is characterized by both value and value-opposite—in each case in one or more modes—the proper procedure is to ascertain the total amount of value—the total amount of value-opposite—and (d) see on which side the balance falls.[21]

It is important to remember the fact that some entities are complex. It has been pointed out[22] that some such are organic wholes characterized by value, or value-opposite, *intrinsically*. In these cases, the amount of value, or value-opposite, is not obtained by a simple summation or two summations and a subtraction. However, the value, or value-opposite, characteristics of the organic whole must be considered in the context of an examination of the value and/or value-opposite characteristics of its ingredients.

For example, the organic whole "awareness of beautiful" has less value than the sum of values of awareness and beautiful. "Hatred of morally good" has more value-opposite than the subtraction of the value of morally good from the value-opposite of hatred. Likewise it must be stressed that, for example, the value of sympathy bears no mathematical relation to the value-opposite of two occurrences of pain. Hence it is well to remember that the *ingredients* in a situation which is an organic whole may on balance be value-opposite despite the value of the organic whole—for example, sympathy. Likewise the on-balance aspect of the ingredient of a situation which is an organic whole characterized by value-opposite, may be value—for example consider: hatred of morally good.

It will have been noted that the details of value or value-opposite characteristics of the organic wholes, in modes other than intrinsic, have not been spelled out, nor has this been done with reference to ingredients which are valuable or value-opposite in modes other than intrinsic. Such complexities will be covered in subsequent chapters dealing with specific entities.

Further complexities remain for examination. Consider a case of high grade morally good behaviour: "Love of a fellow man". It occurs in a specific situation of such a sort that it arouses a great deal of negative reaction, e.g., hatred, disdain, displeasure—such that the thus generated new organic whole is characterized by value-opposite intrinsically, in view of the nature of the reaction to the morally good behaviour. Nevertheless, paradoxically, despite the value-opposite factors, the situation also is an organic whole characterized by value intrinsically. Namely, it is a case of acceptable morally good behaviour persisted in despite violent opposition.

It is important to distinguish between (a) "everything considered" and (b) on balance concerning *ingredients* of an organic whole. The "everything considered" factor includes (b) and as well the intrinsic status of the organic whole.[23] The "everything considered" conclusion may be value-opposite, in a limited situation, despite the fact that the organic whole involved is a case of value. For example, vast suffering arouses sympathy by a few persons, that is pain and an attempt to alleviate the vast suffering. The situation, everything considered is value-opposite, namely the value of sympathy does not over-balance the amount of value-opposite of the pain (suffering). Of course, the time may come when as the result of sympathy by many persons, and very effective means used to alleviate suffering—a situation may come about where there is little suffering and much pleasure. In such an expanded situation, "everything considered" the case is one of value both as to ingredients, and the "sympathy and its results", as an organic whole. Be that as it may, from the beginning sympathy is an organic whole characterized by value intrinsically.

At the end of this outline of modes of value, and problems involved in the evaluation of entities, it is well to be reminded of a fundamental fact: A person, with the relevant background of experience, can and does correctly apprehend the amount (i) of value, or (ii) value-opposite, or (iii) value or value-opposite on balance—status of a large number of entities. The details of *how this skill is obtained* and its precise application have been, and will be, discussed elsewhere. In general it amounts to this: A person of comprehensive experience, who bears in mind the relevant factors introduced in the preceding discussion,[24] is in a position to deal with the problem of accurately reporting the characteristics of many entities which, in human comprehensive experience, are found to be characterized by value or value-opposite. Further, he is in a position to make sound comparison of the various entities on the basis of their relative amount of value or value-opposite characteristics.

VI

It is here suggested that ultimately one should discuss entities only on the basis of what is open to awareness. Disregard what is beyond the range of comprehensive experience, in attempting to understand value. It will be admitted that human beings operate within limits. All characteristics of some entities, in all probability, are not now known. In general, obviously there are some entities which are not now open to awareness. This is indicated by the fact that we are continually finding new ones. However, new entities come within range'', as the result of enlightened effort.

The preceding remarks, as briefly noted, do not rule out the discussion of the value and value-opposite characteristics of what is imagined. (a) In some cases, what is imagined is, an entity simple or complex which is, or has ingredients which are, open to awareness in the non-imaginary realm. The value or value-opposite characteristics they have in the non-imaginary realm are the value- or value-opposite characteristics they have when imagined.

By way of background, it must be realized that a person can think about an entity even though it is not present to awareness at the time. Specifically, (a) using concepts, or images, one can think about wood, pleasure, green, without being aware of these entities, that is, without seeing wood, or green, or experiencing pleasure—at that time. In like fashion, one can imagine wood in an empty fireplace, green characterizing a wooden chair which does not now exist, and the pleasure which will be derived from sitting in such a chair.[25] The "thought about" or "imagined", pleasure has intrinsic value, the wood and green entities have extrinsic values in the situations mentioned. It is essential to note that we are discussing *entities*. The fact that they are being thought about or imagined—though particular occurrences of these entities are not present to awareness—does not deny that the entities do have specified value as well as other characteristics. They have them whether they are now present to awareness or not, though the value in question is not now present in the non-imaginary world in the particular case.

(b) In some cases, the situation is more complex concerning imagined entities. Wood, pleasure, green are entities which persons find. These are not ultimately based on human imagination. On the other hand, men do not find mermaids as objective facts in the non-imaginary world. One is aware of the entities: tail of a fish, head of woman, and the entity "parts joined together". These are imaginatively thought of as being together. This complex object of thought is termed a mermaid. This linkage of head of woman and tail of fish is not found in the non-imaginary world. What is thought of imaginatively is technically speaking "object of imagination". It is an "entity" in the sense that it is what one is thinking about.

The beauty which characterizes the heads of some women characterizes the head of the mermaid if such a head is an ingredient—and so on. However, in all cases—the imagined chair and the imagined mermaid—the value characteristics are not present as an ingredient in the world now—in the fashion indicated by the objects of imagination. To repeat, one can think about, or imagine, entities which are not present. Thinking about them, or imagining them, does not make them present now. But what we think about or imagine are, or have as components, entities which are open to awareness.

One should not confuse (i) the present occurrence of an imagination "image of a mermaid"—an object which is now present to awareness and (ii) the imagined mermaid which can never be present to awareness as far as comprehensive experience (to date) is concerned. The situation is such that: paradoxical as it may seem, one can think about, imaginatively, a complex entity termed "mermaid". This combination of entities is what a person is thinking about, despite the fact that it is not found, that it is never present to awareness.

It will be noted that in discussing the long-range ideal situation (characterized by: "the largest attainable amount of acceptable value in this world")—an imagined object—reference is not being made to the "mermaid" sort of imagined object!

SECTION FOUR

A REPRESENTATIVE SAMPLE OF VALUABLE AND VALUE-OPPOSITE ENTITIES— COMPARISONS

CHAPTER 7

Morally Good—Morally Evil Behaviour

Previous chapters have considered the nature, and modes of presence, of the *value* and *value-opposite* characteristics of entities. It is now appropriate to proceed to examine a representative sample of *entities*, in order to determine their value or value-opposite status,[1] and on this basis, in some cases, to compare them.

I

Before proceeding to an examination of particular cases, a few general background comments are in order, in the form of recapitulation.

The vast complexity of the "modes of value/value-opposite" situation seems to render it impossible to reach a sound conclusion concerning the value, or value-opposite, status of a particular occurrence of an entity. This, however, is not the case. Relatively simple practical procedures are available.

(a) (i) In dealing with entities which are intrinsically valuable, it is to be recalled that they do not draw value-opposite from value-opposite characteristics or consequences. On these bases it is obvious that no value-opposite factors are involved in the possible mode. In some cases an intrinsically valuable entity has value-opposite status because of preventive function, as instrument or cause, and hence in the possible mode. However, this is never enough to overbalance the value of the

149

entity. Hence, simply put, an intrinsically valuable entity turns out to be still valuable after other modes are taken into consideration.

(a) (ii) Concerning entities which are intrinsically value-opposite the same general comments are relevant. Specifically, such an entity does not derive value from any valuable characteristics or consequences which it may have. On this basis no value factor is involved in the possible mode. All intrinsically value-opposite entities have value as ingredients and may have value as instruments, condition or causes. Hence, they are valuable in the possible mode on these bases. However, the amount of value is never enough to overbalance the value-opposite status of such entities. Thus, in brief, an intrinsically value-opposite entity is found to retain the status of value-opposite after all other modes are considered.

(b) In dealing with entities which are neither intrinsically valuable nor value-opposite, the practical procedure is not as simple as with (a) above.

Here a particular occurrence of an entity may be both valuable and value-opposite in some or all of the modes 2—6. Hence one must take all these factors into consideration and strike a balance. On the basis of past experience this is relatively easy in at least some cases.

In making these calculations, it must be remembered that a *person* does not derive value from unacceptable valuable characteristics,[2] while in some cases an inanimate object does—in some cases does not. Further, no entity derives value from unacceptable valuable consequences. It must also be emphasized that acceptable value-opposite entities are not the basis of derivation of value-opposite. In general, the preceding discussion of modes of presence of value and value-opposite must be kept clearly in mind while discovering the value or value-opposite status of any entity (on balance).

It will be recalled that very considerable complexities occur because entities which are characteristics, or consequences, are frequently valuable and/or value-opposite in several modes. Further, in so far as this involves further consequence entities, one seems to be confronted by an extensive regress.

This problem is of chief concern when one is trying to ascertain *the exact amounts* of value, or value-opposite, of entities. On the basis of past experience, and bearing in mind what has been pointed out concerning derivation of value, or value-opposite, in the consequence mode—at least a fairly accurate *rough approximation* can be reached, if sufficient care is taken. In any case, it is well to note that the status of consequences is determined ultimately by entities which are intrinsically valuable or value-opposite. Hence, as we proceed to examine the regress from the first consequence entity to its consequence entity, and so on, there is no shift from, for example, value to value-opposite. Further, it is important to realize that the relevant consequences of consequences are frequently cases of duplication of the first in the series. Hence the problem of evaluation is simplified. It should be noted that in dealing with consequences one tends to concentrate on terminal consequences in a unit of entities (see Chapter 5, pp. 104-6).

As a rule of thumb, for most practical purposes, one does not need to get involved very deeply in the complexities just noted, because of the rapidly diminishing significance[3] of such consequences of consequences.

Attention will be focussed initially on some complex entities which are characterized by morally good, and also some entities characterized by morally evil. There will also be discussion of value, and value-opposite, characteristics of the entity morally good and the entity morally evil. As well, there will be consideration of beautiful, true, pleasure, efficient, fitting, consistent, harmonious—and their opposites. Further, reference will be made to the value- or value-opposite characteristics of situations in which these entities occur. Also, the question of acceptability will be dealt with.

II (A)

Consider an ideal family situation where a parent is *honest* in dealing with his child in a particular crisis situation. That is: desiring and intending to do so—he conveys accurate information. Honesty is valuable intrinsically. Also since it is characterized by morally good, it has value because of the value, in several modes, of this characteristic. As a consequence of parental honesty, the child is honest, and further, he derives pleasure from this parental treatment. Thus additional value is present and accrues to the parent's honesty. Involved in this is the use of honesty as an instrument to arouse similar behaviour on the part of the child. It is valuable when a means.[4] Further, obviously in this situation honesty is valuable in the possible mode, i.e., in view of possible means function and hence future valuable consequences. In any case, the consequence honesty and pleasure are in turn valuable in several modes—intrinsic, as possible and in some cases as means and because of consequences.[5]

It is important to note that the parent's honesty in the ideal family situation, in so far as it is a means to, and has as *consequences*, a favourable environment for the child, hence it helps to prevent morally evil behaviour. In this sense it derives value. In so far as this occurrence of honesty *prevents* possible evil from occurring, it is characterized by value-opposite. However, obviously this amount of value-opposite is infinitessimal in comparison with the amount of value involved. This is a clear case of: on balance valuable. This becomes increasingly clear as we proceed to examine the broader contact in which this case of honesty occurs.

It is well to realize that in the ideal family situation, a parent is motivated by love, intends to facilitate the fullest attainable acceptable value achievement of his child and, in the case before us, therefore behaves in an honest fashion. This is an instance of an organic whole of behaviour termed "love of fellow man"—more specifically, "love of one's child." This latter complex entity is valuable in several modes. For example, it is valuable intrinsically and also because it is characterized by morally good, and has accrued value because of consequences. Honesty in this situation, since it is an ingredient in the organic whole "love of one's child", derives value from its status as ingredient.[6] Further, since honesty is a means (instrument) in achieving acceptable value, this is a source of the value of honesty in the parent-child situation under discussion.

The fact that honesty characterized by morally good is an ingredient in love of one's child, which is also characterized by morally good—may seem somewhat paradoxical. However, this is simply the case. Though both the ingredient and the more extensive organic whole, are characterized by morally good, there is a greater amount of morally good characterizing love of one's child than honesty.

The preceeding discussion of a particular occurrence of honesty is admittedly not complete. A number of additional factors might have been considered. For example, it might have been noted that the occurrence of honesty was characterized by beautiful and efficiency, and that consequences other than those mentioned may have occurred.[7] However, what has been introduced in discussion constitutes a sufficient covering of major factors. Such a coverage serves for practical purposes. Indeed, even the details of coverage here, seems unnecessary later, once a standard pattern of discussion is established.

II (B)

Consider next the case of a man who, on an occasion during World War II, is honest in his reaction to a Gestapo demand for information concerning the whereabouts of a large group of Jews and "downed" allied airmen, hiding in a German-occupied territory. Specifically, this man, motivated by a love of truth and hence desiring to provide accurate information, intends to provide it, and proceeds to do so. This honest behaviour is used by the Gestapo as an instrument which has as a consequence pain for the captured men and women, their families and persons of "like mind". The hatred motivated and deliberately intended infliction of this pain by the Gestapo is a source of great pleasure to them and many fellow Germans.

This occurrence of honesty is intrinsically valuable and derives value from the fact that its characteristic morally good is characterized by value intrinsically. In addition, honesty in this situation is characterized by value when means[8] and as possible means.

Since honesty is intrinsically valuable, it does not derive value-opposite from the value-opposite results of its instrumental function, nor from the fact that it is an ingredient in an organic whole characterized intrinsically by value-opposite.[9] Further, honesty does not derive value from the valuable pleasure consequences because pleasure in this situation is unacceptable. In any case, this honesty, because of the result of its instrumental function, is not an acceptable valuable entity. It therefore is not a case of introduction of acceptable value, or a component in "largest attainable amount of acceptable value" situation, and hence does not derive value from this source.

It is apparent from the preceding discussion that different particular occurrences of honesty (a typical entity characterized by morally good) have vastly different amounts of value when a number of modes are considered. The honesty in the ideal parent is far more valuable than that of the Gestapo information. Its superiority lies in the area of pleasure and other such consequences, and its status as ingredient.

Concerning the ingredients of the "Gestapo situation," one finds that there is more value-opposite than value, that is, on balance it is a case of value-opposite. Likewise as an organic whole the situation is characterized by value-opposite intrinsically. Thus it is obvious that there are situations involving morally good behaviour in which the totality of the ingredients is not a case of value on balance. Further, the situation as organic whole is characterized by value-opposite.

In the "Gestapo situation" it may appear that dishonesty would be characterized by morally good. Indeed, the conveying of false information, coupled with an intention to do so, in this situation, could well be ingredients in valuable behaviour. However, strictly speaking, this would not be a case of dishonesty. Dishonesty would occur if a person is motivated by a desire to convey false information, involving a *basic lack of concern for truth*, and has this intention, and implements it (or tries to). On the other hand, if the intention to, and the providing of false information, are expressions of a concern for the welfare of one's fellow men,—this, because of difference in motive, would be a different sort of behaviour entity. It would indeed be a case of morally good behaviour and also intrinsically valuable.

III

"Love of a fellow man", a behaviour entity characterized by morally good, and by value intrinsically—has been referred to briefly in previous discussion. A more detailed examination is now in order. Incidentally, this will bring into focus some additional general factors concerning entities which are characterized by morally good,—and clarify and expand points already made.

Immediately previous discussion has concentrated on particular occurrences of one entity. In the following illustration the perspective will be broadened to include a consideration of a number of related particular occurrences of the one entity "love of fellow man". In other words, we will examine the entity in the context of a cluster of its particular occurrences.

Consider the case of Albert Schweitzer. He went to Africa motivated by love of fellow man, intending to facilitate the highest attainable level of acceptable value achievement by Africans. He proceeded to try to improve their medical and social conditions by a very large number of different sorts of activities. At first, this "moral behaviour" aroused a great deal of value-opposite reaction. Many of his friends and acquaintances were pained by what they thought of as: the senseless waste of the talents of a great musician, New Testament scholar, medical doctor and philosopher. Some people reacted in various ways characterized by morally evil, e.g., disdain, envy. A few were pleased and inspired by Schweitzer's behaviour. Many of the Africans were painfully disturbed by his presence and its consequences, medical and social. The situation initially was such that as far as its *ingredients* were concerned, on balance the status was value-opposite. Further, on the basis of the negative reaction to acceptable morally good behaviour there was (there were many occurrences of) an organic whole characterized by value-opposite.

It must be stressed, as noted, however, that even initially some consequences of Schweitzer's behaviour[10] were characterized by value which accrued to this behaviour. It was also valuable in the possible mode with reference to possible value consequences. Indeed, there was a high degree of possible value in view of Schweitzer's way of implementing his intentions. Further, his morally good behaviour was an ingredient in an organic whole where acceptable morally good behaviour was carried on in the face of violent value-opposite reaction. Such an organic whole is valuable intrinsically. Thus value accrued to its ingredient. Also by behaving in this fashion Schweitzer was providing what must be present, if an increase in acceptable value is to occur, namely an example and a demonstration of values,[11] morally good and others. Without this there would be no chance that such values would replace value-opposites then present in Africa, and the rest of the world. Thus Schweitzer's behaviour was valuable as a means both actual and possible. It is to be recalled that value-opposite consequences initially, or subsequently, did not produce the slightest diminution of the value of his morally good behaviour. The like to like pattern is relevant here. On the other hand, initially the on balance status of ingredients in the situation was on the side of value-opposite.

By the end of his career, the picture had changed dramatically. Schweitzer's "love of fellow man" behaviour in Africa derived a vast increase of value. Those who once reacted negatively now reacted positively. Thousands were in the positive camp—a relatively small number were on the negative side. Of course, millions were completely unaware of his life in Africa. In later days, the on-balance status of the ingredients in this situation swung from value-opposite to value. Of course, from the beginning the Schweitzer "acceptable morally good behaviour" was characterized by value intrinsically.

It will have been noted that some points made in discussing honesty in the "Gestapo" and in the "ideal family" situation were not repeated in discussing "love of fellow men". For example (a) some characteristics and some consequence entities are valuable in several modes, (b) "the regression of consequences" factor and its problems. The repetition of these points seems unnecessary.

IV

Let us turn now from entities characterized by morally good to those which are morally evil. The behaviour of an individual member of the Gestapo in the situation discussed above, is intrinsically value-opposite, i.e., a case of *hatred of fellow man*. It is characterized by morally evil and hence is value-opposite because of the value-opposite of its characteristics. Such behaviour has as consequence unacceptable pain both for the victims and for those who deplore such behaviour. In so far as pleasure is a reaction to this Gestapo behaviour, no value is derived since such pleasure is unacceptable and, also the "like to like" pattern is relevant. In so far as the Gestapo behaviour is a means to Gestapo ends it has value on that basis. It also is a possible means to future pleasure in Gestapo behaviour on the part of some persons. Hence it has value in the possible mode. In addition to instrumental and causal functions Gestapo behaviour is valuable because it is an ingredient in the situation. However, obviously on balance Gestapo hatred of a fellowman behaviour is characterized by value-opposite.

In order to avoid possible misunderstanding, consider the use of intrinsically value-opposite morally evil behaviour which has a number of wide-spread valuable consequences.

Consider a case of murder. A man kills another, motivated by hatred, intending to kill him and does so in a process of agonizing torture. This morally evil behaviour arouses[12] a great deal of attention. Immediately there is (a) considerable sympathetic pain and (b) a careful examination of the psychology, and sociology, of murder. Because of the desire for improvement, also aroused by the murder, steps are taken to remove the causes of murder—vast beneficial value consequences result. In this situation the ingredients are on balance a case of value. The organic whole of which the murder is an ingredient is characterized by value intrinsically, as far as the constructive reaction aspect is concerned. Nevertheless no value characteristic is derived by this morally evil murder behaviour on the basis of the valuable consequences. Here as elsewhere the "like to like" pattern is relevant. It does derive more value-opposite from its value-opposite consequences, for example pain. The possibility aspect in this respect is also predominantly value-opposite. There is slight accruing of value in the means mode, in the sense that it has the status ingredient and also cause. On this basis it has value in the possible mode. However, the entity is on balance obviously value-opposite.

V

Consider next *dishonesty*. A business man behaves in a dishonest fashion, makes millions and as a result experiences great pleasure. Initially the inferior "short-life" appliances which he produces, and misrepresents with great efficiency, give pleasure to thousands of people. Here, then, is dishonesty, behaviour characterized by morally evil which nevertheless is the means to many entities which are characterized by value. Be that as it may, this situation is not as an organic whole, intrinsically valuable. In any case dishonesty does not derive value from the value of pleasurable consequences.[13]

In due course the real nature of the appliances becomes evident. Pain[14] replaces pleasure in the lives of purchasers. A legal charge is laid. The dishonest business man is finally, despite skilled council, jailed. Here dishonesty on an instrumental basis derives value-opposite from its consequences. Even if dishonesty is not discovered, there is always the possibility that it could be. Hence it has value-opposite characteristics in the possible mode. Further, if as is likely to be the case, his dishonest behaviour is an ingredient in an organic whole: "Lack of concern for fellow man"—then the dishonest behaviour takes on additional value-opposite from the value-opposite characteristics of the organic whole of which it is an ingredient. In any case, "regardless" of the value charac-

157

teristics of dishonesty because of instrumental function actual or possible, and as ingredient,—its value-opposite status remains.

VI

The comparison of different entities which are *reputed* to be cases of the same sort of morally good behaviour—is an important issue. Consider the case of Mr. A. who claims to be motivated by *concern for the welfare*[15] of Africans. He intends to remove rampant diseases which flourish in their midst. He attempts to eliminate witch doctors whose techniques facilitate the presence of the diseases. He proceeds by persuading local authorities to declare witch doctors illegal. He also pokes fun at them and their methods. This causes great enmity and provokes much morally evil reaction. No improvement in the disease situation occurs. Another man, Mr. B. with the same stated concern and ultimate intention, and in the face of strong negative reaction, quietly cures many cases pronounced incurable by witch doctors. In a friendly fashion he offers to discuss with witch doctors: medical techniques. The consequences in this case are characterized by much value.

In view of his unenlightened attitude—above all his lack of success in selecting effective methods, it is strongly questionable whether Mr. A. is really behaving in a morally good fashion (i.e. showing concern) or whether the organic whole of behaviour is characterized by value intrinsically. In the case of the second man, Mr. B., his behaviour is obviously characterized by value in every mode 1-6 and its value-opposite function in thwarting witch doctors does not undermine its value status.[16]

It must be noted that the implementation of a concern for the welfare of a fellow man is appropriate only if there is at least some possibility that the specific technique employed will be effective, and hence later the situation will be characterized by value on balance. If people are, because of, for example, deterioration by drugs, incapable of responding to a rational persuasion, or taking sound advice, it is fruitless to attempt it. That is not to deny that one should deal with such people in a morally good fashion.

A less complicated comparison situation is the following: A young man of limited education, holding a mediocre job, inherits a considerable sum of money. Motivated by concern, intending to help others (a) he gives it all to the poor in the form of "welfare". Much pleasure results and other valuable consequences. Such behaviour is morally good, the organic whole is valuable intrinsically. Suppose, on the other hand, (b) he uses the money to obtain a professional education. Meanwhile he shows his concern for fellow men by acts of friendship. Subsequently he uses part of his greatly enhanced income to assist others financially in a more creative fashion than welfare payments. Thus their status is improved. Case (b) is a more valuable sort of concern behaviour than the former in all modes (1—5). In particular, behaviour (b) is characterized by a higher degree of morally good. Also this provides a greater increase of acceptable value than (a) and is a component of the greatest attainable amount of acceptable value in the world.

The preceding remarks concerning the comparative value of cases of concern for a fellow man can, of course, be paralleled by a similar pattern of analysis with reference to entities which are characterized by morally evil.[17] For example two cases of murder may vary on the basis that one involves more intense hatred, more efficiency, more painful consequences than the other, and so on. In view of the obviousness of this state of affairs it seems unnecessary to spell out the details at this stage of the discussion.

VII

We turn now to a consideration of the entities: morally good and morally evil. These are present to awareness usually as characteristics of other entities. This has an important bearing on the value or value-opposite status.

For example, morally good, as a characteristic of honesty in an ideal family situation, arouses acceptable pleasure on the part of persons who are members of the family and persons of like mind. Here in this occurrence, morally good is obviously characterized by value in the intrinsic, means (causal), consequence and possible modes. The situation in which it is an ingredient is also characterized by value, intrinsically as an organic whole. Hence it derives value on that basis. On the other hand, there are persons such that this occurrence of morally good arouses pain, anger and morally evil behaviour. The situation in which it is an ingredient is characterized, as an organic whole, by value-opposite. However, no value-opposite characteristic accrues to morally good. It is "untouched" by the value-opposite consequences. In so far as morally good arouses a negative reaction and hence functions, as a means to the prevention of value experience, it has value-opposite characteristics actually and in the possible mode. However, this does not seem to change the ultimate value status of the entity in this occurrence, i.e., in this situation in which it is an ingredient.

When an occurrence of the entity morally evil, for example characterizing unjust behaviour, inspires others to engage in morally evil behaviour and has the possibility of more of the same—this occurrence of morally evil is characterized by value-opposite on balance, despite its means value. This is so on the basis of its value-opposite characteristics in the intrinsic, means, consequence, and possible modes. Of course, any valuable consequences of an occurrence of morally evil are not the basis of amount of value for reasons which are now familiar, i.e., like to like pattern.

It must be emphasized that while the entities morally good and morally evil have been referred to in the context of specific occurrences (i.e., what they characterize)—what is of chief concern here is their intrinsic characteristics and their extrinsic status involving the reactions of various persons to the entities morally good and morally evil as such. Specifically, the concern is with the fact that the entity morally good, nor for example honesty, arouses pleasure—the entity morally evil, not for example injustice, causes a person to duplicate it.

Incidentally, it is well to note that an occurrence (A) of morally good which has a relatively low amount of intrinsic value when compared with another occurrence (B)—may well be more valuable (than B) when all modes of value are considered.

It is important to stress that the entities morally good and morally evil, as such, may be considered in abstraction—i.e., not in the context of being the characteristic of an entity. However, here there is involvement in a particular situation, namely a particular person is aware of either morally good or morally evil. Specifically when thought of in abstraction, morally good arouses valuable reactions in some persons and value-opposite reactions in others. The same is the case with reference to the entity morally evil as such. The usual comments about derivation in the means, consequence and possible modes apply here.

160

A

Let us now consider *simple* entities, other than morally good and morally evil, which like them are characterized by value or value-opposite, intrinsically. It will be found that they also involve valuable, or value-opposite, in extrinsic modes. The entities in question are: true, false; beautiful, ugly; pleasure, pain; efficient, inefficient; fitting, inappropriate; consistent, inconsistent; harmonious, discordant.[18]

The entity true, in some situations, arouses unacceptable pain, for example in the case of a person who enjoys the presence of falsehood in human relations. In a situation where a very large number of such persons are contemplating one true proposition, the situation, as far as these ingredients are concerned, is on balance a case of value-opposite and also as an organic whole. However, no value-opposite accrues to true on this basis. On the other hand, if an occurrence of the entity true arouses acceptable pleasure on the part of many people—in that situation true derives additional value. It also derives value from the fact that the situation is an organic whole characterized by value intrinsically. In brief, and without tiresome repetition of preceding analysis, here the entity true "has" value in the following modes: means (cause and ingredient), consequences, possible, intrinsic.

Consider next a beautiful face. If this occurrence of the entity beautiful arouses pain in the case of persons who hate beauty, the situation is a case of value-opposite as an organic whole. However, beautiful does not derive value-opposite characteristics in this situation. On the other hand, when the beauty of a picture gives pleasure to many, inspires others to take up artistic endeavours, is a source of refreshment—in this situation obviously beautiful derives value from these reactions and from its ingredient status in a valuable organic whole. Hence this occurrence of beautiful derives much additional value, namely in the means and consequence modes and possibility. In view of the pattern of analysis and comment already established, it seems unnecessary to repeat obvious details in a discussion of other simple intrinsically valuable entities.

Let us turn now to an examination of entities other than morally evil, which are characterized by value-opposite intrinsically. Consider a case of the entity false (for example, a characteristic of a proposition) which arouses considerable pleasure. The value of this consequence does not accrue to the entity false. Its value as means (cause and ingredient) does not over-balance its intrinsic value-opposite. If it arouses pain and encourages others to be false in their statements, value-opposite accrues to this occurrence of false. Further, value-opposite accrues to false in so far as it is an ingredient in an intrinsically value-opposite organic whole. Also, when false prevents the achievement of value it has value-opposite.

Consider next the case of pain imposed by a parent on a child in the course of preventing him from engaging in activities which will terminate his career, or interfere with his future development. This occurrence of pain is the only means available. The pain is value-opposite intrinsically. It is, value-opposite in so far as it prevents the child from doing certain things. It has as consequences, when the child survives and develops into a superior person, entities characterized by value. In a sense, the pain has value as a means to prevent value-opposite consequences and as a means to further valuable consequences.[19] However, the pain does not derive value from its value consequences—great as they are. An examination of the possible mode does not serve to undermine the on-balance value-opposite status of pain in this situation. However, since the pain is an essential instrumental ingredient in the production of a valuable result, it is an acceptable component in a situation which on balance is a case of value: the pain has a place in an ideal situation.

When an occurrence of pain, for example the suffering of a child ill with polio, stimulates a medical research scientist to discover a preventive innoculation with resultant pleasure and relief, for thousands of human beings—this situation is characterized by value with reference to the on-balance of ingredients. Nevertheless, here again pain on balance is value-opposite. Further, the pain of the child is not an essential component in the total situation involving great beneficial advances in medical research. The research might be stimulated by a desire to know how to keep children healthy. Hence the pain is not an acceptable component in the sense in which the term has been used.[20]

In so far as the medical researcher feels pain when confronted by the suffering of a child, this is an ingredient in sympathetic behaviour which is characterized by morally good (which is characterized by value intrinsically). In this case the doctors' pain is acceptable.

The analysis of the remaining simple entities which are intrinsically value-opposite follows the same pattern as that of morally evil, false, and need not be repeated here.

162

It was pointed out at the beginning of the chapter that attention would be focussed on a particular occurrence, or cluster of particular occurrences, of an entity. No occurrence of an intrinsically valuable entity is on balance value-opposite because of value-opposite extrinsic modes. Likewise no intrinsically value-opposite entity can be valuable on balance because of extrinsic factors. Hence on this basis one can note that all occurrences of some entities (i.e., the entity) will *together* be valuable— all occurrences of other entities *together* will be value-opposite. However, the ascertaining of the total amount of value of all occurrences, to date, of an entity (i.e., the entity), which is intrinsically valuable, involves difficulties. Nevertheless, a rough approximation can be struck in some cases; likewise with reference to intrinsically value-opposite entities.

The preceding discussion of entities which are intrinsically valuable, or value-opposite, is relevant to the forthcoming examination, in chapters 8-10, of the value, or value-opposite, characteristics of entities which are not as such intrinsically valuable, or value-opposite. The point is that such entities frequently have as characteristics or consequences—entities which are intrinsically valuable or value-opposite.

CHAPTER 8

Entities Which Are Only Extrinsically Valuable or Value-Opposite

Value and value-opposite are present in this world quite apart from the existence, or initiative, of human beings. However, it must be emphasized that many entities are characterized by value or value-opposite because of their relation to human beings.

I

Before turning to an examination of the value, or value-opposite, characteristics of entities which are not intrinsically so—it is wise to survey briefly some main features of the human situation, which must be borne in mind in the course of this examination.

All human beings have basic needs: (i) for food, clothing, shelter; (ii) to perform activities significant to them[1], and (iii) for social appreciation. The basic needs are obvious to most persons most of the time. However, on occasion there are individual 'blind spots'. In most cases needs issue in, or involve, relevant desires—that is, one wants to have what is needed. It must be emphasized that there are many cases of a person desiring entities which he does not need, in any basic sense. These basic general needs and desires, in some specific fashion, are present from birth, or very soon after. They continue to the end of life. Satisfaction of these needs and/or desires takes various forms, depending on the age of a person, his abilities and latent potentialities,[2] interests, and the situation in which he is living. The sex urge is also a prominent factor.

In considering needs and desires, it is well to note the dual use of 'need' namely in the sense of (i) having a requirement and (ii) what satisfies the requirement. Likewise, we should distinguish between 'desires' in the sense of (ii) having a strong tendency toward and (ii) the entity toward which this tendency is directed.

Let us turn to a consideration of a representative sample of entities which are not intrinsically valuable or value-opposite, but are characterized extrinsically by value or value-opposite or both,—and one or other, on balance.

The preceding discussion of entities which are intrinsically characterized by value, or value-opposite, provides a basis for this examination. As has been noted, the extrinsic modes of value or value-opposite (with the exception of the means mode) frequently involve the intrinsic mode.

II

It is frequently contended that human life—more specifically any particular living human being—has value intrinsically. In some cases it is claimed that man has value superior in amount to any other entity in the world. These contentions require careful examination.

Let us consider a number of different occurrences of the entity man (living human organism).

Mr. A. is very beautiful. He possesses a great store of knowledge. Specifically he is aware of, or is able to recall quickly, many true propositions concerning the history of human beings, literature, and the subject matter of the natural and the social sciences. He is a successful, efficient, member of the ruling hierarchy of an international cartel. His behaviour is appropriate to his place in this society, and he is consistent. He derives great pleasure from his attainments and activities. He gives pleasure to his considerable group of associates. He is regarded as setting an ideal for enterprising young men to follow. Some attempt to do so. He provides jobs, supports "worthy causes", knows how to "throw a good party". He has a "way with women". Many derive vicarious pleasure from hearing about his exploits. Incidentally, his gaggle of ex-wives and

165

assorted offspring are, for the most part, continuing sources of income for high priced psychiatrists, also gurus and assorted quacks.

On the other hand Mr. A. is dishonest, cruel in his dealings with those inferior to him, unjust in his relations with all men except his "immediate circle of trust". He is thoroughly selfish in the sense that he thinks ultimately only of his own advantage. He is the victim of violent passions and prejudices. Hence he is lacking in inner harmony. As the result of his behaviour, thousands of his employees work under unsatisfactory, and even dangerous, conditions for very low wages. This interferes seriously with the cultivation of the greater values of life, such as: some aspects of morally good behaviour, the enjoyment of beauty, the achievement of knowledge, the pleasure derived from beneficial recreation and employment. Indeed, the employees are characterized by value-opposite in these areas of human experience. Mr. A's industrial empire pollutes the physical environment, and goads his workers into strikes costly to society. He furthers the development of his business by stimulating international tension and, on occasion, actual conflict.

An examination of Mr. A's characteristics: for example, his obvious efficiency, appropriate, and consistent behaviour may seem to lead to the conclusion that he is valuable because of the value of these characteristics. Such, however, is not the case. These intrinsically valuable entities are in practically all cases characteristic of behaviour which is intrinsically value-opposite and characterized by morally evil. As such they are not acceptable values. Hence they do not bestow value on the person whose behaviour they characterize, and in this case characterize him.

On the other hand, the beauty and the knowledge content which characterize Mr. A. are the bases for correctly assigning value to him in the "because of value of characteristics" mode. It is, however, important to note that if Mr. A. uses his beauty and knowledge as an instrument in the context of behaviour which is morally evil, hence such use of beauty and knowledge, i.e., such behaviour, is characterized by value-opposite. In that sense the presence of knowledge or beauty in this situation is unacceptable. On the other hand, his morally evil behaviour in most areas of life, and his lack of harmony "mean" that he is characterized by a very large amount of value-opposite because of his characteristics. On the basis of all these *characteristics* he, on balance, is characterized by value-opposite.

He has value when a *means* to specific ends regardless of what they

166

are. He is characterized by value-opposite when he functions so as to prevent, interfere with, or stop the occurrence of any entity regardless of what it is. It is obvious that in the means mode there is some value involved in Mr. A's behaviour.[3] However, there is more value-opposite.

We turn now to a consideration of the *consequent* mode: It is to be noted that by using his great ability as he does, he is in this sense interfering with the achievement of acceptable value by/for himself and many others. Hence value-opposite accrues to him in the consequence mode. By his morally evil behaviour he brings pain to thousands of people and contributes greatly to the amount of ugliness, ignorance, and inefficiency in the world.[4]

The pleasurable consequences of Mr. A's morally evil behaviour do not provide a basis for the accrual of value to him. On the basis of the "like to like" pattern of accrual, value does not accrue to Mr. A's value-opposite characteristics which cause pleasure. Further a pleasure reaction to such entities is characterized by value-opposite intrinsically. Hence the value of such pleasure is not acceptable. Likewise value accrual is not involved in Mr. A's experience of pleasure because of his value-opposite activities and their value-opposite consequences.

In the mode of the *possible*, the story is the same as in the case of actual occurring modes of value and value-opposite. In brief, considering all relevant modes, on balance Mr. A. is characterized by a very large amount of value-opposite.

It is, of course, possible to provide a more detailed analysis of the life of Mr. A. Attention, for example, might have been paid to the factors: characteristics and consequences of consequences. Likewise there might have been more details concerning the various modes of value and value-opposite relevant to entities which are characteristics. The details of the value of means entities might have been considered. However, this would have involved a tedious repetition of the earlier general discussion. It is assumed that these matters will be borne in mind in dealing with the case before us, and subsequently. In any case, it is suggested that sufficient data have been brought into focus to support the conclusion stated concerning Mr. A. As in other analyses, the procedure is to outline main points and crucial issues in the context of preceding preparatory discussion, and offer a conclusion for the reader's consideration.

Let us now consider *Mr. B*.[5] He is ugly. He possesses a wide range of mechanical "know how", also insight into human nature, business

167

practice, and public relations. He is honest, just and concerned for the welfare of his fellow men. He of course has his defects of character. He, on occasion, is irrascible, naive, and stubborn. He establishes an industry for the making of an inexpensive gadget for human transportation. He is highly successful. He is efficient and consistent in his activities. His workmen receive a more than adequate wage. On the other hand, production methods involve much dull routine. There is frequently a negative reaction to this on the part of employees. However, individual initiative is encouraged. Men who make his product have an opportunity to develop a considerable amount of value experience. His customers, and the public in general, have "new and better worlds opened to them". He derives great pleasure from his activities. Those associated with him, and those who buy his products, do so as well. True, some men are pained by his success. Some men are injured when using his gadget and hence suffer pain. However, in only relatively few of the cases mentioned does pain issue in the accrual of value opposite to Mr. B. Much value accrues on the basis of the pleasure consequences as noted above. Indeed, an impressive amount of value accrues to Mr. B. in the consequence mode. The profits from the business are, in large measure, used for public service in education, supporting the arts, and international peace. It is true that the tycoon's family have a handsome income. Mr. B's family life is on balance characterized by value. In general his behaviour is appropriate and harmonious. In brief, and without spelling out further details of an analysis—it is obvious that Mr. B. is characterized by value. More specifically the amount of value vastly over-balances the amount of value-opposite.[6]

Messrs. A and B are, of course, relatively unusual cases; but they do serve to illustrate the point that the entity man in one occurrence is characterized by value-opposite, in another by value.

Let us now consider other cases. *Mrs. C.* is beautiful, well-educated, possessed of social charm. She has an adoring husband and two children. She uses her beauty to "climb higher" in a social group which is characterized by the presence of pleasures derived from food, drink, dress, undress and sophisticated excitement. In the process she behaves in a dishonest, unjust, unrestricted fashion which prevents her from understanding the basic needs of her husband or children or anyone else. She is very efficient in the pursuit of her goals. Her behaviour is consistent but not harmonious. Her drive for social success invites frustration and inner chaos. Her behaviour is appropriate for a person of her type. In the context of comparison with the largest attainable amount of acceptable value, her behaviour is silly and gauche (that is, inappropriate). The occurrence of efficiency, appropriate, and consistency are almost exclusively in the context of morally evil behaviour. Hence Mrs. C. does not derive any value from the value of these entities which are characteristics of her characteristics. The amount of morally evil characterizing her behaviour over-balances the value of the other personality traits, such as beautiful and knowledge. The lack of harmony also helps to tip the scale in the direction of value-opposite. Mrs. C. does not use her abilities to improve the lot of her ''fellow men'' in such areas as: the extension of knowledge, the enjoyment of beauty, the cultivation of morally good behaviour. Indeed she uses her considerable abilities for the opposite purpose. On this basis value-opposite accrues to her. She derives pleasure, and gives pleasure to a small group of so-called friends, and serves as a source of vicarious enjoyment to many who foolishly admire, or want, this way of life. But as in the case of Mr. A.—no value accrues to Mrs. C. because of these pleasure characteristics or consequences. They are unacceptable entities likewise their values. Obviously Mrs. C. has value and value-opposite in the means mode. For example she facilitates one sort of life and prevents another[7]. The ''picture'' concerning the possible mode is similar to what has been noted above concerning actual modes.

It is evident that—all modes considered—the life of Mrs. C. is characterized on balance by value-opposite, that is, there is far more value-opposite than value.

Miss D. is a university co-ed. She is descended from a long line of ''plain Janes'' with average IQ's. Her paternal heritage is likewise. She works hard at her studies, is honest and fair in her dealings with most people. She devotes her spare time to welfare and reform groups on and off the campus. Most of her behaviour is characterized by morally good. She derives great pleasure from this, on most occasions. Sometimes she feels pain and envy when she looks about her, or in a mirror. The pleasure she experiences in the course of her service behaviour involves an accrual of value to her. A considerable number of those who know her, and benefit from her life style, appreciate the example she sets, derive considerable pleasure from her presence and activities. Hence more value accrues to her. She sometimes arouses pain and derision in those who wish they could manifest her good sense and self-control, or are irritated by it. But no value-opposite accrues to her because of these reactions. The few feelings of envious pain when confronted by her "plain Jane" appearance (and the plain Jane factor itself) and occasional lapses from morally good behaviour into its opposite, do not provide enough value-opposite to over-balance the value of her life—as here considered.[8]

Miss D. is superior to Mrs. C. She, however, is characterized by a smaller amount of value than Mr. B. Incidentally Mrs. C. is characterized by less value-opposite than Mr. A.

The preceding discussion has brought into focus the fact that some occurrences of the entity *life*, specifically "living human being" are characterized on balance by value—in different amounts—other occurrences of this entity are characterized on balance by value-opposite, in different amounts.

A complex problem arises when one attempts to compare the amount of value, or value-opposite, of an adult (A1) and a very young child (C1) who are members of the same social group. This involves the problem of dealing with possibilities and *potentialities*[9] as well as with actualities.

The adult (A1) behaves in a morally evil fashion for the most part. Chances of reform seem slight. He is the source of much unacceptable pain for himself and others. He has no concern for the intrinsic values: beauty and truth. His intelligence is of a relatively low degree. His knowledge is limited. Possibilities of his contributing much to the needs of his fellow men are slight. He possesses few if any worthwhile latent potentialities. Without going into further details of analysis, it is evident that he is characterized by value-opposite. On the other hand, the child (C1) is the descendent of people who have high I.Q.'s, are concerned with all intrinsic values and have manifested this in their behaviour. There is a very high degree of probability that the child (C1) is potentially a high grade adult and that the parents will provide a suitable environment for him so that his potential will be actualized. On the basis of these facts, obviously C1 is more valuable than A1, who as a matter of fact is characterized by value-opposite.

Consider the case (i) of A2, a member of an under-developed society or (ii) A3, a person who has "never had a chance" in a so-called developed society. Some such persons, if given an opportunity to develop characteristics which are valuable, do so.[10] Therefore, in this sense they have possible and potential value. In this sense they are more valuable than people who have had this chance and the results are value-opposite.

III

The preceding discussion provides some indication of how one would proceed to a comparison of the value or value-opposite, characteristics of entities of different types. Consider the question: which is more valuable: (a) a genuine Greek statue (not quite complete) of Aphrodite or (b) the man, Albert Schweitzer? The statue is acceptably beautiful, and it has value on that basis. It has value when it (means mode) is an ingredient in a museum, and is an instrument for furthering the study of Greek culture. It has accrued value due to the pleasure it arouses because of its beauty and as a result of the consequences of its various functions. However, Dr. Schweitzer is[11] more valuable. While the statue is admittedly beautiful and the doctor is not, Schweitzer is characterized by moral goodness— which is superior in intrinsic value to beautiful which characterizes statue. Thus the doctor is more valuable because of his characteristic. Schweitzer satisfies desire for security, moral guidance, medical assistance, philosophical, musical and biblical knowledge and enjoyment. He is valuable as a means for the achieving of all these results. He has value as an ingredient of a society. The value accruing from Schweitzer's contributions are vast when one considers the number of people he influenced.

It is true that the statue also is a means to the satisfaction of many desires and produces valuable consequences for many men. Consider its beauty, its function as a source of knowledge of Greek life and the pleasure which it gives to many thousands of men. Consider its stimulation to an appreciation of greater values. However, it is apparent that despite its very considerable value in the characteristic, means and consequence modes, and likewise also in the possible mode—in comparison with the case of Schweitzer, the statue is lower in the scale of amount of value than is Schweitzer.

In brief: the statue does not have the characteristics and consequences of Schweitzer. It is not Schweitzer. It cannot do for men what Schweitzer did and does.[12]

It will have been noted that in the statue-Schweitzer comparison no reference has been made to value-opposite factors. At this point it is necessary only to be reminded that (as discussed earlier) value-opposite reactions to a morally good man do not accrue to that man. Neither do value-opposite reactions to a beautiful statue accrue to the statue.[13]

It may be argued, in rebuttal, that the statue is the work of a great artist, Praxitelas, and is unique, and is a symbol of the greatness of Greece. However, it may be appropriately pointed out, in reply, that Schweitzer is also unique (there is no great value in uniqueness as such). In any case, the statue derives no value from the value of its creator, in any automatic sense. The creator, on the other hand, places value characteristics in it. Further, the life of Schweitzer is the work of a great artist, i.e., Albert Schweitzer. It is a symbol of the greatness of mankind and human culture, not just (but including) Greek culture. By the way, while in one sense the doctor is ugly, in another he manifests the beauty of holiness.

In comparing the statue of Aphrodite and a drug addict who has passed the point of "no return", and faces death in a few months—the situation seems clear. Here is neither beauty, moral goodness, nor concern for truth. Of course, there is value in the sense of cause, ingredient, condition—but the value is there in a very low degree. The consequences of this man's behaviour involves accrued value-opposite. True, the example of the "speed freak" may have instrumental value in deterring others, but this is not a very high degree of value. On the other hand, the consequences are valuable, but no value accrues to the unfortunate addict. On balance, it is obvious that the drug addict is a case of value-opposite. Though some slight value is present it is overweighted by value-opposite. Hence the statue is more valuable than the drug addict.

The problem is apparently more complex when one comes to compare the statue and a man who "falls" between Dr. Schweitzer and the far-gone drug addict.

Consider Mr. Casper J. Milktoast. He is an ugly man, sometimes morally good in a restricted way, more frequently morally evil. He has some means value as a minor ingredient, and instrument, in a large business firm, and as a member of several clubs of "like persons". He is the source of some acceptable pleasure (of a minor sort) to his few friends, and considerable unacceptable pain to others. This is so because he is bumptious, prejudiced and selfish. He experiences some superficial acceptable pleasures. Some value accrues to him from the consequences

172

of his various functions. On balance, apparently, he is characterized by a small amount of value.

The question arises: Is Casper J. more or less valuable than the statue? Assuming he is a normal human being,—if he is put in a relatively more favourable environment, he will achieve a large amount of value. In the sense that he is capable of being characterized by a larger amount of value, he has value in the potential mode. True, he is now lacking a large amount of actual intrinsically valuable characteristics and actual important effects of the statue. Yet he is a potential source of more pleasure and so on. On the basis of actual performance to date, the statue is more valuable than the man. However, the real issue is the significance of his value in the possible and potential modes. Is this sufficient, along with other factors, to out-value the statue? If the probability of a high level of moral and other attainments of the Schweitzer sort is well based, the value of the man on balance is greater than the value of the statue. If not, the statue is more valuable than the man. The odds here seem to favor the statue.

During this chapter the pattern of discussion has been that of a relatively detailed discussion of particular occurrences—either all of the same entity or of different entities. This has served to underline the point that sweeping generalisations cannot be made concerning a many-occurrence entity. Likewise in comparing entities one must consider particular occurrences.

IV

We turn now to consider a group of entities concerning which it seems unnecessary to undertake as detailed an analysis as in the preceding cases. The same general points of view can be conveyed in more general terms.

There are a number of inanimate entities composing the *physical environment* some particular occurrences of which function as means for the continuing presence of living human organisms. As such they have value when means. In this means context some have additional value depending on degree of: efficiency, fitting, consistent, harmonious (some or all). Further, depending on the value, or value-opposite, *characteristics* of the living organisms (concerning which they are

173

means) the physical entities have accrued values or value-opposites. Also these entities are sources of either pleasure or pain or both. The possible mode must be considered. On these bases, they have on balance value, or value-opposite, characteristics.—Among such entities in the physical environment are: fresh air, pure water, light, moderate temperature, food, clothing, shelter.

Incidentally, air, water, light, heat are means for the production of food, clothing, shelter, that is they are means to means.

It is essential to note that entities customarily regarded as food, clothing, shelter, are not only means to the presence of life—they are in some cases means to death. Specifically some items of food have poisonous effects on some people, and kill them. Some items of clothing, specifically in the case of very young children, may result in strangulation. Some shelters, for example, a closed car with engine running in a blizzard, may result in death from carbon monoxide poisoning. It must be admitted that normally this sort of result is not the case. But, in the interests of a comprehensive treatment of such entities, variations from normal should be noted. Hence in cases where food, clothing, shelter are means to death, they have value as means. But these occurrences are, on balance, characterized by value-opposite if the results which they produce is the death of a valuable person and hence the elimination of values which the living organism has, and is able to produce. Further, the occurrence of death usually gives rise to unacceptable pain.

The physical and social environment situation is very complex. The value or value-opposite characteristics, for example, of clothing, that is occurrence of specific garments, are not based only on the means-end relation concerning the preservation, or elimination, of living human organisms. Items of clothing also are in the means-end relation to many other ends or results. For example, a specific style of clothing may be a means instrument used to express (i) a certain view of life, (ii) the desire for a specific place in society (iii) a desire to be comfortable, (iv) dissent, and so on. Insofar as the style of clothing is a means to such ends, it is valuable. If it is a case of efficient means, in some cases, its value is enhanced. Here, however, obviously results must be considered. If the style of dress brings acceptable satisfaction (pleasure)[14] the value is further enhanced. If it results in snobbish pride or stands in the way of the attainment of ends which are characterized by high degrees of value[15], then the style of dress may be characterized in its overall aspect by value-opposite, even though it does serve as a means to preserve life and has value because it is a means to other goals mentioned above.

Consider variations from "the establishment" in dress as a symbol (means) of dissent. There are other less stereotype, and more constructive, symbols of dissent. However, be that as it may, the dissent style of dress may serve as a good "contact device" between those who, while dissenting yet have constructive ideas and techniques, and are prepared to implement them, on the one hand, and those who on the other, while dissenting, cannot see their way to go beyond the more destructive negative type of dissent. In other words, one cannot judge an entity merely by its package. Interestingly enough, some young dissenters "take a dim view" of older people who dress like young ones, even if they (the elders) are in the dissent group. In other words, seniors regardless of anything else, are expected to dress in a somewhat conservative fashion! It is of course the case that styles of dress change from time to time—quite apart from the issue of dissent. Hopefully comfort is a viable factor.

In addition to all these considerations of value, and value-opposite, characteristics based on some means-end relation, one must also note the importance of intrinsic values in addition to efficiency. Obviously beautiful or ugly are factors to be taken into consideration in some cases of clothing, and as well food and shelter. [16]

The preceding remarks about clothes and dissent serve to shift attention from the physical to the social environment. In general a social environment is a means for the bringing into existence, and development of living organisms and indeed, to prevent the destruction, or deterioration, of living organisms. They, of course, may have exactly the opposite effect. Further, social institutions are a context in which all modes of value, or value-opposite, are "in effect". It is of course obvious that there are many different sorts of social institutions. There are many different occurrences of each sort.

V

Before proceeding to comment on the value, or value-opposite, characteristics of various social institutions, it is well to stress the point that among the most general[17] means to many entities are: physical and

175

mental health. On the other hand, physical and mental illness have the opposite function.

Physical and mental health are conditions (means) for the production and continued existence of living organisms. Likewise they are means to the efficient functions of many social institutions. They are also causes of pleasure. Physical and mental illness interfere with, or prevent, the achievement of these goals. Also they are causes of pain.

As in the case of other means entities discussed above, health has value when it is a means to anything. But the total value picture varies from particular occurrence to particular occurrence—of health. Referring back to Mr. A and Mr. B (and the discussion of value or value-opposite of a particular occurrence of life), let us assume, for example, that both men are physically healthy. Physical health in the Mr. A particular occurrence is valuable when a means, i.e., a condition of his body which facilitates the performance of his many activities physical and mental. The same is true for Mr. B.

It will be recalled that Mr. A's behaviour, in its many versions, has accruing to it a great deal of value-opposite. It is characterized on balance by value-opposite. Since the behaviour is a consequence of health, it may appear that health derives value-opposite from the value-opposite characteristics of the behaviour. This, however, is not the case. On the other hand, in the case of B, health is a condition for valuable behaviour. It is valuable not only when a condition but also because of value of its consequences.

Ill health interferes with the occurrence of some valuable entities, and hence is value-opposite. It is characterized by value-opposite in proportion to the amount of value which it prevents. However, ill-health as a condition, or cause, of such interference is valuable in the means mode. Value-opposite accrues on the basis of pain which results. On balance it has the status: value-opposite.

It is to be stressed that there are complex means-end relations concerning means entities. Food, clothing, shelter are means (some or all of cause, instrument, condition) to physical and mental health and vice-versa. The social environment has a bearing on physical and mental health as does the physical environment. On the other hand physical and mental health of people lead to effects in the physical and social environment.

176

CHAPTER 9

Major Social Institutions and Related Matters

Let us now turn to an examination of the value, or value-opposite, characteristics of some major social institutions.

I

The entity *family*, in some of its particular occurrences, is a means (condition) for the production of living human organisms. Some families are also means (cause and/or conditions) for facilitating the continuance and growth of human beings in a value oriented fashion. Specifically, such a family is a means to food, clothing, shelter and the satisfaction of most needs and desires of its members. In general it is a context in which values are achieved and experienced. Hence particular families have value as (when) means and because of consequences of the sorts mentioned above. It is to be noted that some of the consequences are personal characteristics.

Of course, there are some cases where a family is not a means to the production of life. There are instances where this institution does not facilitate the preservation of life or, for the most part, the achievement of valuable consequences. Indeed, the opposite is the case. Likewise there are some families with no characteristics which are valuable as such.

Thus some occurrences of family are on balance a case of value, others value-opposite. In part, this is determined by the way in which the family organization functions. Obviously there are many sorts of organization: tyrannical, democratic, permissive, and so on. Even more basic are the personality traits of the members of a family. It is clear that it is incorrect to generalize about value, or value-opposite, characteristics of the entity family as such. References must be made to particular occurrences.

The preceding somewhat cryptic remarks require clarification and expansion.

Concerning the entity: family—it is, of course, a complex entity constituted by its individual members in specific relationships. The *characteristics* of a family are (a) some of the characteristics of its individual members and (b) the characteristics which, in addition, it has because it functions as a unit, that is, as an organic whole.[1] These latter characteristics do not belong to any one individual. For example (a) if all members of a family are individually morally good, the family will be characterized likewise. However, if the members of a family are heterogeneous in their behaviour, the family will be characterized accordingly. Consider a family business in which the advertising group is composed of dishonest rascals, while the service staff is honest. In such a situation the family is characterized both by morally good and morally evil.[2]

Consider also (b) the case of a family "functioning as a democratic committee". Each member contributes what information he has concerning a problem. After considerable rational discussion, a conclusion is reached which is characterized by more justice and wisdom than characterizes any individual "on his own".

In view of preceding detailed discussion in Chapter 5, it seems unnecessary to engage in a more extensive analysis of all the *consequences* of behaviour of the sorts just mentioned, and the issue of the accrual of value or value-opposite on these and other bases (e.g., means, possible, potential).

Before proceeding to a consideration of the next, related topic, it is necessary to give further development to a point already briefly mentioned "in passing". It was noted that in some particular occurrences, a family is the context in which a person finds satisfaction for many of his desires and needs. In general, a family also can be a situation in which a person develops a large amount of value achievement and experience. It is of course the case that the same sort of favourable comments can be made concerning other social institutions.

However, it is here reported that some particular occurrences of family are superior to all other social institutions as means for the satisfaction of some desires and needs and in general for the achievement of some values. Here under discussion is what may be termed an "ideal family". Specifically one male and one female are in love with each other and married, in the full sense of the term. These persons are united in all aspects of their behaviour. The dominant characteristic of their relationship is: love of a fellow human being. These founders[3] of the ideal family, apart from exceptional cases, are "joined" by children. The needs and desires for significance and social appreciation are satisfied in such a family in an amount which can not be closely approximated in any other social group. Likewise such a family provides a superior environment in which a person (parent and child alike) develops a concern for morally good behaviour, beauty, truth and other intrinsic values. Further such a family is the best context in which the needs for food, clothing and shelter can be met. Of course only some families can be described as "ideal". The fact remains that at least a few merit this evaluation.

The superiority of the ideal family to other *social organizations*, in the respects noted above, will not be "spelled out" in detail, before other entities have been discussed. The main point however, is this: In the ideal family the basic foundation is "love of fellow men". This is not involved in other *social institutions* to the same extent. In most cases it is not involved at all. As noted previously the love of fellow man involves a way of life which is superior to what other patterns of behaviour involve in human affairs.[4]

Of course, it is clear that the goals of the founders of some families fall far short of those of the ideal family. In many cases a man and a woman come together as a unit, i.e., constitute a family, in order to facilitate the satisfaction of a relatively restricted set of desires and needs. They do so in a superficial and even gross fashion. There is little or no genuine concern for any of the great values. Any children are of like sort.

There is an accrual of value-opposite if a person uses the family situation in such a way as to interfere with the achievement of value by other members of the family. Specifically if parents bring children into the world on a purely selfish basis—have no real concern for the children's value achievement—this is a case of a very large amount of value-opposite characterizing the behaviour of the parent. The value-opposite characteristics and consequences of course accrues to the family as well.

In view of the place of sex in the life of the founders of a family, it is appropriate to introduce some comments on sex, with reference to adult males and females.

II

The question of the value, or value-opposite, characteristic of specific occurrences of sexual interaction must be examined in the context of specific situations. At this point attention will be focussed on a number of relevant factors. The sexual relation between a man and a woman is a very complex one. It can be mental as well as physical, involving shared goals, emotions and cooperative activities of various sorts.

Physical sexual interaction, ranging from "play" to intercourse, is a means of satisfying a basic desire and is valuable in the means mode. If characterized by efficiency further value is derived. The pleasure aroused by physical sexual interaction has intrinsic value. It is a source of value accrual. When physical sexual interaction is an aspect of "high grade" love it has value not only as ingredient, but also because of its ingredient status in the consequent mode.[5] This activity can be a means to produce children. Also it can be a basis of family unity and stability as far as its founders are concerned. Sexual intercourse, on this basis, obviously is characterized by very considerable value.

In many instances sexual physical interaction is part of a process whereby one person "takes advantage"[6] of another. This behaviour is a case of injustice and narrow selfishness, and thus is morally evil. Hence the activity of sexual intercourse acquires value-opposite because of its ingredient status. (Strictly speaking, the *activity* as such is not morally evil.) While there is considerable pleasure, if it is a reaction to morally evil behaviour, it is unacceptable. There is also usually a large amount of present and/or subsequent pain in this situation. Hence sexual interaction, despite its pleasure, is value-opposite because of the greater amount of pain. Further there is the very important factor of setting an example and so influencing some other people to engage in the same value-opposite behaviour. There is value in the means mode. Efficiency also may be present.[7] But the value aspects are relatively negligible. In such a situation obviously sexual interaction is characterized by value-opposite on balance.

By way of clarification of the preceding comments concerning sex, it is here reported that sexual intercourse between male and female has more value in the context of the ideal family situation than in any other form of association. Specifically, the ideal family is predominantly a relation between two persons such that the behaviour of each to the other is a case of love of a fellow man. The vast majority of items of behaviour are organic wholes, intrinsically valuable, and characterized by morally good, to a very high degree. Hence more value is derived by sexual interaction from this source, *on the basis of ingredient status*, than from any other source.

Further any means value, efficiency, or acceptable pleasure which may occur in any other context, with reference to sexual interaction, can at best be equal to that in the ideal family context. In most cases it surpasses its competitors in these regards. Hence everything considered, the superiority of the ideal family context, as far as the value of sexual behaviour is concerned, is increasingly obvious—as one considers previous remarks and subsequent ones.

At this point, it seems appropriate to attempt at least an outline consideration of the value, or value-opposite, characteristics of some sex-based forms of association.

It will be recalled that the love of fellow man (woman) relation of which the ideal family is a case, involves a deep and enduring bond of affection, i.e., devotion to the welfare of the loved one. In particular, there is an attempt to facilitate the fullest attainable amount of value achievement and enjoyment. On the other hand a more superficial and *temporary* association has less, or little, concern for many values,[8] or the welfare of another person. They obviously have less value than the ideal family pattern of behaviour.

As a matter of fact, some informal temporary episodes are very brief. Their termination is painful if, as usually happens, one member of the pair does not favour termination. In such associations, very frequently indeed, the "take advantage of the other person" factor is clearly present, or at best thinly disguised. Of course, it is possible for the associates to part by mutual consent and without excessive emotional upset. Be that as it may, the value content is slight in comparison with that which characterizes members of the ideal family. A reputed common concern for some greater values in some cases is genuine—particularly in the field of aesthetics. But to repeat, the range of value concern, and achievement, is relatively restricted.

It must be admitted that some informal associations last during a considerable period of time, and involve a common interest in a wide range of some of the greater values. However, such an association, except in cases of genuine religious, philosophical or legal barriers, is usually symptomatic of lack of complete devotion to mutual maximum value achievement. (There is of course the possibility of mental illness to be considered.) There is the cherished possibility of a convenient escape when "the going gets a bit tough", or "something better comes along".

It is to be noted that both the very brief, and the relatively longer, informal associations—in a considerable number of cases—result in the production of infants. These children, in many cases, have a poor environment in which to grow up. The sorts of association under consideration, of course derive value-opposite from the resultant value-opposite behaviour.[9]

III

Social institutions such as educational, political, economic ones, religious organizations, recreational groups, cultural organizations and so on, are valuable, when means to the satisfaction of desires and needs. They are value-opposite when functioning as frustrations of such desires and needs. In general, and most significantly, they, on occasion, are means to the attainment of entities which are valuable, or value-opposite, intrinsically and/or extrinsically. Depending on their characteristics, means function and results,[10] the overall (that is, on balance) status of particular occurrences of these institutional entities will be either value or value-opposite. What has been reported concerning particular occurrences of the entity family indicates a general pattern of discussion relevant to other social institutions. There is, however, an exception. They are not directly means to production of living organisms! Nevertheless they are means to the continuation of life, or in some instances, its termination.

The immediately preceding remarks require some expansion and clarification.

(A)

A *religious* organization (church) is valuable if it is a means to satisfy its members' desire for social approval and a significant pattern of life. If its component members are concerned with morally good behaviour and the organization fosters the achievement and enjoyment of morally good beautiful, true and other intrinsically valuable entities—further value accrues to this occurrence of religious institution.

However, it is obvious that some particular religious organizations, while valuable as means to social approval etc., are on balance cases of value-opposite. Some churches hold views of God, and practice religious observances, which involve, and encourage, such morally evil behaviour as pride, hatred and a bigoted approach to many entities which are characterized by morally good, beautiful, true and so on. Their reputed concern for "good works" is suspect.

Incidentally, even though such an institution is efficient in satisfying a devotee's desire for social approval and a significant pattern of life, no value is derived because of the nature of the pattern of life.

(B)

We turn now to a consideration of a number of social organizations and institutions which are concerned with *recreation*. Here again the crucial issue is: what kind of activities take place in, and result from, such organizations, i.e., clubs, theatre groups, and other less closely knit associations. A few general remarks will serve the immediate purpose.

Some recreation-oriented activities are characterized by beautiful, moral goodness, true, efficient, fitting, consistent, harmonious. Likewise they encourage the presence and appreciation of these entities.[11] Thus these activities acquire value on the basis of the value of their characteristics and the consequences mentioned, as well as others. For example, a theatrical presentation, and hence "the theatre", can be efficient etc. means to "catharsis" and thus mental health, provide factual information, facilitate development of moral goodness, give pleasure, provide for social unity, be causes of beautiful objects, provide relaxation. Further, these activities may be means for expressing frustration because of the thwarting of needs and desires. Also, they may serve as means for escaping from entities which are characterized by value-opposites. The same is true of some cases of sport, or some hobbies.[12]

On the other hand, sport, theatre, hobbies, etc. may serve as means for escaping from the problems of achieving intrinsic or extrinsic values. Some occurrences of these activities do not result in genuine recreation and are on balance value-opposite. For example some people who engage in sport, theatre and other art forms, and hobbies, involve themselves in morally evil, false and ugly behaviour. Their "recreations" are characterized by inefficient, silly (inappropriate) inconsistent and discordant behaviour. Thereby men and women distract themselves from the pursuit and attainment of the largest attainable amount of acceptable value. Consider some participants in professional sport, and some members of the viewing public, "looking for blood". Some people "go in for" theatre, or music, as a means to narrow self-aggrandisement. Some men's hobbies are a disgusting cultivation of a reputed status symbol, at the expense of other more valuable activities. Consider the tycoon who collects "objets d'art"—which he "enjoys"[13] in the selfish privacy of his own home. He spends millions which might be put to use in improving the lot of thousands of fellow men who are in desperate want. In all cases, when a recreational activity takes place in the context of morally evil behaviour it derives value-opposite, because of its ingredient status in an intrinsically value-opposite organic whole.

Incidentally, extreme concern for means of any sort will defeat the ultimate purpose of having means, namely to provide for great intrinsic and extrinsic values. For example, intense concern with the instruments of transportation and communication may result in a situation where there may be "nothing" (worthwhile) to say, and not much point in going anywhere. Thus, for example, freedom of speech, under some conditions, has little or no value, that is, a person who claims the right, and exercises it, has nothing worth saying.

IV

Turning now to a consideration of political institutions, some remarks are in order concerning the entity: *nation*.

A nation is characterized by great value when its component citizens cooperatively endeavour to achieve the largest attainable amount of acceptable values.[14] This will involve many ingredients—human, inanimate and relational—a harmony of many individually contrasting elements. It should be obvious that a spirit of nationalism, in this context, is not a case of narrow in-turning. It is not a snobbish attitude of "see how wonderful I am." Rather, it is a matter of legitimate pride in the effort to make the best use of available opportunities, at a specific "point" in space and time, for the maximum attainable benefit of the people living within the nation, and also for those outside its borders. There may well be emphasis on a few *distinctive* activities, some of great value and some not so great. One should not down-grade something just because it is "local".

When a national group does not seriously concern itself with these "ideals", rather it flouts them—then of course it is characterized by value-opposite.

These very general comments will be clarified, and illustrated, in the context of a discussion of some of the less inclusive institutions which are ingredients of the complex entity: nation—also relevant techniques and ideals.

However, before proceeding to these matters, further background comments are in order.

V

One of the forms of national life, i.e., one form of political institution, is *democracy*. The term "democracy" is notoriously ambiguous. Hence it is important to examine, with care, the various senses in which the term is used—in order to keep clearly in mind what is under discussion.

It must be realized that any social group may be a democracy; that is not just a nation but also an industry, a club, a church, a family, an educational institution. Initially, attention will be focussed on the "nation in general" case of democracy. But the following comments are relevant to smaller social groups as well.

A

In its broad sense, democracy is (a) a set of *ideals* and (b) relevant *techniques* involved in the achieving, or manifesting, of the conditions under which men should live. Prominent among such ideas are: liberty, equality, fraternity. Appropriate techniques are, for example: friendly

185

discussion, rational analysis and decision, persuasion rather than force. There are other techniques which are frequently mentioned. Consider for example: government of the people, for the people, by the people; one man-one vote, majority rule. Democracy in its narrow sense involves a concentration on such techniques. The ideals, which the techniques are designed to implement, are sometimes neglected. Hence in some cases worship of techniques interferes with the achievement of the ideal goals of democracy (as more broadly conceived). In any case, some of the techniques of democracy differ in different situations. For example in a small Greek city (state)—direct participation in government is in order. However, even here top offices can only be held by candidates, though selected by ballot or lot, who have special qualifications. Democracy in larger countries, more appropriately involves representative government, in the sense that a few people are selected by the rest to undertake technical decisions, and implement them. In any case, techniques have no autonomy, nor are they self justifying. They have instrumental and consequence value in the context of some situations.

More detailed comments concerning liberty, equality and fraternity[15] are now in order. They indeed function as ideals, goals. But basically they are *conditions* which make possible the attainment of the supreme goal of democracy: the fullest attainable amount of acceptable value achievement by each individual human being within the social group.

Liberty (freedom) has a "from" and a "to" aspect. In general it means either (a) escape from some value-opposite entity or (b) the absence of obstruction or restriction of behaviour, so that a person can perform actions in which a human being would normally propose to engage. There are, of course, some natural restrictions on our behaviour. These do not constitute a denial of freedom. Consider, for example, speed of running, time one can stay awake, the fact that a person cannot fly without mechanical aids.

Many occurrences of the entities from which a person wishes to be free, here under consideration, arise from other people either directly or indirectly. For example: consider freedom from the threat of death, hunger, fear, pain.[16] The causes of death and hunger, in some cases, may seem to be primarily non-human. But as a matter of fact, going far enough back, the causes turn out to be human. In any case, some of them can be removed by human initiative.

186

The "to" aspect of freedom, for example: act, speak, assemble, worship, involves the absence of what interferes with, or prevents the occurrence of, such activities. Various forms of political or social oppression are obvious "cases in point". It must be emphasized that freedom, in both its "from" and "tó" aspects, is not confined exclusively to social situations. The factor "freedom" is relevant to the mythical single man on a desert island.

In the context of the "to" sense of freedom: in all instances, freedom when a means (condition) has extrinsic value. However it is essential to note that it does not have intrinsic value, as such. Human behaviour in a freedom (liberty) situation, *on occasion*, is characterized by beauty and moral goodness. Also truth, (in the context of knowledge,) and pleasure, are involved in some particular occurrences of free behaviour. Since liberty is a condition for the presence of these valuable entities, values accrue to it in the consequence mode.[17]

Of course the exact opposite results may occur in some cases of the presence of the liberty (in the "to" sense) condition. A man uses his freedom to behave in a morally evil fashion—bringing pain to many, and so on. Here, obviously, value-opposite on balance accrues to an occasion of freedom. Thus the entity liberty (freedom) as such (intrinsically) is neither valuable or value-opposite. In the extrinsic sense, it is both (i) on occasion valuable and (ii) on other occasions value-opposite.

The same general state of affairs is in effect with reference to the other aspect of freedom. The *escape from* the threat of death, hunger, fear, pain, is not valuable as such. In some cases an escape from these entities derives value from the consequences of the escape, or from the characteristics of the escape. Other particular occurrences of escape from these entities have value-opposite consequences.[18] When a man's "time has come" it is impossible, hence silly, to even consider escape from death. In some situations hunger, fear, pain are appropriate and have beneficial consequences. Consider, for example, fear when confronted by serious risk in a traffic situation, or pain when it serves as an ingredient in athletic training. The absence of fear in a battle situation has obvious value-opposite consequences. If one does not accept the pain implied in training he misses the full value of athletic achievement. It is to be noted that only pain, of the group of entities here under consideration, is intrinsically value-opposite. Despite that fact, its absence in some cases, as noted, is not intrinsically valuable. In other words in some contexts, i.e., some particular occurrences of it are acceptable.

In general, it is important to realize that in discussing freedom from death, hunger, pain and fear, one, strictly speaking, is concerned with unacceptable occurrences of these entities. Such unacceptable occurrences are characterized by value-opposite. The absense of unacceptable value-opposite is of course a resultant which is intrinsically valuable.

Equality is a state of affairs which exists when justice is done (see earlier comments concerning justice).[19] While just behaviour has intrinsic value, its ingredient, equality, is characterized only by extrinsic value, or value-opposite. When, for example, equal opportunity, or equality before the law, is a means (a condition) for the development of acceptable values, value accrues to it because of this consequence. However, it is to be noted that, in some situations equal opportunity, equality before the law, are involved in results which are characterized by value-opposite. Hence, these cases of equality have value-opposite accruing to them and are on balance value-opposite, despite their value when means and possible value. Consider the criminal who profits from equality of treatment with reference to a "no wire tap" law. Equality of opportunity to own and drive a car, on occasion, leads to disastrous results as in the case of an alcoholic, or a person who is mentally ill. It may be replied in objection that these are "unfair" illustrations. Ideally "opportunity" and "the law" should be such that value-opposite consequences do not occur. However, as a matter of fact, in many cases "the law" does have such unfortunate results. It is clear that "equal opportunity" must be set in a wider context of qualifying controls, if full value is to be derived from this social means. As in the case of liberty—equality is neither intrinsically valuable or intrinsically value-opposite.

Fraternity in the political context is "roughly" a synonym for: mutual appreciation and liking. This constitutes a situation that is a condition for the achievement of value, in some cases. The fraternal feelings of members of a genuinely dedicated service group are means to the removal of much misery and pain and a source of much pleasure. Hence, in such a case, value accrues to fraternity.

On the other hand, in some situations it is the basis of extreme value-opposite consequences. Consider the case of fraternal feelings among the execution squad of a terrorist gang. It is the basis of successes in carrying out a number of cruel and ruthless murders.[20]

B

Liberty, Equality and Fraternity are not only "ideals" stressed by Democracy, in the sense of being recommended means. They are also, in the context of some democratic theory, referred to as *rights*—at least liberty and equality are so regarded.

Other entities also have the status of democratic ideals, and are deemed to be *rights*, "along with" liberty and equality. These are: Life, Happiness, Prosperity. All five are regarded as inalienable rights, which democratic men will recognize and honor. The notion of inalienable rights seems to "amount" essentially to this: there is no justification, in terms of sound value considerations,—for depriving a man of life, liberty, equality, happiness, or property (at least a certain amount of it).[21] In some contexts it is further contended that each man as such is characterized by liberty and equality—that is each man is born free and equal. As a matter of fact, it must be admitted that hereditary factors favor some and not others—as well as variations in environment leading in the same direction. It may, of course, be contended that what we have here is the statement of an ideal—not of fact. Hence an appeal to the so-called inalienable right is a claim that all men ought to have: freedom, equality of opportunity, happiness, property and no danger of early termination of life.

Be that as it may, there are cases where, in the interest of achieving the largest attainable amount of acceptable value, it is necessary to deprive "a man" of some, or all, of these "rights". Consider the case of a drug-crazed individual who is intent on killing a normal human being in the context of a robbery attempt. There is no other way to stop him except at the risk of killing him by shooting. Or to take a less extreme illustration—it is the case that, in terms of acceptable value considerations, one is justified in removing an alcoholic's property, if he insists on using it in a dangerous fashion, for example, driving his car when he is drunk. He is thus deprived of equality of opportunity and liberty to travel in this fashion—and so of attendant happiness.

Incidentally, none of these so-called rights is intrinsically valuable except happiness (that is, pleasure). All except happiness, on occasion,

189

are characterized by value-opposite extrinsically, as well as, on occasion, by value, on balance. This has been shown in the case of life, liberty and equality. It is obvious also in the case of property.[22]

There is no ultimate justification for these entities in terms of the "nature of man". The justification of rights is their means function with reference to ultimate value consideration. That is, a claim to have rights involves a concern for value consequences for others and oneself as well.

These "so-called" rights do not have different degrees of means value. However, life is most basic for the reason that without it the others means are not even present.[23] Liberty, in some sense of the term, is next in importance. A person can experience intrinsic value or extrinsic value without property or equality as a means, for example St. Francis of Assisi. Happiness is not a necessary condition for value achievement.

It is well to note that the term "right" is also used to refer to the fact that a person is capable of performing specific activities and this fact is appropriately certified. For example a person has the right to practice medicine as his College of Physicians diploma states.

VI

Law. The *laws of society* in some cases are deliberately planned, and formulated, to deal with specific problems—for example: traffic laws. Other laws develop by a process of trial and error. In any case, they are instruments used to facilitate valuable life in society. There is no evidence of divine creation of civic laws, or of any independent status in nature for them. At best, they reflect the nature of human beings and their environment, and what is required if human beings are to live together in such a fashion as to achieve specific goals. These laws are characterized by varying amounts of value on the means basis and that of other characteristics, and their consequences (and in the possible mode). When laws are codified and enforced in order to unjustly favour a minority of the population, or in any way function to serve, on balance, value-opposite goals—they are, characterized by value-opposite. It must be admitted that, on occasion, laws designed to further value ideals, on balance are characterized by value-opposite because of their characteristics or total consequences.

190

INDUSTRY: The earlier discussion of two industrialists labelled Mr. A and Mr. B., indicates very obviously that industry, in some occurrences, is characterized, on balance, by value, in other occurrences by value-opposite. The fact that an industry provides jobs, pays taxes, supports or provides community recreation facilities—does not, as such, constitute the industry a valuable entity *on balance*, though these are relevant factors. Other characteristics and consequences must be considered in order to reach a sound evaluation. Consider industry A. It is run purely for the sake of high profits which are used in a narrowly selfish fashion by a few entrepreneurs. Consequently the product is shoddy, wages are just slightly above the subsistence level. The environment is polluted and the industry leaves when profits fall below a large figure. Despite favourable factors noted above, on balance, such an industry is characterized by value-opposite.

On the other hand, consider industry B. It functions in such a fashion that it produces a sound product. It is directed by men who are satisfied with a moderate return from their investment and labors. Employees and employers both at work in the community, have an opportunity to appreciate and reach high levels of major value achievement. Also the industry tries to improve the community, as best it can, and avoids polluting the environment. In times of difficulty the industry acts in such a fashion that all involved: management, employees, the community in general,—suffer the minimum loss of values. Such an industry is characterized by value on balance. It may seem "too good to be true". However, at least a few enterprises fit this blue-print of a valuable industry.

As with management, so with labour unions. Some unions try to serve the best interests, (that is, the achievement of maximum attainable amount of acceptable value) of their members, the industry as a whole, and the wider community. This does not imply a gullible acceptance of "sugar-coated" injustice, by members of the union. Specifically, in some cases the members of the union are enlightened and their behaviour is characterized by moral goodness. The consequences are likewise valuable. The leaders are the same. Here obviously we have very valuable occurrences of the entity: union. On the other hand, some unions are composed of men who, at least the majority of them, are narrowly self-seeking. Their leaders are characterized by value-opposite as much as any robber baron tycoon. The activities of the union are such that the industry suffers, and much misery is periodically brought to the wider community. Thus, here as elsewhere in dealing with social institutions, one can not generalize concerning value or value-opposite.

VIII

Money is valuable, not only when it is used as an instrument (means) for the acquiring of many other entities. Also, it is valuable if it is characterized by beautiful, value-opposite if ugly. However, means and other characteristics are not the only factors to be considered in determining whether or not a sum of money is characterized by value, or value-opposite. Accrued aspects (i.e., because of consequences) are far more fundamental with reference to overall (that is, on balance) value, or value-opposite. The possible mode is also very important.

When a particular sum of money (e.g., a person's income) is used to provide a beautiful home, nourishing food and drink, comfortable and beautiful clothes,—an environment which encourages the appreciation and development of moral goodness and a concern for truth and many other valuable entities, in an acceptable fashion,—that particular occurrence of money has a high degree of value. Even if it is not so used at the moment, the money has value in the possible mode. On the other hand, if a person uses the same amount of money as a means to gross self-indulgence which issues in misery for his family and danger to others— the money is characterized by value-opposite on balance even though some temporary pleasure results to some people. Consider the case of a man who buys a prestige automobile which he cannot afford, drinks too much in celebrating his purchase, takes his family for a drive and crashes into a loaded school bus. The money also has value-opposite status in the possible mode.[24]

192

CHAPTER 10

Educational Institutions and Social Techniques

Education: Like any other social group, an educational institution, in some occurrences, is characterized on balance by value, in other occurrences by value-opposite.

I

Let us consider "Z" university.[1] In the Z.U. faculty there are a number of men and women who have, or pretend to have, vast knowledge in their various disciplines. A very few of them produce numerous learned articles and some definitive books. The vast majority claim to be so engaged—but seldom "appear in print". Some of the productive scholars are leaders in their fields and receive appropriate recognition. Some of the faculty are bloated with extreme self-satisfaction. Some are driven by an overwhelming craving for self-aggrandisement and ruthless power. They "wheel and deal" for a place in the academic sum. Honesty, justice, genuine concern for the welfare of others, sympathy, are for the most part lacking. Indeed in general—behaviour characterized by moral goodness, has little, or at least only a restricted, place in their dealings with their colleagues, their students or those who are so unfortunate as to be temporarily members of their families. Many of these men and women regard undergraduate teaching as a waste of "their valuable time". Any student, or colleague, indeed anyone, who does not share such a person's "professional interests" is regarded as "beyond the pale".

There are, of course, even at Z.U., a considerable number of faculty members who "gladly teach" large numbers of undergraduates. Graduate courses rarely fall to their lot. Their bibliographies are brief, or non-existent. But they strive to keep alive the spirit and practices of liberal education. Many students consider their classrooms and offices to be oases of refreshment and inspiration in an otherwise barren desert. Such faculty members are among the so-called "non-professional", "unpromotable", "nameless" men and women of the academic community of Z.U.

Also among the "nameless ones" is a considerable group of "sad souls" for whom a Ph.D. degree is an elusive "will o' the wisp". Likewise, present are those decorated by a doctorate. Many of these persons succumb to the pressures of domesticity, laziness, incompetence, or lack of nerve and so shrink into an uninspired, dull routine. Their feelings of inferiority are expressed in fashions which interfere with the best interests of those with whom they come in contact.

Fortunately, Z.U. has the good luck to be blessed by the presence of a few 'odd ones' who do not fall into the above categories. They are sound and productive scholars in the best sense. They achieve excellence in the realm of the intellect and in their personal lives as well. They teach skillfully on all levels of instruction. They serve the university, and its community, with dignity, good humour and impressive efficiency, despite the distractions of an uncongenial environment. They are honored abroad and for the most part "not appreciated" at home, except by those who are concerned with liberal education.

The administration of Z.U. gives lip service to the cause of: "education of the whole man"; not just intellect, but excellence in all aspects of behaviour, in accordance with lofty value ideals. However, harassed by many pressures, in their actual procedures they are usually concerned only to "apply grease to the wheel with the loudest squeak".

The community looks to Z.U. for wise leadership, and frequently is disappointed. The advanced students, with the exception of those who wish to emulate the intellectual "prima donnas", are seriously frustrated. Not only do they not obtain relevant information from the intellectual non-communicating myopic elite, they are led to believe that one need not bother with value in the categories: morally good or beautiful. Sophisticated "scholarship" money, and narrow intellectual specialization, are the goals officially held up for emulation at Z.U. Any attempts by students, or those staff members, who are involved in liberal education, to institute reforms—are discouraged.

The procedures of those in power generally are supported by men and women who owe their place in the university to them. These "camp followers" lack the drive and know-how of the leaders. They on occasion do not genuinely approve the guiding principles and techniques of their masters, but in the interests of personal security and peace—they support them.

Some members of the university, the establishment or dominant "in-group", experience considerable pleasure.[2] Some of these add, impressively, to the store of data in some fields. Some of this information is of the "make work" variety. Much of it is duplication of what is being done elsewhere. The point is to get it published first, or again—in superficially different form. Much of the behaviour of some members of the so-called elite is characterized by morally evil, ugly, silly, inconsistent, discordant. As such it interferes with the achievement of values in relevant areas of behaviour. The frustration of student and community needs and desires is of course characterized by a large amount of value-opposite. This major value-opposite state of affairs is partly countered by the behaviour and influence of the so-called "nameless" devotees of liberal education, and "odd ones". On balance, the ingredients of the educational situation of Z.U. is a clear case of an educational institution characterized by value-opposite. Further, as an organic whole, this University is characterized by value-opposite intrinsically. Also as a social institution it suffers from ugliness. inefficiency, inappropriateness, inconsistency and discord.

It is well to note that the devotees of liberal education, and in particular those who are concerned with morally good, true, beautiful and other intrinsic values, do not derive value-opposite from their ingredient state in an organic whole so characterized. The "like to like" function is not operative here.[3]

II

On the other hand, consider I.U.[4] In theory, and in practice, it is concerned with providing an environment in which all its members can develop their possibilities and potentialities of value experience in all major areas of human experience. This occurs in the context of an attempt to achieve the largest attainable amount of acceptable value. Members of the administration and the faculty are characterized by continuing acquisition and dissemination of information and skill in their fields of specialization. They also continue to acquire a grasp, or general understanding, of at least the main data in other fields of knowledge. In their behaviour they manifest moral goodness and a genuine appreciation of truth, beauty, efficiency, appropriateness, consistency and harmony. By example, and by percept, they encourage their students to develop along those lines. In like fashion they participate in the general life of the University. They engage in a cooperative activity of dealing with the basic problems which confront all human beings, either on or off the campus of a University. All members of the University,—administration, staff, students, old grads, members of the community—in the best sense of democracy, function together for the common good.

It is obvious that the ingredients of this educational situation are on balance characterized by value beyond question. On this basis, its status as an institution is the same. As an organic whole the social group is intrinsically valuable. It is also beautiful, efficient, appropriate, consistent and harmonious. Its ingredient members derive value on the basis of their status in such a valuable organic whole.

It may be objected that such a university is a "pipe dream". The reply is: there have been universities which approach this ideal goal. Of course no man is perfect in all his activities. If it be contended that Z.U. is the price we must pay for the increase of knowledge—this is simply not the case. Highly valuable human beings have made, for example, great scientific discoveries. Indeed the "narrow specialist" is less likely to make a break-through in human knowledge than a truly civilized hence, more broadly based and flexible human being.

A few additional comments, concerning *knowledge* are relevant here. As in the case of many other entities, it is important to note that, for example, a particular occurrence of knowledge is sometimes used as a *means* to the production of some other entity. When this is done, on this basis it is valuable. If the consequences are acceptably valuable, value accrues to knowledge. Consider the case of specific chemical information which is used to remove disease from a human body and hence, with the restoration of health, pleasure is derived. Further, since the chemical knowledge is an ingredient in a complex sort of behaviour, it has value on that basis. Also, if it is an ingredient in behaviour which is characterized by value intrinsically, it derives value from that fact.

On the other hand, consider the case of a person who motivated by hatred of fellowmen, intentionally includes a pain producing ingredient in a soft drink which is widely used. Such behaviour is, of course, intrinsically a case of value-opposite. However, the knowledge ingredient, in this situation, does not derive any value-opposite from its value-opposite consequences. This is in accordance with the "like to like" pattern. Specifically, knowledge of the proposition type involve essentially the factor: true, which is intrinsically valuable. The sort of knowledge which is skill (know how) involves essentially the factor: efficient. This likewise is intrinsically valuable. What is essentially[5] characterized by something which is intrinsically valuable does not derive value-opposite from a consequence which is characterized by value-opposite.

Related issues must now be considered, namely the question of the value or value-opposite characteristic of (a) reasoning and (b) a rational approach to a problem. Those issues are complex because the terms "reasoning" and "rational" do not coincide in their meanings.

Reasoning is a mental process of proceeding from one or more entities in an *attempt* to reach another entity which has the status of: conclusion. This attempt may or may not be successful. The entities involved in reaching the conclusion are usually concepts, simple or complex, or images (memory or imagination). In a few cases attention may be focussed, in part, on mental activities or on physical objects. Conclusion entities are of the same sorts. For example a person proceeds from the concept Socrates to the concept man, from the concept man to the concept mortal and hence to the proposition: "Socrates is mortal". Present in the process of reasoning there may be a memory image of Socrates rather than a concept. Also a person himself may be present to awareness.

Any process of reasoning is valuable in the means mode when it is successful in reaching a conclusion (as in the illustration). Particular occurrences of reasoning differ in degrees of efficiency in reaching conclusions. For example, some take more time and effort or are more complicated than others. When a process of reasoning is concerned with facts and is in accordance with facts (illustration above) it is characterized by accurate (true) and has value on that basis. If the opposite is the case, it is characterized by value-opposite. When a process of reasoning is consistent it is valuable because of the value of this characteristic. Otherwise it is not.

If a particular process of reasoning results in a valuable conclusion (e.g. a true one) it derives value from the value of its consequence, i.e., the conclusion. (It should be realized that a true conclusion is usually a case of knowledge.) On the other hand, if the consequence is value-opposite (e.g., false) it derives value-opposite on this basis. Thus it is also so when the process of reasoning is inaccurate and/or inconsistent.

It must be realized that in some cases a process of reasoning is either inaccurate or inconsistent, or both (at least in part) and yet a true, i.e., valuable conclusion is reached. For example: Round is a figure superior to all others. The head is round. The mind is located in the head (i.e., mental activities are linked with the brain). Conclusion: The mind is the superior part of man.[6]

As in the case of any other particular occurrence of an entity, one must consider the various modes in which it is valuable, or value-opposite, and ascertain the "on-balance" characteristic.

The term "*rational*" is here regarded as synonymous with: "in accordance with relevant facts and/or consistent". Thus rational is a characteristic of some processes of reasoning.[7] The entity rational, i.e., accurate (true) and/or consistency—is characterized by value intrinsically. When a process of reasoning has a valuable conclusion, because of the rationality of its process, value accrues to rational. If value-opposite consequences occur, the reasoning process being consistent, value-opposite does not accrue to the rational reasoning involved (as noted in the preceding discussion of the "like to like" pattern).

V

At this point it is appropriate to refer briefly to *persuasion* and *violence*, which are sometimes used in attempting to bring about social change, or in the course of social relationships.

"Persuasion" in the sense here employed, refers to a process (rational or emotional) which is designed to lead a person to accept a conclusion or engage in action, on his "own volition". The use of violence, on the other hand, is an attempt at overcoming a person's resistance to some proposal—and make him, "against his will" agree and/or act. In some cases, it involves the use of physical activity resulting in the destruction of, or damage to, physical objects inanimate and animate (that is, a person's body). Violence may also occur in the realm of mind. In any case the use of violence casts the recipient in the role of victim.[8]

The preceding summary comments now require clarificatory illustrations. To begin with, persuasion may take a rational form. When it does, it is characterized by value because of the value of its characteristic: rational. Consider a community which is persuaded to accept the rejection of a favourite form of relaxation and sociability, namely the smoking of cigarettes. This was done by pointing out, in a purely factual fashion, the bad effects on health. Another case of persuasion took a predominantly emotional form. People who are greatly admired, for example sports or theatre personages, were presented as advocating the abandonment of cigarette smoking as being the "in thing".

The persuasive process with rational characteristics had more value in the characteristics mode than the emotional one. In both cases the consequences of instrumental function were characterized by value. Both methods derived further value since they were in the context of an organic whole of behaviour which was a case of concern for the welfare of one's fellow men. In these modes (including means) the two techniques were equal in value. Rational persuasion however, is superior because of its rational characteristic. Rational persuasion, because of its essential characteristic does not derive value-opposite, for example from pain,

199

which may be its consequence. Consider the case of a person who is thus persuaded to face up to his own great defects of personality. However, if emotional persuasion has value-opposite consequences, value-opposite is derived. The point is, as noted in the previous discussion of rational, that while rational is intrinsically valuable and hence does not derive value-opposite from consequences, this is not the case with emotional persuasion.

When *violence* is used in the context of hatred of members of another social group, with the intention to damage or destroy, obviously it is value-opposite. It derives much value-opposite because of its ingredient status in an organic whole which is morally evil, and a case of value-opposite intrinsically. There are, of course, other value-opposite consequences such as pain, fear,[9] and so on. These value-opposite consequences far out-balance the efficiency and means value which characterize it.

On the other hand, consider a case where violence is the only means available to break the hold on a society of a morally evil tyranny. The violence is used in the context of a concern for the welfare of fellow men. Then it derives thereby enough value to over-balance all the painful value-opposite consequences of using violence as an instrument. This is particularly the case when the violence as means produces salvation from tyranny.

When violence in the sense of destructive force, is used as a means to give vent to pent-up pressures, and expresses itself in a fashion which does not harm other persons, it is characterized by value. Consider, for example, the harassed business man who smashes a decrepit and useless chair and as a result feels much better (and incidentally replenishes his supply of kindling wood)!

As in the case of other instances of the use of force of a destructive nature, some occurrences of *war* have value on balance. This is so when it is a means to the existence, and preservation, of a larger amount of acceptable value than unacceptable value-opposite. Consider, for example, war against the Nazis. There is an analogy with killing a mad intruder who is about to rob and kill members of one's household. Similarly war should be used only if no other alternative is available. Most (other) wars are forms of aggression or selfishness—economic or jingoistic. Obviously, such wars are contrary to the requirements of the largest attainable amount of acceptable value, and in general are characterized by value-opposite.

A number of entities which have a prominent place in the personal and social life of a human being require consideration at this point: (a) drugs and liquor, (b) art, (c) a philosophy of life.

These are claimed by many people to have value because they are efficient means to some or all of the following: (i) escape from institutional, or other, oppression or restriction, and resultant frustration, (ii) expression of frustration—and also (iii) achieve such ends as self-development, the enjoyment of intrinsic values,—in general the satisfaction of thwarted needs and desires. Such claims will be kept in mind in the course of an attempt to ascertain the value, or value-opposite, status of these entities.

(A)

Let us consider the value, or value-opposite, status of *drugs*. A mild drug like aspirin, used with care,[10] is valuable as a means for escaping pain resulting from physical illness and social pressures, as far as many situations are concerned. It is valuable because efficient in leading to these results. Also it is valuable because of these results. Hence the overall characteristic is that of value. On the other hand excessive (for a period) use of aspirin, while it relieves some pain, etc. has as a long-range result: deterioration of health and hence will have accrued value-opposite characteristics. In this situation the overall, that is, on balance, status is that of value-opposite.

LSD when first used, is an effective means for producing some results which are characterized by value—for example, beautiful hallucinations, and pleasure. More specifically it is the case that a hard drug can function as an instrument to achieve the results claimed: escape sources of frustration, express frustration, satisfy some needs and desires, for example social recognition, etc.

It is frequently claimed that the frustration of needs and desires leads to many sorts of value-opposite results. However, it is essential to note that the use of hard drugs, to any considerable extent produces results which are far worse than those of the original frustration, i.e., the denial of satisfaction of needs and desires. Indeed, the user of such drugs usually puts himself under a worse restriction and frustration than those from which he is trying to escape. All this is very obvious in the case of use of drugs to the point of extreme misery resulting from serious deterioration of physical and mental health.

If it be objected that attention should be focussed on a few occurrences, or the occasional user—a serious difficulty still remains.[11] The use of hard drugs, even in such cases, results in a considerable restriction of the range of value expression. To this extent the drug is characterized by enough value-opposite to overbalance any valuable characteristics it may have. If this is not entirely clear, consider the case of a person who in the context of "lack of self-control" behaviour uses a hard drug. This behaviour is an organic whole characterized by value-opposite intrinsically. It is also value-opposite because of its morally evil characteristic. Because of its ingredient status in this organic whole, the drug derives additional value-opposite. A further comment is relevant concerning the satisfaction of desires. In certain situations LSD, or any hard drug, does function as a means of achieving social recognition and approval, and provides the basis for one kind of self-development. However, when one examines, carefully, the nature of those who approve—and the self in process of development—there is no basis for the claim that such drugs derive value because of such consequences, sufficient to over-balance value-opposite aspects.

In order to avoid possible misunderstanding, it is well to note that the particular occurrences of pleasure and of beautiful referred to above are unacceptable values. That is so because the price to be paid in terms of subsequent misery and deterioration, and restriction in range of value-experience, is too high. Nevertheless in so far as this drug produces the pleasure and beautiful images, on that basis it derives value. However, the unacceptability characteristics indicated that such occurrences of pleasure and beautiful have no place in the situation which involves the largest attainable amount of acceptable value. In the case of efficiency— if the result is pleasure and beautiful the drug has value because of the value of efficiency. If it is efficient in producing misery and deterioration the drug derives no value on that basis. In either case such efficiency has no place in the ideal situation.

The preceding discussion of drugs provides a pattern of analysis which is applicable to *liquor*. In view of the obviousness of this point, it seems unnecessary to engage in the details of a repetitious analysis.

We turn now to a consideration of art and a philosophy of life.

B

The Last Supper by Leonardo da Vinci is valuable because of its characteristic: beautiful. It also derives value from the insight which it gives into moral and religious facts. In so far as it inspires people to aesthetic, moral and religious achievement,[12] and the search for truth, it derives further value. Its causal efficacy in producing pleasure is of course highly significant. In all this it serves to satisfy a number of needs and desires in an efficient fashion. It is the basis of the development of a value-oriented self. In so far as the painting occurs in the context of behaviour characterized by a concern for higher value, it derives value from its ingredient status in an intrinsically valuable organic whole. No value-opposite is derived from any value-opposite consequences which may result from its value status in general, or characteristics or consequences in particular.

A man who engages in artistic activity of painting such a picture finds it to be a means of avoiding the frustration which results from restrictions which interfere with the satisfaction of basic needs and desires. Such artistic activity also is the basis of social approval by men and women of like mind. It is to be noted that this sort of escape does not involve worse frustration and related value-opposite results. It is a sort of escape which provides refreshment and stimulus to greater, rather than less, value achievement.

Consider next a more complicated case. A novel portrays a group of ugly, morally evil, persons who ride rough shod over morally good individuals in an ugly environment. Pain is a dominant factor in the experience of all the characters. The name of the book is "Legion". As a result of reading this novel, a cynical lack of concern for morally good behaviour and beauty is engendered in many persons. There is the possibility that others will be likewise affected. On the other hand, some people, on thinking about it, are inspired to improve the lot of such human beings. In any case, it has the possibility of producing that result. On these bases, and because it is an accurate report of the life of some people, the novel is characterized by value.

203

In so far as the volume satisfies a desire to be informed concerning value-opposite phenomena it has value as means. But since it serves to blind some readers to the existence of the value of morally good and beautiful, it strengthens the hold of the value-opposite way of life. This of course is a value-opposite consequence. In any case, immersion in the novel is not a refreshing and stimulating escape from value-opposite data for its readers. The pleasure generated by the contemplation of the morally evil, ugly characters portrayed in the novel is not the basis of value accrual to it. However, in so far as the novel is an efficient (and true) presentation of some of the facts of life, it derives value. Further pleasure reaction to this characteristic is the basis of value derivation. Incidentally, it is important to note that the novel as such is not morally evil or ugly. More specifically, it is not necessarily ugly just because it discusses ugly persons and things. Further lack of concern for morally good or beauty which result from reading it are not bases of value-opposite derivation.

Everything considered—the novel on balance has the status: valuable.

(C)

It is now appropriate to examine the entity: *philosophy of life*. Under consideration is a general view of the nature of men and the environment, and in particular a consideration of: what, if anything, is valuable, and why.

A view concerning the main ingredients of the world, if true, derives value from that characteristic. Further, and more specifically, a philosophy of life should involve a sound logic. This provides what may be a useful instrument with valuable consequences. A philosophy of life which identifies major valuable entities is valuable in the means mode. If all this information is put to acceptable use in the business of living, the philosophy, of course, has greatly enhanced value. In the context of concern for value achievement, such a philosophy derives value because of its ingredient status.

On the other hand, a philosophy which stresses only some of the main ingredients of the universe, and denies the presence of some entities which are there, is characterized by value-opposite because of its false-hood. Possible, or actual, consequences of the implementation of this view are the bases of value-opposite accrual. Such a philosophy of life, if implemented, may well serve as a means of escape from some difficulties, but its consequences indicate the value-opposite nature of such escape. In so far as a defective philosophy of life is an ingredient in behaviour which is a case of narrow self-interest, snobbish arrogance, or lazy lack of concern for the welfare of self or others—it derives value-opposite from its ingredient status.

However, such a philosophy has value in so far as it is a means to satisfying the desire to manifest even the attitudes mentioned above. Further it may be a means of expressing frustration and achieve social recognition and hence derive further value. Its escape value has already been noted. Because it is an ingredient in that world it has value on that basis. However, all those value aspects are completely overwhelmed by its numerous value-opposite characteristics and consequences.

VII

At the end of an evaluation of a number of familiar, every-day entities, it is well to ''look briefly'' at: an excellent man in an excellent society. The term ''excellent'' is here used as a substitute for the cumbersome phrase: characterized by the largest amount of acceptable value attainable by a man or a society in this world. This examination will serve to give more specific detail concerning the so-called: ''long-range ideal situation''.[13]

An excellent man is concerned with a wide range of intrinsically valuable entities and is familiar with the main sorts of extrinsically valuable ones. But as a member of the human race, as we now know it, he has extensive limitations. For example, he experiences and enjoys many cases of pleasure, beauty and truth. Yet no human being, so far known, is aware of all true propositions or all occurrences of beautiful. Some excellent people are not characterized by beautiful. No person achieves the highest degree of morally good in all his behaviour. An excellent person makes effective use of many (but not all) entities, and functions as a means in an effective fashion in many instances. He produces many valuable consequences. Here again there are limitations. For example an excellent person may be relatively inefficient in producing works of art and in investigating the structure of a very difficult dead language. He simply lacks ability in these areas. In general a (any) man is limited by the situation in which he as an individual finds himself, that is: by his heredity and environment.

Some further explanatory comments are in order: Being outstanding, or even highly competent as a professional in some one specialized branch of science or art, or business, politics, education, or any other social organization or institution is an essential but not the most fundamental characteristic of an excellent human being. A high level of attainment of morally good behaviour is more fundamental. It has already been emphasized that an excellent man will be competent in a wide range of areas of knowledge and aesthetic experience. He will also be competent in a number of social organisations (but it is not humanly possible to be so in all) in which he is not professionally involved. It must be stressed that it is in the course of his life as a member of society in general, and in various social organisations in particular, that much of a man's morally good behaviour occurs. Thus an excellent human being will be concerned with the welfare of his fellow men. He will be sympathetic, tolerant, honest, just, merciful, self-controlled—all in the interests of increasing the amount of acceptable and appropriate value in the world.

His relations with his fellow men in this context, guided by calm intellectual analysis, will be characterized by persuasion as the preferred instrument. Force will be used only as a last resort, and only when justified by the requirements of retaining or increasing the amount of acceptable and appropriate value.

As previously stressed, individual men and women differ markedly in interests, capacities[14] and abilities. In an excellent society, each person will live in a physical and social environment such that his *basic* needs will be satisfied. Further he will have an opportunity to achieve a large amount of the intrinsic and extrinsic values[15] which are open to him in view of his interests, capacities and abilities. However, since an 'excellent' society, in the sense here employed, falls short of unlimited conceivability, there will not be full satisfaction of all appropriate needs and desires.

Nevertheless, this excellent society is composed of a considerable number of excellent men and women who give leadership and set an example, cooperating with those of lesser capacity, ability and achievement. Educational facilities will provide a good (not perfect) opportunity for each person to find out what his capacity and abilities are,—and prepare himself for valuable use of them. Each person will have adequate

206

food, clothing, shelter and recreational facilities. In the context of family, vocational, educational (continuing through life), religious and recreational activities (the term is broadly used to cover sports, hobbies, club membership)—each person will receive respect for what he is, and is trying to become (of value). He will have a sense of being a significant member of his group. All this implies the use of the physical environment as a "resource" in the best sense of the term. Pollution and in general selfish exploitation will not occur.

The complex problem of how this state of affairs can be brought about, specifically how physical and social resources can be managed in such a fashion as to achieve this complex pattern of goals, has been in part indicated by some of the preceding comments in this section. At this point, one general comment is in order. The question as to method required—does not have a simple readily available answer. In other words, there is no simple formula referring to a simple technique. It is neither doctrinaire, in any of the well known variations, capitalism or socialism. It implies a concern for the welfare of all men in the social group, which ultimately is world wide. To this extent it resembles socialism, or a type of enlightened capitalism. However, it does not imply a so-called "democracy" which interferes with that individual initiative which is productive of "high level" value. In one sense of the term, this is a form of democracy—that form which stresses and implements the ideals of civilized living.

VIII

At the end of this discussion of the value, or value-opposite, status of a number of representative entities, it is well to bring into summary, and supplementary, focus a group of very significant related factors.

The question of (a) the *amount* of value[16] which characterizes an entity and (b) the *comparison* of the value of different entities, have received considerable attention. In the context of comprehensive experience a person, with due care, can compare many pairs of entities (specifically particular occurrences of them) and gradually come to be aware of a series of increasing amounts of value as one moves, for example, from a pen to an occurrence of the entity beautiful, to a morally good and beautiful occurrence of behaviour, to the life of Schweitzer, to the ideal goal of human experience,—with many intervening stages. However, as noted previously, one must be very careful to avoid the error of hasty over-generalization.

Even though amounts of value of entities can not be expressed in exact numerical terms, the increasing amount of value of a series of entities from little value to maximum attainable, can be stated in the following fashion, which fits the varying distinguishable grades of amounts of value of entities. The following labels are convenient and appropriate: (1) slight; (2) considerable; (3) very considerable; (4) great; (5) very great— amount of value.[17] All these are stages in a series leading up to (6) the amount of value of the long range ideal situation (i.e., that characterized by the largest attainable amount of acceptable value in this world). Expanding and revising the previous reference to such a series, consider (1) a pen, (2) an occurrence of the entity morally good, (3) an occurrence of love of a fellow man, (4) Schweitzer, (5) the organic whole: "Friends of Albert Schweitzer", the world wide group of people associated with Schweitzer, who supported his work by a vast range of activities.

The series 1—5 may be described technically speaking as

(1) inanimate objects which are not intrinsically valuable;
(2) simple entities which are intrinsically valuable;
(3) some complex entities which are organic wholes;
(4) some persons
(5) some intrinsically valuable complex organic wholes involving at least 2 persons.

However referring back to the danger of hasty generalizing, it must be remembered that some physical objects, for example, the statue of Aphrodite, are more valuable than some men. In some cases a simple intrinsically valuable entity is more valuable than an organic whole which has an intrinsically valuable characteristic. For example the entity beautiful, if present to a very high degree, is superior in value to some cases of cooperation or to reciprocation of benefits. Thus the description of the 5 stages (above) must be understood as a rough sketch, applicable in many cases, but not to be used uncritically. This involves also the recognition of the fact that within each so-called stage there is a very significant variation in the amount of value characterizing entities which belong to the same stage (i.e., group). For example, in Chapter 2 it was pointed out that morally good, true, beautiful, pleasure etc. vary in value to a noticeable extent though all are members of the "same" group. Obviously this variation is the case with reference to different physical objects—all belong in the "slight" class.

As a supplementary comment, it is well to note that entities which have been termed "operational resultants"[18] are characterized by varying amounts of value.—They fall within one or other stages 1—5 depending on the amount of value involved in the introduction, increase, etc. of value. However, it is essential to note that the amount of value of the operational resultant is much less than the value of the entity which is involved in the operation—despite the fact that both are in the same value group. On the other hand, in cases of removal or prevention of value-opposite the amount of value of the operational resultant is the same as the amount of value-opposite of the entity involved in the removal or prevention.

The general status of *means* entities is that of slight. The fact that there is variation in value among causes, instruments, etc. has already been discussed (Chapter 5, pp. 92-93). It was found that some cases of, for example, cause functions are more valuable than some inanimate objects, e.g., a lump of mud (in some situations). It has been obvious from previous discussion[19] that amounts of value can be compared with reference to what is involved in various modes in terms of the labels here employed, i.e., varying from slight to very great. For example, the amount of value derived in a means mode is slight. On the other hand, entities which are characterized by acceptable beauty or acceptable courage derive considerable or very considerable value thereby. Thus one can compare the amount of value derived in various different modes as well as compare entities on the basis of their total value status (in all modes together).

The preceding comments concerning value can be paralleled by others of the same general pattern concerning value-opposite—in view of the relevant situations.

EPILOGUE

EPILOGUE: Replies to some possible criticisms

It is obvious that this book is not exclusively concerned with the meaning of the terms "value" and "value-opposite" or more specifically "morally good", "morally evil", "beautiful", "ugly", "true", "false" and so on, and their use in the context of value[1] discourse. It has little to say about the logical structure of value discourse. Nor does it discuss obligation or the free will issue.

This state of affairs should not be interpreted as an indication that the author considers these topics unimportant. Such most definitely is not the case. There is a genuine concern for the effective use of value language. This arises from a more basic concern for the understanding of the nature of value, and value-opposite, and the ways in which value or value-opposite are present in this world. This involves an examination of value, or value-opposite, characteristics of a representative sample of entities which are frequently of interest to human beings.

Some of the topics not covered or fully covered or fully discussed, in this volume have been dealt with in *Experiential Realism*.[2]

Roughly speaking, in general scope but not in detail, this study is in the tradition of Plato, the Stoics, Dewey and Whitehead—whose approach to value involved both rational analysis and practical concern for the solution of specific human problems. In some details it has kinship with G. E. Moore.[3] It is in agreement with C. L. Stevenson in thinking that when the logic of evaluation has been attended to, the main problem of value study remains to be faced.[4]

In *Modes of Value* there are a few references to contemporary and traditional treatment of value issues in order to clarify the orientation of this book. Otherwise there is no direct "by name and book" discussion of the contemporary or traditional literature in the field. This should not be interpreted as neglect by the author of this important material. The "many voices" have been heard. Their messages have been pondered.

In brief, this book does not engage in detailed controversy covering the vast range of ingenuous comments concerning value (and value-opposite) issues. Its main concern is to outline the results of comprehensive experience in this field—carefully bearing in mind the work of others.

It is here contended that in so far as alternate views try to identify, or account for, value (value-opposite) in terms of some other entity—they are open to very serious criticism. The same is true of those who neglect some modes of presence of value (value-opposite). If it has defects in these senses, an alternate philosophy will not be in a sound position to discuss the meaning of value (value-opposite) terms or the methodology, or logical structure, of such discourse.

It will have been evident from previous discussion that *Modes of Value*, in its approach to meaning, stresses as primary the referential (denotative) aspect. But the emotive (or prescriptive) phase of meaning is not overlooked. However, its status is—associated.

In using value (value-opposite) concepts (or terms) in a process of reasoning—since value is one sort of factual entity—the logic of its discussion is that of any other fact. However, in so far as value (value-opposite) concepts and terms have an emotional (prescriptive) aspect, the logic of their use, for example in expressing and arousing attitudes—is different from that of simply referring to, or reporting, the existence of facts.

It may be objected that since *Modes of Value* reports that in comprehensive experience there is direct awareness of value (value-opposite)—it is open to all the standard objections to intuitionism—subjectivism, relationism—hence the impossibility of objective proof and intellectual respectability. Since these matters have been dealt with in *Experiential Realism*[5] the discussion will not be repeated here.

The evaluation "here offered" of various familiar entities, and in particular of some sorts of behaviour, will strike some readers as being incredibly, naively, irrelevant—in view of the present state of affairs.[6]

214

However *Modes of Value* deals with the evaluation of particular occurrences of actual human behaviour. Some very valuable behaviour is not at the moment wide-spread (i.e., common). This does not cast aspersions on its value.

A very basic question has perplexed many persons: Why bother with value and value-opposite? It sometimes takes the form: Why be morally good? There is a set of related questions: Why prefer[7] a larger amount of value to a smaller? Likewise why prefer a smaller amount of value-opposite to a larger? Indeed, why prefer value to value-opposite? The final answers to these related questions, as far as comprehensive experience is concerned, are very simple: As a matter of fact human beings are concerned with value and value-opposite. As a matter of fact they prefer value to value-opposite. Likewise they want and strive for as much value as they can obtain and endeavour to have as little value-opposite as "they can".

It is obvious that value and value-opposite are not always in clear focus of attention. The degree of concern etc. varies from person to person and from "moment to moment". Men and women are concerned with, and express preference for, many entities which they believe are characterized by value or are more valuable than others—but as a matter of fact such is not the case.

This book involves an attempt to be of assistance in dealing with the situation.

NOTES

Notes

CHAPTER 1

[1]For the significance of the term "external" here see Chap. 5, pp. 101-02.

[2]The terms "characteristic" and "external consequence" are here, and elsewhere, used in the plural form in order to avoid possible misunderstanding. If singular forms were employed it might be assumed that only one sort of characteristic or external consequence is relevant. This is not the case. Illustrations of these modes will cover a wide range of different particular characteristics and external consequences.

[3]The terms "beautiful", "true" are used rather than "beauty", "truth", because the entities to which they refer have the status: characteristic of some entity.

[4]The terms "accrue" and "derive" are used to make clear the point that the value which an entity has is not present intrinsically but as the result of relation to other entities.

[5]It is to be stressed that the form of expression "modes of value" is a convenient abbreviation for "modes of presence of value" and will be employed on this basis.

[6]In a sense, "what it takes" is a *consequence* of an entity being present.

[7]See R. B. Perry, *The Theory of Value*, Harvard University Press, Cambridge, Mass., 1950, pp. 115-16.

[8]T. Hobbes, *Leviathan*, Clarendon Press, Oxford, 1909, p. 41.

[9]or interest, or desire, or pleasure.

[10]The entities mentioned in the immediately preceding paragraph are not.

[11]and entities characterized by it.

[12]specifically: See: Chapter 5, fn. 69.

[13,14]See discussion of "acceptable" and "unacceptable" in Chap. 3, pp. 33-38.

[15]A so-called "physically based resultant" is an entity such as a shadow or mirror image or the elliptical shape seen when looking at a penny from an angle— which through the result of interaction of physical entities is, as such, not

physical. Neither are such entities characterized by mental, nor are they concepts. Indeed many entities have this status, i.e., not physical, mental, etc. Consider the entities green, length, between.

[16]Consider the preceding and subsequent discussion of a particular pen.

CHAPTER 2

[1]"Entities which are Intrinsically" is a convenient and usual abbreviation for "entities which *are characterized by* value or value-opposite intrinsically."

[2]As a matter of fact, beautiful is not generated by desire or pleasure. These entities frequently are present and beautiful is absent, or vice versa. In general, see the preceding discussion of the nature of value.

[3]It may not be very obvious that beautiful has value because of the value of its characteristics. But in a technical sense this is so. Beautiful in this situation has relational and numerical characteristics. These entities being ingredients have value on that basis. The entity beautiful derives value from the value of these characteristics. But here again, the extrinsic mode of presence of value is obviously distinct from the intrinsic.

[4]In this sense it differs from morally good, beautiful and true. These entities as such are neither mental, physical, concepts or physically based resultants, i.e., do not have these entities as characteristics.

[5]If this "raises hackles" because of the apparent introduction of unnecessary, additional, entities—use the term "different"!

[6]This sort of supplementary comment will be dealt with in subsequent discussion.

[7]Though synonymous terms may be used, e.g., "appropriate" or "meet requirements of situation".

[8]It is to be noted that like fitting, efficient occurs in either a natural or a conventional context.

[9]i.e., valuable intrinsically.

[10]See detailed discussion in Chapter 4, pp. 75-78.

[11]It is to be noted that the term profound (pain) refers not only to intensity but also to depth, complexity and pervasiveness.

CHAPTER 3

[1]The term is here used in a considerably broader sense than that of G. E. Moore, *Principia Ethica*, pp. 27-31, Cambridge U. Press, 1929.

[2]See pp. 30-33 for a discussion of operational resultants.

[3]pieces of wood which may function as legs and top.

[4]Likewise in the carpenter's shop, pictures on the wall, dust on a lamp bulb, wood shavings—are all components of an aggregation.

[5]Indeed to be aware of any entity in the universe. See subsequent discussion, pp. 31-32.

[6]It is essential to realize that the behaviour entity "pleasure reaction to morally good behaviour" does not take on, or have, the value of the morally good behaviour. For example, when Mr. X. is profoundly pleased by a case of love of a fellow man behaviour on the part of Schweitzer—Mr. X's reaction behaviour does not thereby have the value of Schweitzer's morally good behaviour. Hence

the value of Mr. X's behaviour is not the sum of the value of Schweitzer's behaviour and X's feeling of pleasure. In any case, X's behaviour is not an aggregation. It is an organic whole. As a matter of fact, the reaction of pleasure to a case of morally good behaviour is less valuable intrinsically than the case of morally good behaviour. This is so even though morally good behaviour is an ingredient (i.e., focal object, with reference to which the pleasure reaction occurs).

It is assumed that the occurrence of morally good behaviour with reference to which the pleasure reaction occurs—is acceptable. See this chapter, pp. 33-37 for an explanation of the term 'acceptable'.

[7]and hence the difficulty in becoming aware of them.

[8]in distinction from entities which are so characterized.

[9]The phrase "the occurrence of" is, it is hoped, a convenient synonym for "the presence of".

[10]There are also cases where the associated entities are value-opposite extrinsically.

[11]There are also cases where the associated entities are value-opposite on balance.

[12]In some cases there is delayed payment of price. The beauty of drug induced images is unacceptable because of the eventual personality deterioration.

[13]See comments on page 34.

[14]In other words, being an ingredient of an intrinsically value-opposite organic whole is one thing—being unacceptable is another. Indeed the unacceptable situation, as illustrations indicate, is not always an organic whole.

[15]See subsequent discussion (for illustrations) chapters 8-10.

[16]unacceptable value-opposite.

[17]It is important to emphasize *internal*. Positive external reactions to acceptable valuable entities is not intrinsically valuable or value-opposite as such. For example, consider merely physically approaching an acceptable occurrence of beautiful, or an acceptably valuable book. However these actions, in certain sorts of behaviour, may well have extrinsic value—in others, extrinsic value opposite.

[18]See discussion of pleasure reaction to morally good, pp. 39-40.

[19]It should be obvious that a positive reaction to the entity value as such is an intrinsically valuable organic whole.

[20] there was an over-balancing loss.

[21]See discussion, pp. 28-31, and chapter 4.

[22]In the context of the immediate situation.

[23]People, as the result of a process of development, acquire characteristics which they previously did not actually have, but the basis for development was there, i.e., latent potentiality. See Chapter 1, p. 9.

[24]When a person has learned how to do something, he has the ability to do so even if he is not actually doing it at that time. For example, though I am sitting in my study writing, I have the ability to drive a car.

[25]The preceding very general introductory outline will be filled out by subsequent discussion.

[26]i.e., entities available to function as conditions.

[27]A few men, on occasion, measure up to the requirement of these ideals.

[28]Specifically it is a case of pleasure and book functioning as instruments. However, it is well to note that this is not the sort of instrument which most frequently occurs. Namely an entity is used in the production of another entity which is not its characteristic. In the case immediately before us the value has been introduced because it is characteristic of what has been introduced into the situation. The latter being the instrument for the presence of value.

[29]tearing down is a "sort" or removing.

[30]It must be admitted that there are similarities in illustrations of (b) and (c).

[31]The same general point applies to prevention.

[32]It is essential to note that "depends on"—is not.

[33]In general, these operational resultants, other factors being equal, are ranked in order of amount of value from introduction—to increase—to progress. However, in the "last analysis" individual cases must be the basis for comparison.

[34]or any other relation involving calculation using other symbols, e.g., large, small.

[35]It is to be noted that this state of affairs will involve the occurrence of some cases of value—not only when means, but also value in other modes.

CHAPTER 4

[1]See Chapter 3, pp. 29-30.

[2]The term "entity" is used in the phrase "the entities morally good and morally evil" in order to stress the fact that morally good and morally evil *as such* are being discussed—not the behaviour which they characterize.

[3]The apparently cumbersome phrase "*behaviour* entities" is used here, and elsewhere, to emphasize that there are a number of different specific organic wholes of the same general sort here under discussion.

[4]In referring to behaviour entities which are intrinsically valuable and also are characterized by morally good, it seems convenient to abbreviate, as in this case, by referring only to "characterized by morally good". It will be understood that one is dealing with behaviour entities which are intrinsically valuable. This procedure will usually be followed in subsequent discussion. Occasionally, for clarification, the fact of intrinsic value will be mentioned as well.

In this chapter attention tends to focus on the morally good aspect of these behaviour entities. However, when relevant the relation between the intrinsic value of an organic whole and the intrinsic value of its ingredients (or their value-opposites) will be discussed.

[5]i.e., an entity which functions as a motive and hence is "named after" its characteristic. Hence this behaviour ingredient is identified not by its nature but by its function.

[6]It will be noted that choice and acts of will are technically speaking not here termed "motives", despite the fact that they do have a dynamic function. This is so because feelings, emotions and desires are more fundamental as causes of intentions and actions. This is indicated by the fact that there are cases of morally

222

good behaviour which do not involve choice or acts of will. See discussion this chapter.

⁷Or at least an attempt to act.

⁸Components and their relations.

⁹If this statement seems unduly technical, consider Hegel's definition of love: "It is the identity of the relativity of an infinitesimal portion of the absolute totality of Infinite Being"!

¹⁰Specifically the desire factor must have maximum intensity. In working out the means (contributory) goals leading to the ultimate goal, full use must be made of a person's intellectual resources. In translating plans into action, here again full use must be made of available resources internal and environmental. In the face of obstacles attempts at action must be unrestricted as far as the lover is concerned.

¹¹See Chapter 10, pp. 207-09.

¹²It is not necessary to continually spell out this aspect of nature of intention, in all subsequent discussion.

¹³Thus implementing the contributory intention.

¹⁴It is essential to emphasize that there are two sorts of so-called selfish behaviours: (a) the focus is on obtaining value for the actor alone (narrowly selfish) at the expense of value effect for others; (b) the focus is on achieving the largest attainable amount of acceptable value for each person in the context of just (see later discussion, this Chapter, pp. 58-61) treatment. Thus a self is involved who is concerned with the fair sharing of values rather than getting them for himself. The behaviour of such a self is in a sense selfish, i.e., the goals of the self are present but these are not the goals of a self who is prepared to flourish at the expense of others.

¹⁵An illustration involving two males is now in use.

¹⁶"Love of a fellow man" is of course available as an alternate phrase.

¹⁷See subsequent discussion, Chapter 5, pp. 92-93 and fn. 7.

¹⁸i.e., involved in the basic ultimate intention (goal).

¹⁹In view of the obvious parallels between sympathy and love of another human being, it seems unnecessary to engage in more detailed comment concerning sympathy.

²⁰Sympathy falls somewhere between the two in the matter of degree.

²¹It is well to note that "just" refers to (is basically) a *relation* (of fair, i.e., sameness). When the relation *just* is in effect, a human situation is a case of justice. However, it must be emphasized that "same" is not exactly a synonym for "just". Some cases of sameness are not cases of just, e.g., one apple is the same as another—fair play is a matter of following the rules of the game—by all. However, here no special privileges are permitted, but there is not equal opportunity, etc.

²²For example, a person does everything in his power to ensure fair treatment for an accused person—but a corrupt judge prevents it.

²³i.e., it results in justice.

[24]Further detailed comment along the lines of now well established patterns of analysis would involve repetition of the obvious. It is important to note that the subsidiary (contributing) intentions and resultant actions in the case of love of, or concern for, another human being, or sympathy—are means to entities characterized by value intrinsically but are not necessarily intrinsically valuable themselves. Concerning just behaviour it is a case of intention and relevant actions characterized by just, or intentions and actions leading to a just situation. In the case of cooperation, the subsidiary intentions involve sorts of the activity of working together—not merely means to entities characterized by working together.

[25]This chapter, pp. 52-53.

[26]It is essential to note that a person may manifest concern, sympathy, justice and cooperation, in some situations and withhold it in others. This is not the case with reference to love of another human being.

[27]Here more detail is provided, than in the immediately preceding case, to remind the reader of basic factors—and in view of the importance of this behaviour entity.

[28]An expression of the tendency to feel fear.

[29]An alternative locution for "another human being".

[30]See discussion of selfishness, this chapter, fn. 14.

[31]Self sacrifice must be evaluated in the context of what is required for an increase of acceptable value in the world in accordance with an ideal situation.

[32]It must be reiterated that without a specific minimum of ability, e.g., knowledge of various sorts (information and skill), a person will be unable to formulate a relevant intention (plan) or translate it into existence. In other words, without a relevant ability, a person is unable to behave in a morally good fashion in a specific situation.

[33]See this Chapter, p. 72.

[34]Here "specific" means "sort of"; "particular" means "individual instances".

[35]Speaking technically, concern for a fellow man is a many occurrence entity. Contributions to the Red Cross and friendly greeting are also many occurrence entities. These latter two are subordinate entities to the former. A particular activity of contributing to the Red Cross, or giving a friendly greeting, is a particular occurrence both of concern for a fellow man and also of the relevant subordinate entity.

[36]See pp. 54-55 for earlier reference to these illustrations.

[37]In other words the specific cases involved in the particular occurrences are equal in status.

[38]In the interests of simplified presentation, references to latent potentiality will be omitted here and subsequently, unless necessary, likewise in some cases: use of available facilities.

[39]an alternate expression for "concern for another human being".

[40]providing, of course, the person has adequate ability, in the situation.

[41]Of course the way in which a person tells the truth may well have a bearing on: love of or concern for a fellow man.

[42]Assuming they are in the same financial circumstances. This is not a case of making more use of facilities.

[43]The brief reference occurred on p. 57 of this chapter.

[44]with the exception of: love of a fellow man.

[45]The term "hatred is also used in this context. See this chapter, p. 78.

[46]In any case the paralleling mentioned has to do with the relation as to degree between the intrinsic value of an entity and the *morally good* which also characterizes it. But this relation does not hold with reference to the intrinsic value of entities and beautiful, true, and so on which they may have as characteristics.

In brief, the relation of relative degrees of intrinsic value of morally good, true, beautiful, etc. as discussed in Chapter 2 has no bearing on the comparison of the intrinsic value of entities of which morally good, true, beautiful etc, are characteristics.

[47]See this chapter, p. 72.

[48]i.e., has more value intrinsically.

[49]It is not constituted by the entities it characterizes nor does it derive its intrinsic value-opposite from them. In these senses it is similar to morally good. See discussion, this chapter, pp. 55-56.

[50]It is very important to note that the term "hatred" is here used in the sense of (a) "irrational enmity". The term also has the sense of (b) "strong aversion, or dislike, based on rational grounds." See p. 74. At this point "hatred" is used in sense (a).

[51]The term "intention" here, as previously noted, covers the ultimate goal of a behaviour entity plus subsidiary plans or goals.

[52]See discussion of specific cases in the context of love of another human being, fn. 6 of this chapter.

[53]That is: concern for another human being. It is to be noted that hatred for another human *being* is different in several important senses from love of another human being (fellow man). There is not the same sort of ultimate goal. In the case of "love of" the goal is the achievement of the largest attainable amount of acceptable value. In the case of "hatred" it is mainly an increase of unacceptable value-opposite. Other differences will be noted later.

[54]And of course abilities and as well the attempt to develop latent potentialities.

[55]See this chapter, pp. 54-57.

[56]Obviously much of the detail mentioned with reference to hatred of a fellow man need not be repeated here.

[57]It seems unnecessary to continually point out that such behaviour is also intrinsically value-opposite.

[58]That is, behaviour which is characterized by excess which is one sort of inappropriate. Roughly speaking, excess so understood is the opposite of self-control. It may be referred to by the label: "lack of self-control".

225

[59]See later discussion of the term. In general, it means acceptable value-achievement.

[60]It will be noted that the medieval "seven deadly sins" here are covered—along with other specific cases of excess.

[61]It will have been noted that all the details, in particular contributory intentions, have not been "spelled out".

[62]In the interests of simplified presentation, |his obvious point will not be studied in each subsequent case.

[63]Here and subsequently it seems unnecessary to continue calling attention specifically to the minimum-maximum distinction.

[64]There are also cases of value-opposite in an extrinsic mode. For a full discussion, see Chapter 7, pp. 156-58.

[65]Not just different particular occurrences of a specific behaviour entity.

[66]Also involved is the degree to which a person develops his latent potentialities and makes use of available resources. The difficulty overcome factor is also important.

[67]But not equivalent to.

CHAPTER 5

[1]Modes of value (i.e., mode of presence) will be numbered in accordance with the notation established in Chapter I.

[2]See pp. 91-93 for the meaning of this term.

[3]In other words: entities have the status means—when they function as instrument, or cause, or operational condition or ingredient.

[4]More generally, the term "situation" refers to any entity, or group of entities, under discussion.

[5]Technically speaking this is a statement concerning a many-occurrence complex entity (situation) in which the entity pen is sometimes involved. It is stated in terms of reference to *a* pen. This locution should be understood as referring to *each* of the particular occurrences of the entity pen—in the specific situation under discussion. This is far less cumbersome than the more technically exact version. This locution (and procedure) is in general use in subsequent discussion.

[6]This is a simplified analysis of cause, concentrating on cause in the "presence" sense (see discussion in *Experiential Realism*, Chapter 7, pp. 170-91).

[7]It is well to note that sometimes an entity is functioning as a cause even though the end has not yet been achieved. The point is that some causal processes require the lapse of a period of time from initiation by the cause to achievement of the effect. This sometimes involves a series of intervening subsidiary (contributory) causes. In some cases the cause continues to produce a specific effect. In others, having produced the effect the entity ceases its causal function.

[8]It is important to realize that in producing its effect the stimulus function is linked with a generative function. See later discussion.

[9]See p. 90.

[10]The term is not here used as a synonym for "value", rather it refers to status in the matter of: contributing to effects.

[11]For example, in the context of a committee situation, the members of the committee may have the status: essential ingredient. A particular pen used by a member is not an essential ingredient.

[12]See Chapter 3 for discussion of acceptable and unacceptable, pp. 33-38.

[13]See later discussion, Chapter 6, pp. 136-39.

[14]See this Chapter, p. 94.

[15]Chapter 3, pp. 33-38.

[16]It will have been noted that examples of characteristics of persons considered here are all intrinsically valuable. There are of course entities which are unacceptable and are valuable only in extrinsic modes. However, the most obvious and common personal characteristics concerning which the question of derivation of value arises, i.e., the question of acceptability is raised—are those which are intrinsically valuable.

[17]For example, pleasure in the unacceptable misery of others.

[18]See this chapter, p. 113.

[19]For example pleasure in morally good behaviour.

[20]Incidentally qualification (a) applies here. The occurrence of efficiency in this context is intrinsically value-opposite. Hence efficiency is unacceptable.

[21]The term "condition", as the context indicates, is not here used in the sense of: "operational condition".

[22]On the basis of self control. This of course must be done in an acceptable fashion, i.e., when self-control is not a mere means to some value-opposite end.

[23]See reference to qualifications, p. 102.

[24]The term "have" is sometimes used with reference to modes (3) and (4). But in order to point to the difference between characteristics and consequences just noted, the term "accrue" is ordinarily used with reference to mode (4) but not applied to (3). "Derive" is employed in both cases.

[25]The complex term will be used initially in order to familiarize the reader with the point at issue.

[26]Of course, if a consequence is such that no intrinsic mode is involved, and (i) no value-opposite is involved or (ii) is valuable on balance (in one or more extrinsic modes), it is acceptable in one sense of the term. The acceptability of intrinsically valuable entities is what requires special consideration, as noted above.

[27]This term is a variation of "accrue", or "derive".

[28]More specifically, the information it provides.

[29]It seems unduly cumbersome to keep stressing the point that the value must be acceptable. Further, in the interests of simplified exposition, subsequent illustrations, except when it is necessary to make the point clear, will operate in the context of acceptable value.

[30]Henceforth the term "external" will be omitted. It should be "understood" unless otherwise indicated.

[31]See previous discussion of importance and variations of amount of value in the means mode. This chapter, pp. 92-93.

[32]This, of course, must be done since specific means entities function with reference to specific ends, in a specific environment. Particular occurrences of specific entities must be considered because of variations among specific many-occurrence entities.

[33]The preservation of acceptable value is characterized by value intrinsically. (See Chapter 3, pp. 46-47.)

[34]It must be emphasized that here, as elsewhere, it is not claimed that value is literally taken from the consequences. Rather because of the value of consequences a means entity becomes valuable.

[35]It will be well to distinguish carefully (a) valuable because ingredient and (b) valuable because of ingredient status in an organic whole. The former (a) is a case of valuable in the means mode. The latter (b) comes under the heading: valuable because of consequences. An entity is valuable in the ingredient means mode in the sense that it, by its presence, contributes to the fact that things are as they are. On the other hand (b), as noted above, brings into focus another fact—that of the consequences of ingredient status. Specifically, it involves cases where an entity is a constituent ingredient of an organic whole. This organic whole has distinctive value characteristics. The constitutive ingredient derives some value on the basis of its status in the valuable organic whole.

[36]Simple or complex.

[37]See this chapter, pp. 92-93.

[38]The points just mentioned concerning cause-effect *series* of entities raise the question as to whether similar situations exist involving instruments, conditions, ingredients and their consequences. This topic will be dealt with briefly at this point. Attention will be focussed on representative cases. Consider an instrument situation. A knife is used by a surgeon as an instrument in performing an operation. The operation is an instrument for bringing about the consequence: health. In this case the knife is not, strictly speaking, an instrument with reference to health. Consider next a situation involving: air, a living organism and morally good behaviour. Here also, while air is a condition for the presence of the living organism—strictly speaking only the living organism is a condition for morally good behaviour. However, it is essential to note that the *absence of air* is a *cause* for the removal (absence) of morally good behaviour. Air does not have that status. On the other hand, turning to an ingredient situation, consider: literature, a liberal education, the good life. Here literature is not only an ingredient in a liberal education but also in a good life. A liberation education is not only a consequence of literature but also a condition for a good life.

[39]In the context of this discussion the term "initial" refers to the temporary first entity in a specific causal series. The term "decisive" refers to the member of the specific causal series which starts (initiates) the causal process of development

228

leading to the terminal effect. It will become obvious from later discussion that *not all initial causes are also decisive.*

⁴⁰This is technically speaking an organic whole of the reaction sequence sort. See Chapter 3, pp. 29-30.

⁴¹The knife in this case is a mediating cause which is actually not the effect of a preceding cause. This sort of complexity occurs, in many cases, in a causal series which, in general, are primarily ones in which mediating entities are in turn effect and cause.

⁴²It is interesting to note that while an actual situation which is intrinsically value-opposite which is an initial cause—does not derive value from valuable consequences—a description of it, say in a novel, does derive value from such consequences. Consider an ugly slum which as initial cause arouses a reform group to replace it by an at least slightly beautiful new housing development. The slum as initial cause derives no value from the consequences. However, a story about the slum which results in a valuable replacement does derive value. It is essential to realize that while the actual slum is ugly, the story about it is not; indeed it is true. On this basis there is value derivation. Of course, the reform group as decisive cause derives much more value.

⁴³The terms "initial" and "decisive" have been used previously in the context of situations which are relatively complex, extensive, causal series. The entity which gets the specific causal process actively under way is termed "decisive". Implicit in the immediately preceding discussion of group pressure and feeling of frustration is the suggestion that one might appropriately use "initial" or "prior" and "decisive" in a reaction situation, which is, in at least some cases, much less complex than the ones already investigated.

⁴⁴The term "standard" here refers to patterns of behaviour such that they are possessed by all normal human beings. In this sense these patterns are part of the "make up" of (nature) of human beings. Given the relevant stimulus a sequence of events automatically occurs leading to a specific conclusion.

⁴⁵In this context one can understand the luring or inspiring function of great men. In order to avoid confusion it is well to note that technically speaking, a stimulus operates by contact, a lure operates by appeal or attraction. The result of a stimulus is a reaction by an organism; the effect of a source of inspiration is imitation, i.e., the transfer of a pattern of behaviour from the inspirer to the inspired. However frequently the term stimulus is used in the more general sense of a synonym for initial cause.

⁴⁶It is very important to note the distinction between "conditioning" process and status: "condition". What satisfies the desire for social approval, and hence is involved in the conditioning (i.e., process) is relevant because of the condition: it is desired.

⁴⁷See discussion of the surgeon and his teachers.

⁴⁸For example, what religion or moral code, or vocation, or political system etc., should be adopted.

⁴⁹And obviously not a robot-like creature.

[50]as the result of conditioning and/or internally initiating factors.

[51]If, however, for such a person this pattern of behaviour becomes habitual, i.e., automatic, he does not cease to derive value. The habit is based on original causal initiative on the part of the reactor.

[52]In situations where they are not. Of course in other situations instruments may well have a causal function, i.e., with reference to a specific entity.

[53]This brings into focus a very important point: an entity which is not intrinsically value, or value-opposite, derives value, or value-opposite, in the consequence mode, on the basis of those of its characteristics which are decisive in the producing of consequences. If the characteristic, as in this case, rules out derivation of value-opposite, the same is the case with reference to the entity which has the characteristic. See discussion of "characteristic dependent", this chapter, pp. 94-95. See also subsequent discussion this chapter pp. 115-16.

[54]as in the cases of *ingredients*. See this chapter, p. 93.

[55]Likewise if pain is an ingredient in an intrinsically valuable organic whole—sympathy-pain despite its ingredient status in relation to sympathy as consequence—does not derive value from this consequence.

[56]Of course, we are dealing here with characteristics of the proposition, face, etc. hence the because of characteristics mode is involved. See pp. 94-100. Further, this parallels the preceding discussion of a value-opposite reaction to a valuable entity, pp. 109-15.

[57]See later discussion, Chap. 8, pp. 165-71.

[58]i.e., its valuable characteristics and hence its extrinsic value.

[59]It should not be assumed that in all cases where an external entity is the initial and decisive cause of pleasure—the pleasure is acceptable and hence the basis of derivation of value. A poisonous toad stool causes pleasure when eaten. However, this pleasure is not acceptable. This is because of its essential association with pain resulting from the poisoning process.

[60]The misery may continue long after the structure is completed. It may take centuries to pay for it. There is also the problem of upkeep.

[61]See Chapter 3, pp. 46-48.

[62]bearing in mind the issue of acceptable and unacceptable. See previous discussion.

[63]in view of the nature of its ingredients.

[64]Up to a certain point in history (World War II) *no* Somali had been a motor mechanic, but as human beings, men of this race had the potentiality of developing these characteristics.

[65]and means, possibility, potentiality status.

[66]See discussion of pleasure, this chapter, p. 113.

[67]See discussion of pain in the context of sympathy.

[68]It must be reiterated that (a) and (b) are not *arbitrary*, or *legislating*, *principles*. They are merely statements of facts concerning the non-accrual of value-opposite to an entity, despite the value-opposite characteristics of its consequences. However, they are sometimes loosely referred to as "principles".

[69]See this chapter, pp. 124-25. The situation with reference to condition function is more complex than that concerning causal and instrumental function. In the case, for example, of the tapping finger, a table is a *specific* condition—and derives value-opposite therefrom. On the other hand a relevant degree of health is a *general* condition for finger tapping—and many other activities. On the basis of the generality of condition factor, health does not derive value-opposite in the tapping situation. Paradoxically, in the case of an entity which has valuable consequences—health does derive value on the basis of its condition function.

[70]See this chapter, p. 125.

[71]This includes even honesty in the lynching situation.

[72]A complex entity which is intrinsically value-opposite. See other examples, this chapter, p. 119.

[73]In view of preceding discussion of value in these modes—detailed exposition seems unnecessary because of the generally similar state of affairs.

CHAPTER 6

[1]For the most part subsequently the term "mode" will be used as an abbreviation for "mode of presence".

[2](2) when means, (3) because of value of characteristics, (4) because of value of consequences, (5) as possible, (6) as potential.

[3]Here obviously point (iii) above is being considered.

[4]Some of the foregoing comment on the means mode is a repetition of points already made, see Chap. 5, pp. 90-94. It is repeated here in the interests of emphasis and completion of discussion of extrinsic modes.

[5]This qualification is to be assumed in subsequent illustrations unless otherwise s ated.

[6]Not just the physical object but essentially the information which is "provided by it".

[7]Any occurrence of it.

[8]See Chap. 5, pp. 122-23.

[9]This is a very loose way of referring to causal, instrumental etc. functions whereby prevention, or interference occur.

[10]See pp. 10-11.

[11]As noted previously behaviour which is characterized by morally good (which is intrinsically valuable) is also characterized by value intrinsically.

[12]It is to be understood here and subsequently, unless otherwise noted, that the value is acceptable and the value-opposite unacceptable.

[13]It must also be pointed out that entities, either many-occurrence or particular, in some cases have several characteristics, several consequences, have several means functions, also several possible, several potential aspects.

[14]In all cases the value of consequences must be acceptable. For more detailed exposition see pp. 137-38.

[15]See examples in Section 4.

[16]The term "evaluation" is used to refer to the finding of the value or the value-opposite characteristics of an entity.

[17]See previous discussion of cause-effect units, Chap. 5, pp. 104-06.

[18]indeed any end or goal.

[19]These differences are based on differences in intensity of beautiful or pleasure as the case may be.

[20]See Chapter 1, pp. 13-15.

[21]For specific examples, see Section 4.

[22]However, the analysis is repeated (see Chapter 3, pp. 28-41) and expanded here because of its very great importance. These points must be clearly in mind as we proceed to the practical business of evaluating entities in Section 4.

[23]It should be noted that "everything considered" refers as a matter of fact to the on balance factor in a total situation which is in contrast to the on balance factor involving only the ingredients of the organic whole, when they are considered as separate entities.

[24]and a few to be noted subsequently. See *Experiential Realism*, Chapters 6, 8, 16, 18—and this volume, Section 4.

[25]Fireplace and chair of course are entities open to awareness like wood, green, pleasure.

CHAPTER 7

[1]The common locution which refers to valuable entities as "values" will not usually be employed in this discussion. But on occasion this occurs.

[2]or from those which are not decisively initiated by the person. See Chap. 5, p. 113.

[3]i.e., "more and more" means factors are involved.

[4]not only when instrument but also as ingredient.

[5]and of course in the case of honesty—because of its characteristic morally good.

[6]In any case it has value as ingredient. See distinction between "as ingredient" and "because of status as ingredient in a valuable organic whole" (Chap. 5, p. 104).

[7]Further, it might have been noted that this behaviour is involved in both the immediate and long range ideal largest attainable amount of acceptable value situation.

[8]when instrument. It is also valuable as an ingredient.

[9]However, it is characterized by value-opposite since it is instrumental in preventing the experience of value by the victims of the Gestapo.

[10]i.e., a related cluster of occurrences of: love of a fellow man.

[11]i.e., valuable entities.

[12]It must be emphasized that it has the causal status: initial, not decisive. See Chapter 5, pp. 104-06.

[13]The "like to like" pattern is not applicable here, i.e., pleasure is a reaction to what is characterized by value-opposite.

[14]It should be obvious by now that the consequent pain is not only value-opposite intrinsically but also in the possible mode. Further, when it is a means to more pain it is value-opposite because of that consequence.

[15]This section supplements discussion of the topic in Chapter 4, pp. 57-59.

[16]In view of preceding discussion it seems unnecessary here, and subsequently, to spell out further detail.

[17]and by value-opposite intrinsically.

[18]It is important to note, that entities such as honesty and "love of a fellow man" are invariantly characterized by morally good while, for example, dishonesty is invariantly characterized by morally evil. Further, they are characterized by value or value-opposite intrinsically. The status "invariantly characteristic" is not the case with reference to entities characterized by true or false, beautiful or ugly, pleasure or pain, efficient or inefficient, fitting or inappropriate, consistent or inconsistent, harmonious or discordant. Specifically, for example, the entity proposition is not always true or always false: the entity human face is not always beautiful or ugly. Human experience is not always characterized by pleasure or pain and so on.

[19]It of course has value as ingredient.

[20]See also preceding discussion of initial and decisive cause Chapter 5, pp. 104-06. In the case before us the child's pain is initial cause. The doctor is decisive cause.

CHAPTER 8

[1]It is to be noted that for most adults, "activities significant" covers not only a job but also hobbies and other forms of recreation and in general a wide range of social activities.

[2]In this book the term "ability" is used to refer to the fact that a person now can do or has done something. The term "latent potentialities" refers to the fact that though a person is not now able to do something—yet after a process of development or training, if all goes well, he will be able to do so.

[3]It will be recalled that in addition to instrumental causal means function there is also the ingredient one.

[4]All these value-opposites are unacceptable.

[5]That is, another particular occurrence of the entity: human life.

[6]The same comment is relevant to the means and possible modes.

[7]and of course she has value as ingredient.

[8]And "so on" concerning means and possible modes.

[9]It will have been noted that in the preceding discussion the potential aspect when relevant has not been mentioned. This has been done in the interests of simplification.

[10]It was found during World War II, for example, that "ordinary native tribesmen" living on the shore of the Red Sea were able to profit from expert instruction and very quickly became competent motor mechanics.

[11]A specific human entity. The time notation—is in the present tense to indicate continuing importance.

[12]still does, on the basis of reports concerning his life and work.

[13]The preceding remarks are based on the point that the characteristics morally good and beautiful are most frequently the causes of value-opposite reaction—to such entities as men and buildings.

[14]That is, it occurs in the context of an organic whole of experience which is not characterized by value-opposite intrinsically.

[15]For example, a brilliant specialist in some field of knowledge "loses out" for a university appointment because of his style of dress.

[16]The preceding comments on clothing indicates a general pattern of analysis of such cultural entities as art, literature, theatre, i.e., food and shelter for the mind.

[17]Entities which function as means to a larger number of entities are termed "general". For example, life is a means to many entities. The physical and social environment are means to many entities. Thus they are also cases of very general means though, of course, not quite as general as life. Hence, life may be termed a "foundation" means and to only a slightly lesser extent so may the physical and mental environment. Less general (again) are such means as food, clothing, shelter and physical and mental health.

CHAPTER 9

[1]In the case of many entities which are organic wholes, item (a) is not relevant, e.g., pain is value-opposite, sympathy is not.

[2]This is a very flimsy organic whole. In view of the two main behaviour patterns it comes close to being two organic wholes in loose association.

[3]It is appropriate, and efficient, for a male and a female who undertake to found an ideal family—to make known their intention to achieve the results for which the family can be a means. The commitment to this project is of course basically a private matter involving the founding partners. However, the use of public ceremony and even of legal recourse serves to certify the seriousness of commitment. These also provide an opportunity for others of like mind to offer encouragement and support. Likewise when two people take a stand in favour of specific values and techniques, others are encouraged to do so.

[4]It is essential to note that it is not being claimed here, or elsewhere, that love of a fellow man can occur only in the context of an ideal family. It may occur in relations between any two persons. It may be involved in the function of other *social institutions*. The point being emphasized here is that among social institutions the ideal family provides the most extensive achievement of love of a fellow man. It is involved in all phases of the life of an ideal family. At best, it appears in a very few phases of the life of other social institutions. Of course not all activities of an ideal family are cases of love of a fellow man. However, a greater proportion of them are than in the case of other social institutions. Also there is more concern with the implementation of this pattern of life. Obviously parents will manifest the pattern more frequently than their young children, but the latter are progressing steadily in that direction.

[5]See Chapter 5, p. 104.

[6]Desiring and intending as well as doing so.

[7]In order to avoid possible misunderstanding, the complexities of this situation must be borne in mind. When A engages in sexual interaction in an efficient fashion, this activity derives value because it is characterized by efficiency. If A uses his efficient sex-interaction behaviour as an instrument whereby to take an

unfair advantage of B—value does not account to A because of the efficiency of his behaviour. Its occurrence in this context is unacceptable. But nevertheless the sexual interaction, because efficient, is valuable on that basis.

In general it is well to realize that there is a difference between efficient as such and efficient in providing results. A toadstool is efficient in producing death. Because of the nature of its results the efficiency is not the basis of derivation of value to the toadstool. The situation is different in the case of the efficiency of a sharp knife. As such it is efficient.

[8]i.e., valuable entities.

[9]It will have been noted that discussion has focussed on the male-female sex relations of adults. No attempt has been made, or will be made, to deal in any detail with male-female sex relations between children, or homosexual relations. As stated earlier, this book proposes to examine only a representative group of entities, and in some cases only some particular occurrences of an entity.

[10]and possible and potential aspects as well.

[11]i.e., some particular occurrences do.

[12]Sport and hobby are, in a sense social institutions, with varying degrees of organization.

[13]Such pleasure, as in other similar cases, is unacceptable and hence not the basis of value derivation.

[14]This involves both the so-called "immediate ideal" but also the "long-range ideal", see Chapter 3, pp. 41-46.

[15]It is important to note the status of liberty, equality and fraternity. These are what may be termed "state of affairs" entities—which involve at least two other entities. It should be emphasized that liberty, equality and fraternity are not complex entities like justice or courage, nor are they characteristics of persons in the same fashion that beautiful, morally good or efficient are. Liberty, equality and fraternity are sorts of relations between persons and/or persons and things. In so far as a person is in one of these relations he is characterized by the fact that he is in that relation—in this sense one may be said to be characterized by that relation. (Some characteristics are not relational, for example, beautiful.) Among those which are, in any sense related (i) some cases are a-symmetrical, for example true, efficient, liberty, also some are (ii) symmetrical, for example equality, fraternity.

[16]A person wishes to escape not only such entities but also those obstructions and restrictions which interfere with freedom in the "to" sense.

[17]But to repeat, they are not characteristics of freedom as such. As in other cases reference is made to acceptable entities and their value.

[18]In both cases the entity is valuable when means.

[19]See Chapter 4, pp. 58-61.

[20]It is obvious that "fraternity" and "concern for the welfare of a fellow man" are not here regarded as synonymous terms.

[21]The proviso: having worked for it, and such that he uses it—is sometimes stressed.

²²This comment also covers the related "medium of exchange" entity—money. Here the means function is that of instrument, not condition.

²³See Chapter 5, pp. 93-94.

²⁴In view of the extensive nature of previous discussions it seems unnecessary to spell out the supporting details for the rather general analysis and conclusions outlined here.

CHAPTER 10

¹A sample of a seriously defective university.

²but it is unacceptable.

³The tone of this description of ZU will remind some readers of Plato's technique (in the *Republic*) in dealing with defective forms of social (political) organization. The same is true of the following description of the opposite type of university.

⁴"I" stands for "ideal".

⁵This, however, does not mean that anything which on occasion is characterized by efficient is characterized by value. See Chapter 3, pp. 33-34.

⁶In this case the process of reasoning does not derive value because of the value of its consequences. This is so because of the inaccurate and/or inconsistent nature of the reasoning. In short, the like to like pattern is relevant, i.e., what is essentially value-opposite does not derive value from valuable consequences.

⁷The term "rational" is also applied to the conclusion of some process of reasoning. Further, the term "rational" is used in the context of discussion of ethical to mean "what is in accordance with self interest".

⁸In this context "force" is *usually* a synonym for violence, but it *may be used* in the context of "pressure". More exactly "force is a synonym for 'energy' or 'exertion of energy' ".

⁹in some cases.

¹⁰a small cluster of particular occurrences of aspirin.

¹¹in addition to pointing out the risk of addiction after a very few exposures.

¹²all being acceptable.

¹³See Chapter 5, pp. 41-42.

¹⁴in the sense of latent potentialities.

¹⁵i.e., value present in these modes.

¹⁶In the interests of simplification, attention will be concentrated on value—the same general pattern of analysis applies to value-opposite.

¹⁷It will be noted that the terms here used for purposes of general summary are not widely used elsewhere. However, the distinctions they register must be kept constantly in mind.

¹⁸See Chapter 3, pp. 43-46.

¹⁹See Chapter 5.

EPILOGUE

¹and value-opposite.

²See obligation, pp. 221-24, knowledge, pp. 145-69, 340-69, responsibility, pp. 187-8, 215-9, free-will, pp. 188-90; 375-81; 387-8, meaning, pp. 110-44, 284-97. (A- H. Johnson, *Experiential Realism*, George Allen & Unwin, London, 1973.)

³i.e., concerning the naturalistic fallacy.

⁴See *Ethics and Language*, Yale University Press, New Haven, 1944, p. 336.

⁵See pp. 65-70, 153-56, 220-21, 347-55.

⁶It is to be hoped that a waspish reviewer will not neglect the following context!

⁷"Preference" means, in this context, not only selection from among alternatives but also as in the case of "concern" not only "interest in" but as well "an attempt to achieve".

INDEX

241